CLASSICS IN PSYCHOLOGY

CLASSICS IN PSYCHOLOGY

LECTURES

ON THE

Experimental Psychology
of the Thought-Processes

BY

EDWARD BRADFORD TITCHENER

ARNO PRESS

A New York Times Company
New York ★ 1973

Reprint Edition 1973 by Arno Press Inc.

Reprinted from a copy in
The Princeton University Library

Classics in Psychology
ISBN for complete set: 0-405-05130-1
See last pages of this volume for titles.

Manufactured in the United States of America

————◆————

Library of Congress Cataloging in Publication Data

Titchener, Edward Bradford, 1867-1927.
    Lectures on the experimental psychology of
the thought-processes.

    (Classics in psychology)
    Reprint of the 1909 ed. published by Macmillan,
New York.
    1.   Thought and thinking.   2.   Psychology,
Experimental.   I.   Series.
[DNLM: BFT618L   1909F
BF455.T62   153.4   73-2995
ISBN 0-405-05167-0

A NOTE ABOUT THE AUTHOR

EDWARD BRADFORD TITCHENER was born in England in 1867. He graduated from Oxford and then spent two years in Wundt's laboratory, receiving a Ph. D. from Leipzig in 1892. Titchener immediately emigrated to America and accepted a position at Cornell. He became full Professor in 1895 and remained at the Ithaca institution until his death in 1927.

Despite his Anglo-American ties, Titchener devoted his academic life to the clarification and dissemination of the structural psychology he had learned from Wundt. He believed that psychologists should study the normal adult mind, and that the point of departure for such a study must be the experience of an individual. He viewed feelings as independent elementary states, and attention was related to specific aspects of sensory experience. In a number of major textbooks and outlines, Titchener contrasted his point of view with the American psychology which was gaining in prominence during his time. He inveighed against functionalism, claiming that the uses to which mental processes were put were not of major concern for the psychologist; and he could not accept the behaviorist rejection of introspective and conscious phenomena. Titchener's point of view did not lead to the formation of a structuralist school in America, but his scholarship, grasp of the field of psychology, brilliant pedagogy, and personal integrity inspired the many students and colleagues with whom he came into contact.

LECTURES

ON THE

Experimental Psychology
of the Thought-Processes

BY

EDWARD BRADFORD TITCHENER

New York
THE MACMILLAN COMPANY
1909

THE MASON-HENRY PRESS
Syracuse, N. Y.

To
MADISON BENTLEY

PREFACE

IN a course of lectures on the elementary psychology of Feeling and Attention, published last year, I remarked that "the system of psychology rests upon a threefold foundation: the doctrine of sensation and image, the elementary doctrine of feeling, and the doctrine of attention." This statement, which formed the basis of my whole discussion, was promptly challenged by reviewers. I was misled, they affirmed, by a sensationalistic bias; I should have taken account of current experimental work upon the thought-processes; I had no right to assume that all intellection is imaginal in character.

I could not but acknowledge the essential justice of this criticism, although I could not either accept my critics' point of view. I was, indeed, engaged in writing a brief defence of psychological sensationalism, when I received an invitation to deliver a series of lectures at the University of Illinois. Here was an opportunity, of which I gladly availed myself, to treat in some little detail of the recent experimental contributions to the psychology of thought. The present volume is the result.

I have printed the lectures as they were written for delivery at the University of Illinois, in March, 1909. In the appended notes, I have allowed myself a freedom of reference and comment somewhat wider than before. The presence of the notes at the end of the book need not disturb the general reader, while their fulness may prevent certain minor misunderstandings to which the *Feeling and Attention* has been exposed. I have, however, made it a rule to leave out of consideration all experimental work that is concerned simply with association and reproduction, and all purely theoretical studies of the thought-consciousness. Where the dividing line is at all obscure, I have, it is true, not hesitated to transgress. Still, the psychological reader will miss much that, without this limitation of purpose, he might reasonably expect to find.

My thanks are due to my wife; to Professor S. S. Colvin, of the University of Illinois, whose invitation gave occasion for the writing of the lectures; to many friends, at Urbana and at Ithaca, among whom I may name Professor J. W. Baird, Dr. L. R. Geissler, and Dr. W. H. Pyle; and especially to my colleague, Professor I. M. Bentley, who has read the manuscript of the book, has constantly assisted me during its

preparation with criticism and positive suggestion, and by his sacrifice of time and energy has
made it possible for me to bring my task to early
completion. In dedicating the volume to Professor Bentley, I wish to express my gratitude
for the help that he has generously rendered, not
only in this particular case, but in all my literary
undertakings of the past dozen years.

Cornell Heights, Ithaca, N. Y.
        July 15, 1909.

CONTENTS

LECTURE I
IMAGERY AND SENSATIONALISM

LECTURE I

IMAGERY AND SENSATIONALISM

IF I chance to be reflecting on the progress of science, there is likely to arise before my mind's eye a scene familiar to my childhood,—the flow of the incoming tide over a broad extent of sandy shore. The whole body of water is pressing forward, irresistibly, as natural law decrees. But its front is not unbroken; for the sand is rock-strewn and uneven, so that here there are eddying pools of unusual depth, and there, again, long fingers of the sea stretched out towards the land. My mind, as I shall presently show in more detail, is prone to imagery; and this image, of check and overflow in the van of a great movement, has come to represent for me the progress of science.

You will take my meaning, even if you do not see my picture. Scientific knowledge is steadily and continuously increasing; but the men who stand for science are likely, at any given time, to be dominated by a few particular interests. Sometimes a brilliant discovery or a daring theory opens up a certain line of investigation;

sometimes suggestion seems to spring of itself from the mere accumulation of facts. Striking illustrations, under both of these heads, are furnished by the physics and the biology of the past decade. Illustrations at least as striking, although less generally known, are furnished by our own growing science of experimental psychology. A few years ago, it seemed that everybody was interested in kinæsthetic sensations. Then the geometrical illusions of vision had their day. Then we were all running to the study of memory and association. Then the affective processes came to the forefront of discussion. And all the while the experimental method was doing its appointed work over the whole face of the science.

Just now, it might fairly be argued that the centre of interest for the experimental psychologist lies in the field of thought. Current tendencies are oftentimes difficult to explain, simply because we lack perspective; and I do not find explanation easy in the present case. Yet there must have been, at the beginning of the twentieth century, something in the psychological atmosphere that was peculiarly favourable to thought.[1] We may point, perhaps, to the gradual and increasing recognition of the value of introspection, with its promise of a wide extension of the experimental method: for if the psychological experiment is, in essentials, a controlled introspection, and if our instruments of precision are but means to that control, the method may evidently be carried into every region of consciousness.[2] We may think, also, of the publication of Wundt's great work on language, and of its challenge to the experimentalists.[3] "Fortunately for the science," Wundt writes, "there are sources of objective psychological knowledge, which become accessible at the very point where the experimental method fails us. These are certain products of the common life, in which we may trace the operation of determinate psychical motives: chief among them are language, myth and custom."[4] Here is a limit set to the applicability of experiment; and to set a bound is directly to challenge a trespass. We may think, once more, of the stimulus received from workers in neighbouring fields of logic and *Gegenstandstheorie,* from Lipps and Erdmann, from Husserl and Meinong.[5] We may remember that the human mind is for ever swinging between extremes, and we may suppose that the time had come for a reaction against 'sensationalism.'[6] Here are motives enough, if we could trace their several influences,—and if we could be sure that they are motives: if, I mean, we could be sure that they are not themselves symptoms of a general movement, which has involved experimental psychology as it has involved the mental sciences at large. However that may be, the fact is there. Binet in France, Marbe and his successors in Germany, Woodworth in the United States, have all sought to bring the processes of thought under the control of the experimental method. And all alike have reached the conclusion, each independently for himself, that the experience of thought is not adequately described in the orthodox textbooks of psychology.

It is of these men, of their views and their work, that I am to speak in the lectures now begun. I shall report, as impartially as I may, their results and their interpretations; and I shall then outline my own understanding of the whole matter. But we cannot come, all in a moment, to close quarters with the experiments. There are certain prior questions that must be asked and answered; and I devote this and the following Lecture to their discussion.

I

First of all, there is the question of individual differences, differences of mental constitution. The creation of a scientific psychology of these

differences is, in my opinion, one of the principal achievements of the experimental method;[7]
and I believe that a frank acceptance of the
teachings of differential psychology will go
far to allay some of the perennial controversies
of the text-books. At all events, I do not see
how one can fairly approach the psychology of
thought, whether as critic or as expositor, without taking account of the machinery of thought
in one's own case. I said just now that I should
try to be impartial; and I can offer no better
guarantee of good faith than to confess my
constitutional bias. I propose, therefore, to turn
out my mind for your inspection. I can give
you nothing systematic, nothing that has been
verified by experiment; but the account will be
correct, so far as it goes, and will suffice for our
present purpose.

My mind, then, is of the imaginal sort,—I
wish that we had a better adjective!—and my
ideational type is of the sort described in the
psychologies as mixed. I have always had, and
I have always used, a wide range and a great
variety of imagery; and my furniture of images
is, perhaps, in better than average condition,
because—fearing that, as one gets older, one
tends also to become more and more verbal in
type[8]—I have made a point of renewing it by

practice. I am able now, for instance, as I was able when I entered the class-room nearly twenty years ago, to lecture from any one of the three main cues. I can read off what I have to say from a memory manuscript; or I can follow the lead of my voice; or I can trust to the guidance of kinæsthesis, the anticipatory feel of the movements of articulation.[9] I use these three methods under different circumstances. When it is a matter of preparing a lecture on a definite plan, of dividing and subdividing under various headings, I draw up in the mind's eye a table of contents, written or printed, and refer to it as the hour proceeds. When there is any difficulty in exposition, a point to be argued *pro* and *con* or a conclusion to be brought out from the convergence of several lines of proof, I hear my own voice speaking just ahead of me: an experience which, in the description, sounds as if it should be confusing, but which in reality is precisely the reverse. When, again, I come to a piece of straightforward narrative, I let my throat take care of itself; so that I am able to give full attention to blackboard drawing or to the manipulation of instruments on the table. As a rule, I look to all three kinds of prompting in the course of a single hour. At times, however, some one method is followed exclusively: thus, when I am tired, I find that vision and audition are likely to lapse, and I am left alone with kinæsthesis.

When I am working for myself, reading or writing or thinking, I experience a complex interlacing of imagery which it is difficult to describe, or at any rate to describe with the just emphasis. My natural tendency is to employ internal speech; and there are occasions when my voice rings out clearly to the mental ear and my throat feels stiff as if with much talking. But in general the internal speech is reduced to a faint flicker of articulatory movement. This may be due, in part, to the fact that I am a very rapid reader, and have tried to acquire the power of purely visual reading.[10] But it is also due, I am sure, to the fact that I have vivid and persistent auditory imagery. If I may venture on a very sweeping statement, I should say that I never sit down to read a book, or to write a paragraph, or to think out a problem, without a musical accompaniment. Usually the accompaniment is orchestral, with a preponderance of the wood-wind,—I have a sort of personal affection for the oboe; sometimes it is in the tone-colour of piano or violin; never, I think, is it vocal. Usually, again, it is the reproduction of a known composition; on rare occasions it is wholly unfamiliar. I am not aware that I make any use of this musical imagery, though I should be sorry to lose it, and I can offer no explanation of its arousal.[11] However, the important point in the present connection is, simply, that its freakish appearance has, without doubt, tended to repress the auditory factor in internal speech.

These musical and verbal images crop up of their own accord. I have never sought to control the former; I have, as I said just now, somewhat weakened the latter by my effort after purely visual reading. I turn now to the topic of visual imagery, which is always at my disposal and which I can mould and direct at will.[12] I rely, in my thinking, upon visual imagery in the sense that I like to get a problem into some sort of visual schema, from which I can think my way out and to which I can return. As I read an article, or the chapter of a book, I instinctively arrange the facts or arguments in some visual pattern, and I am as likely to think in terms of this pattern as I am to think in words. I understand, and to that extent I enjoy, an author whom I can thus visualise. Contrariwise, an author whose thought is not susceptible to my visual arrangement appears to me to be obscure and involved; and an author who has an arrangement of his own, which crosses the pattern that

I am forming in my mind, appears to me difficult and, to that extent, unenjoyable. Hence
my standard of clarity and consistency is, in the
last resort, visual. A writer may be discussing
a highly complicated question; but if he is what
I call clear, I can follow and understand him;
his pattern is complex, but it may be traced. On
the other hand, a writer may be discoursing in
the easiest popular fashion; but if he is what I
call obscure, if I cannot trace his pattern, I am
baffled by him. I must then go to my friends, or
to printed reviews of his work, and try to pick
up a pattern at second hand.[13]

You will understand that this visual frame-
work of thought is both an advantage and a
limitation. What I know, I know clearly; and
what I have once understood, I am likely to remember. But there are disadvantages. The
task of composition, for example, is for me
extremely laborious. Words come quickly and
readily enough; I have only to let them come, in
terms of internal speech. But then the words
are apt to switch me off the visual track, to
entangle me in secondary arguments, to bring
up irrelevant associations; I cannot trust myself
to think simply in words; indeed, I sometimes
doubt, as I read over my rough draughts, if there
ever was a psychologist who could make so many

loose-ended statements in so few pages as I can.
This defect prescribes its own remedy. More
serious is the temptation to allow one's visual
schemata to harden, to become rigid. I have
constantly to fight against the tendency to premature systematisation.

The term 'visual schema' is, of course, itself
equivocal. Those of you whose minds are built
on the same general plan as my own will know
well enough what it means. But I must warn
the others, to whom this sort of imagery is unknown, not to think of a geometrical figure
printed black on white, or of anything a hun-
dredth part as definite. I should be sorely
puzzled to say what colours appear in my schemata, and I certainly could not draw on paper my
pattern of a particular writer or a particular
book. I get a suggestion of dull red, and I get
a suggestion of angles rather than curves; I get,
pretty clearly, the picture of movement along
lines, and of neatness or confusion where the
moving lines come together. But that is all,—
all, at least, that ordinary introspection reveals.
The hardening and rigidity, against which I am
always on guard, is not a fixation of the schema
as visual outline, but its fixation as meaning, as
the meaning of something read or heard or
thought. I wish to be clear on this point: the
visual pattern does not indifferently accompany,

but is or equals, my gross understanding of the matter in hand.

My visual imagery, voluntarily aroused as for Galton's breakfast-table test, is extremely vivid, though it seems bodiless and papery when compared with direct perception. I have never, so far as I am aware, experienced a visual hallucination; I have no number-form; I know nothing of coloured hearing. On the other hand, my mind, in its ordinary operations, is a fairly complete picture gallery,—not of finished paintings, but of impressionist notes. Whenever I read or hear that somebody has done something modestly, or gravely, or proudly, or humbly, or courteously, I see a visual hint of the modesty or gravity or pride or humility or courtesy. The stately heroine gives me a flash of a tall figure, the only clear part of which is a hand holding up a steely grey skirt; the humble suitor gives me a flash of a bent figure, the only clear part of which is the bowed back, though at times there are hands held deprecatingly before the absent face. A great many of these sketches are irrelevant and accessory; but they often are, and they always may be, the vehicles of a logical meaning. The stately form that steps through the French window to the lawn may be clothed in all the colours of the rainbow; but its stateliness is the

hand on the grey skirt. I shall not multiply
instances. All this description must be either
self-evident or as unreal as a fairy-tale.[14]

It leads us, however, to a very important
question,—the old question of the possibility of
abstract or general ideas. You will recall the
main heads of the controversy. Locke had maintained that it is possible to form the general
idea, say, of a triangle which is "neither oblique
nor rectangle, neither equilateral, equicrural, nor
scalenon; but all and none of these at once."[15]
Berkeley replied that "if any man has the faculty
of framing in his mind such an idea of a triangle,
as is here described, it is in vain to pretend to
dispute him out of it, nor would I go about it. . . .
For myself, I find indeed I have a faculty of
imagining, or representing to myself, the ideas
of those particular things I have perceived, and
of variously compounding and dividing them,
. . . [but] I cannot by any effort of thought
conceive the abstract idea described above. . . .
The idea of man that I frame to myself must be
either of a white, or a black, or a tawny, a
straight, or a crooked, a tall, or a low, or a
middle-sized man."[16] The dispute has lasted
down to our own day. Hamilton calls the
Lockean doctrine a 'revolting absurdity.'[17]
Huxley finds it entirely acceptable. "An anat-

omist who occupies himself intently with the examination of several specimens of some new kind of animal, in course of time acquires so vivid a conception of its form and structure, that the idea may take visible shape and become a sort of waking dream. But the figure which thus presents itself is generic, not specific. It is no copy of any one specimen, but, more or less, a mean of the series,"[18]—a composite photograph of the whole group.

All through this discussion there runs, unfortunately, the confusion of logic and psychology that is characteristic of the English school. It is no more correct to speak, in psychology, of an abstract idea, or a general idea, than it would be to speak of an abstract sensation or a general sensation. What is abstract and general is not the idea, the process in consciousness, but the logical meaning of which that process is the vehicle. All that we can say of the idea is that it comprises such and such qualities; shows these and these temporal and spatial characters; has a certain degree of vividness as focal or marginal, clear or obscure; has the vague haziness of distant sounds and faint lights or the clean-cut definiteness of objects to which the sense-organ is accommodated; is arranged on a particular pattern.[19] Locke and Huxley, now, believed

that abstract meaning is represented in consciousness by abstract or composite imagery;
Berkeley and the other Nominalists believed that
imagery is always individual and concrete, and
that abstract meaning is accordingly represented
by the abstract term, the general name.[20]   But
here is no alternative for psychology.   Imagery
might be strictly reproductive in form, and yet—
for a certain type of mental constitution—be the
psychological equivalent of an abstract meaning;
and, again, imagery might be vague and indefinite, and yet be the psychological equivalent of
an individual, particular meaning.   The issue, in
its psychological formulation, is an issue of fact.
Is wordless imagery, under any circumstances,
the mental representative of meaning?   And if
it is, do we find a correlation of vague imagery
with abstract and of definite imagery with particular meaning?

The first of these questions I have already
answered, for my own case, in the affirmative.
In large measure I think, that is, I mean and I
understand, in visual pictures.   The second question I cannot answer in the affirmative.   I doubt
whether particularity or abstractness of meaning has anything essentially to do with the degree
of definiteness of my images.   The mental vision
of the incoming tide, which I described at the

beginning of this Lecture, is no more definite when it recalls an afternoon's ramble than when it means the progress of science. We must, above all things, distinguish between attentional clearness and intrinsic clearness of definition, —sharpness, precision, cognitive clearness. A process may be transversing the very centre of consciousness, and therefore from the point of view of a psychology of attention may be maximally clear: yet it may be so weak, so brief, so instable, that its whole character is vague and indefinite. In my own experience, attentional clearness seems to be the one thing needful to qualify a process for meaning. Whether the picture as picture is sharply outlined and highly coloured is a matter of indifference.

Come back now to the authorities: to Locke's triangle and Huxley's composite animal. My own picture of the triangle, the image that means triangle to me, is usually a fairly definite outline of the little triangular figure that stands for the word 'triangle' in the geometries. But I can quite well get Locke's picture, the triangle that is no triangle and all triangles at one and the same time. It is a flashy thing, come and gone from moment to moment: it hints two or three red angles, with the red lines deepening into black, seen on a dark green ground. It is not

there long enough for me to say whether the
angles join to form the complete figure, or even
whether all three of the necessary angles are
given.   Nevertheless, it means triangle; it is
Locke's general idea of triangle; it is Hamilton's
palpable absurdity made real.   And the composite animal?   Well, the composite animal
strikes me as somewhat too even, too nicely bal-
anced.   No doubt, the idea in Huxley's mind
was of that kind; he, as an anatomist, was interested to mark all the parts and proportions of
the creatures before him.[21]   But my own ideas
of animals are sketchier and more selective: horse
is, to me, a double curve and a rampant posture
with a touch of mane about it; cow is a longish
rectangle with a certain facial expression, a sort
of exaggerated pout.   Again, however, these
things mean horse and cow, are the psychological
vehicles of those logical meanings.

And what holds of triangle and horse and cow
holds of all the "unpicturable notions of intelligence."[22]   No one of them is unpicturable, if you
do but have the imaginal mind.   "It is impossible," remarks a recent writer, "to ideate a meaning; one can only know it."[23]   Impossible?   But
I have been ideating meanings all my life.   And
not only meanings, but meaning also.   Meaning
in general is represented in my consciousness by

another of these impressionist pictures. I see
meaning as the blue-grey tip of a kind of scoop,
which has a bit of yellow above it (probably a
part of the handle), and which is just digging
into a dark mass of what appears to be plastic material. I was educated on classical lines; and it
is conceivable that this picture is an echo of the
oft-repeated admonition to 'dig out the meaning' of some passage of Greek or Latin. I do
not know; but I am sure of the image. And I
am sure that others have similar images. I put
the question not long since to the members of my
graduate seminary, and two of the twelve students present at once gave an affirmative answer.
The one reported the mental unrolling of a white
scroll: what he actually saw was a whitish lump
or mass, flattened and flattening towards the
right. The other reported a horizontal line, with
two short verticals at a little distance from the
two ends. The suggestion in these two cases is
plain enough: meaning is something that you
find by straightening things out, or it is something that is included or contained in things.
There was, however, no such suggestion in the
minds of my informants: for them, as for me,
the mental representation of meaning is a simple
datum, natural and ultimate.[24]

I have dwelt at some length upon this visualisation of meanings because the point in dispute is of great importance, historically and systematically, and because visual imagery offers, so to say, the most substantial materials for its discussion. Let me repeat, however, that my mind, the mind which I am trying to describe to you, is by no means exclusively, is not even predominantly, of the visual type. I have, as I have said, a great deal of auditory imagery; I have also a great deal of kinæsthetic imagery. The former needs no further discussion, since it plays no active part in my thinking; but I must speak briefly of kinæsthesis.

As recently as 1904 I was not sure whether or not I possessed free kinæsthetic images.[25] I could not decide whether my kinæsthetic memories were imaginal, or whether they involved an actual reinstatement, in weaker form, of the original sensations. I had no criterion by which to distinguish the sensation from the image. However, as so often happens, I had hardly recorded my difficulty when the criterion was found: a ground of distinction so simple, that one wonders why there should have been any difficulty at all. It may be roughly phrased in the statement that actual movement always brings into play more muscles than are necessary, while ideal movement is confined to the precise group of muscles concerned. You will notice the difference at once—provided that you have kinæsthetic images—if you compare an actual nod of the head with the mental nod that signifies assent to an argument, or the actual frown and wrinkling of the forehead with the mental frown that signifies perplexity. The sensed nod and frown are coarse and rough in outline; the imaged nod and frown are cleanly and delicately traced.[26] I do not say, of course, that this is the sole difference between the two modes of experience. On the contrary, now that it has become clear, I seem to find that the kinæsthetic image and the kinæsthetic sensation differ in all essential respects precisely as visual image differs from visual sensation. But I think it is a dependable difference, and one that offers a good starting point for further analysis.

We shall recur to this kinæsthetic imagery in a later Lecture. All that I have to remark now is that the various visual images, which I have referred to as possible vehicles of logical meaning, oftentimes share their task with kinæsthesis. Not only do I see gravity and modesty and pride and courtesy and stateliness, but I feel or act them in the mind's muscles. This is, I suppose, a simple case of empathy, if we may coin that term as a rendering of *Einfühlung*; there is nothing curious or idiosyncratic about it; but it is a fact that must be mentioned. And further: just as the visual image may mean of itself, without kinæsthetic accompaniment, so may the kinæsthetic image occur and mean of itself, without assistance from vision. I represent the meaning of affirmation, for instance, by the image of a little nick felt at the back of the neck,—an experience which, in sensation, is complicated by pressures and pulls from the scalp and throat.[27]

II

I said at the outset that I should confess my constitutional bias; and if you were now asked to name that bias, you would doubtless agree that a mind which thinks in the manner described must have a strong leaning toward sensationalism. I do not think that such a tendency is matter for praise or blame, is anything to be proud or ashamed of; it is a natural fact. What I would ask you to remember, however, is this: that the constitutionally impartial mind does not exist, or at any rate is infinitely rare. Every one of us has his natural inclinations to overcome; and if I lean towards sensationalism, why, the imageless minds, the minds of the extreme verbal type, lean just as strongly in the opposite direction. A critic will often begin—fairly enough—

by charging his author with bias, but will then proceed to state his own views in complete unconsciousness of a very robust counter-bias. Well! it is from the clash of these individual psychologies that a generalised psychology of thought must arise. The individual psychologist can avoid misrepresentation and unfair imputation; to that extent he can and must achieve impartiality; but he cannot wholly transcend the limits of his mental constitution. Philosophy itself, we have recently been told, is in no negligible degree a question of temperament.

I am ready, then, to acknowledge a tendency toward sensationalism, if that is the logical inference from my mental type. But it is important to know precisely what the sensationalism of experimental psychology connotes. Otherwise, we shall be unable to trace its consequences, and we shall be in danger of reading into it historical implications, perhaps of an epistemological sort, which are entirely foreign to its psychological meaning.

Sensationalism is succinctly defined, in Baldwin's *Dictionary,* as "the theory that all knowledge originates in sensations; that all cognitions, even reflective ideas and so-called intuitions, can be traced back to elementary sensations."[28]   It is thus, primarily, a theory of the origin of knowledge, not a theory of the genesis of thought. "Historically,"—the *Dictionary* continues,—"it is generally combined with Associationalism." Turning to Associationism, in the same work, we find the following definition: "The theory which, starting with certain simple and ultimate constituents of consciousness, makes mental development consist solely or mainly in the combination of these elements according to certain laws of association. According to this theory, rigidly carried out, all genesis of new products is due to the combination of pre-existing elements."[29] Here is psychological formulation. But it would be a great mistake, though it is a mistake not seldom made, to confuse the sensationalism of experimental psychology with the doctrine of associationism. Let us see wherein the two kinds of sensationalism differ.

In the first place, the associationists did not distinguish the theory of knowledge from the theory of thought. "The British thinkers of the past"—I am quoting from a British thinker of the present—"were far from keeping their psychology unadulterated. . . . They gave us, in general, psychology and philosophy inextricably intermingled." "Their work often shows a crossing of interests and of points of view. Questions of logic and theory of knowledge were mixed up

with the more properly psychological inquiry."[30]
In fact, the associationists dealt, on principle,
with logical meanings; not with sensations, but
with sensations-of; not with ideas, but with
ideas-of; it is only incidentally that they leave
the plane of meaning for the plane of existence.
The experimentalists, on the other hand, aim to
describe the contents of consciousness not as they
mean but as they are. An admirable illustration
of this change of standpoint is furnished by the
doctrine of association itself. We were formerly
taught that the idea of Napoleon calls up the
idea of Julius Cæsar because both men were
great generals: it is a case of association by similarity; and that the idea of church calls up the
idea of state because the two ideas have often
been conjoined in experience: it is a case of association by contiguity. But when Ebbinghaus
began the experimental study of memory and
association, he chose as his materials nonsense-
syllables, verbal forms that lacked verbal meaning, contents that presented themselves simply
as existential. These syllables, he points out, are
qualitatively simple and homogeneous: "out of
many thousand combinations of letters there are
only a dozen or two that make sense, and of these
again there are only a few that arouse the
thought of their sense or meaning during the

process of learning"; and they are also quantita-
tively variable, "whereas to break off before the
end or to begin in the middle of a verse or a
sentence entails manifold disturbances of the
sense and so introduces all sorts of complica-
tions."³¹   It is, indeed, these nonsense-syllables
that have mainly helped us to our present knowledge of the mechanics of reproduction.   You
may roughly measure the advance by comparing
Ebbinghaus' chapter on *Die Aufeinanderfolge
der seelischen Gebilde* with Bain's chapters on
Intellect.   I do not say, of course, that experimental psychology ignores meaning; in so far
as meaning is a phase or aspect of conscious
contents, it is taken account of; but it is taken
account of *sub specie existentiæ.*   And where
existence is the form to be considered, we sim-
plify our task and hasten our progress by select-
ing, as the first materials of experiment, contents
to which that form is natural and adequate.³²

Locke's ideas, then, and James Mill's ideas,
were meanings, thought-tokens, bits of knowledge; the sensations and ideas of modern
psychology are *Erlebnisse,* data of immediate
experience.   And the change of standpoint
brings with it a second principal difference
between the older and the newer sensationalism.
Meanings are stable, and may be discussed with-

out reference to time; so that a psychology whose elements are meanings is an atomistic psychology; the elements join, like blocks of mosaic, to give static formations, or connect, like the links of a chain, to give discrete series. But experience is continuous and a function of time; so that a psychology whose elements are sensations, in the modern sense of the term, is a process-psychology, innocent both of mosaic and of concatenation. This is a point which Wundt, the father of experimental psychology, never tires of emphasizing. In a well-known passage, in which he is appraising the value of the experimental method for his own psychological development, he says: "I learned from it that the 'idea' must be regarded as a process, no less variable and transitory than a feeling or a volition; and I saw that, for that reason, the old doctrine of association is no longer tenable."[33] And again, in protesting against the hypostatisation of ideas, he writes: "The ideas themselves are not objects, as by confusion with their objects they are supposed to be, but they are occurrences, *Ereignisse,* that grow and decay and during their brief passage are in constant change."[34] Now I dare say that you have heard or read dozens of statements to this effect. What I want you to do, however, and what I want some of our philosophical critics to do, is to realise what the statements mean; to realise that those who do their business in the laboratories are always operating and observing in terms of process. The realisation is not quite easy: first, because language is discontinuous, and our descriptions must substitute a word-mosaic for the moving pictures of experience; and secondly, because the terms which we are obliged to use for these descriptions are already stamped as meanings by their use in previous systems. Even so modern a psychologist as James has not worked out to entire clearness in this matter. In his chapter on *The Stream of Thought* he speaks, you will remember, of the varying rate at which successive psychoses shade gradually into one another. "When the rate is slow," he goes on, "we are aware of the object of our thought in a comparatively restful and stable way. When rapid, we are aware of a passage, a relation, a transition *from* it, or *between* it and something else." Consciousness, "like a bird's life, seems to be made up of an alternation of flights and perchings." So he distinguishes the substantive from the transitive parts of the stream of thought. "Now it is very difficult, introspectively, to see the transitive parts for what they really are. . . . The rush of the thought is so headlong that it

almost always brings us up at the conclusion
before we can arrest it. . . . The attempt at
introspective analysis in these cases is in fact like
seizing a spinning top to catch its motion, or trying to turn up the gas quickly enough to see how
the darkness looks."[35] But is there not here a
confusion between what is transitive in function
and what is transient in experience? Does it
not often happen that the flight is steadier and
lasts longer than the perching? I think that a
good deal of the mystery which attaches to the
feelings of 'if' and 'but' is due to sheer confusion
of logical meaning and psychological process, of
transitive and transitory. The conditioning and
the excepting consciousnesses may, in fact, move
more slowly than the object-consciousnesses to
which they refer. And if James had looked
away from 'awareness of object' and 'awareness
of relation,' and had looked toward the actual
contents of consciousness, we should not have
heard of the top and the gas-jet. Contrast, for
instance, his treatment of the 'feeling of the
central active self.' "It is difficult for me to
detect in the activity any purely spiritual element
at all. Whenever my introspective glance suc-
ceeds in turning round quickly enough to catch
one of these manifestations of spontaneity in
the act, all it can ever feel distinctly is some bod-

ily process, for the most part taking place within the head."[36]   Why cannot the introspective glance do as much for the feelings of relation?

But we must return for a moment to associationism. I said that the psychology of meanings left us with mosaic arrangements or with discrete series. You may reply that this characterisation is unfair. James Mill speaks, for instance, of the coalescence of ideas: "where two or more ideas have been repeated together, and the association has become very strong, they sometimes spring up in such close combination as not to be distinguishable"; the idea of weight—to take a single illustration—involves the ideas of resistance and direction and the "feeling or feelings denominated Will," and resistance and direction are themselves compounded of simpler ideas.[37] And John Mill writes, in the same spirit: "When impressions have been so often experienced in conjunction that each of them calls up readily and instantaneously the ideas of the whole group, those ideas sometimes melt and coalesce into one another, and appear not several ideas, but one, in the same manner as, when the seven prismatic colours are presented to the eye in rapid succession, the sensation produced is that of white. . . . These therefore are cases of mental chemistry, in which it is proper to say that the simple ideas generate, rather than that they compose, the complex ones." That is from the *Logic*.[38] There is a similar passage in the *Examination of Sir William Hamilton's Philosophy:* "If anything similar to this [that is, to colour mixture] obtains in our consciousness generally (and that it obtains in many cases of consciousness there can be no doubt) it will follow that whenever the organic modifications of our nervous fibres succeed one another at an interval shorter than the duration of the sensations or other feelings corresponding to them, those sensations or feelings will, so to speak, overlap one another, and becoming simultaneous instead of successive, will blend into a state of feeling, probably as unlike the elements out of which it is engendered as the colour of white is unlike the prismatic colours."[39] It seems to me, however, that associationism has here fallen out of the frying-pan into the fire. The principle of association, which was to be in the world of mind what the principle of gravitation is in the world of matter,—"Here is a kind of attraction," said Hume, "which in the mental world will be found to have as extraordinary effects as in the natural, and to show itself in as many and as various forms,"[40]—this principle has broken down, and composition has been supplemented by generation, mechanical mixture by chemical combination. I see no gain; I see rather an equal misunderstanding of chemistry and of psychology.[41] It is, however, a misunderstanding which has been fruitful of bad consequences, and of which we are not yet wholly free. I believe, nevertheless, that experimental psychology has, in the main, transcended the doctrine of mental chemistry. Colour mixture— the illustration chosen by the two Mills and before them by Hartley[42]—is, as we all know, not a mixture of visual sensations, but the sensory resultant of the interplay of excitatory processes in the retina. That is a minor matter. But, in general, we have better means than a false chemical analogy for explaining what cannot be explained in terms of a straightforward associationism. We have learned, for instance, to make allowance for complication of conditions; we do not expect, if two sensations are put together, to obtain a simple concurrence of their two qualities; we expect that the synergy of the underlying physiological processes will, in some way, become manifest in consciousness. We may speak of general attributes of sensation, as Ebbinghaus does; or we may speak of *Gestaltqualität,* form of combination, funded character; or we may speak of the organisation of elements in the state of attention. Different systems deal with the facts in different ways, and one psychologist entertains possibilities that another rejects; but at all events there is no need of a mental chemistry. We have learned, again, that physiological conditions may produce their effect not within but upon consciousness; that nervous sets and tendencies may direct the course of conscious processes without setting up new and special processes of their own. We have learned, also, that such formations as perception and action can be understood only in the light of their history and development; the life of mind is, throughout, subject to a law of growth and decay, of gradual expansion and gradual reduction; what is now, so to say, a mere tag or label upon a dominant formation may, a little while ago, have been itself a focal complex, and the formation to which it attaches may, a little while hence, sink to the parasitic level. We have all this knowledge, and much more, to supplement what we know of the mechanics of reproduction, the modern substitute for the laws of association; and there is, surely, good hope that we may work out a psychology of thought without taking any such leap in the dark as John Mill took when he added generation to composition.—

I have mentioned two principal differences between the older and the newer sensationalism.

3

The experimental psychologist deals with existences, and not with meanings; and his elements
are processes, whose temporal course is of their
very nature, and not substances, solid and resist-
ant to the lapse of time.   These differences
illustrate, as they follow from, the more fundamental difference of general attitude.   Current
sensationalism is a result to which we are led by
empirical analysis, and its sensations are simple
processes abstracted from conscious experience,
last terms in the psychological study of mind.
The associationism of the English school is a
preconceived theory, and its sensations are,
accordingly, productive and generative elements,
first terms in a logical construction of mind.
Associationism, in other words, puts sensations
together, as physical atoms or chemical molecules,
while modern psychology finds sensations together in the given mental process.

This wider consideration brings us now to a
third principal difference between the two stand-
points which we are comparing.   The sensationalism of modern psychology is simply an heuristic
principle, accepted and applied for what it is
worth in the search for the mental elements,—
whereas the older sensationalism, just because it
was a preconceived theory, required that the facts
conform to it, whether they would or whether

they would not. The *Dictionary* from which we have already quoted defines the 'composition theory' of mind as "the hypothesis that our mental states are the resultant of the varied combinations of certain primitive elements. In its extreme form it assumes that the ultimate units of composition are all of one kind."[43] I suppose that the older sensationalism is, strictly, an extreme form of this theory; that the units which it postulates should all be sensations or the ideal derivatives of sensations. James Mill is, then, only playing the rules of the game when he speaks of pleasure and pain as sensations, and of desire and aversion as the ideas of these sensations.[44] But, in this matter of the affective processes, the majority of present-day psychologists have abandoned the strict letter of sensationalism; they have placed pleasantness and unpleasantness under a separate rubric. No doubt, there are some who, for psychological reasons, identify feeling with sensation. The demand for that identification comes, however, in its most insistent guise, from the outside,— from physiology and philosophy. I wish that I had time and occasion to speak of our debt to physiology, a debt which, in this sphere of sensation, is especially heavy. But it is clear that the physiologists themselves have had no need of more than a popular psychology, the mixture of faculty-psychology and associationism that passes as common sense; if they psychologise on their own behalf, they do so in terms of the organs of sense and the sensory and associational areas of the cortex; and sensationalism appears to them to be both logical and adequate.[45]   The philosophers, the theorists of knowledge, are concerned with the presuppositions of science, which it is their task to classify and to criticise; naturally, then, they lay greater stress upon formal consistency than the psychologist dares or can afford to do.[46]   For the actual problem before psychology is, not the discovery of sensations, but the disentanglement of the mental elements.

What I wish you to remember, therefore, in this third place, is that sensationalism is an heuristic principle and not a creed.   If modern psychology is to be termed sensationalistic, that is not because it is wedded to sensation.   It must mean simply that psychology prefers to work with as few tools as possible, and that sensation alone, or sensation and affection together, seem to give it all that it requires for the work of analysis. Wundt, for example, will hear nothing of a thought-element; his whole psychology, including the psychology of thought, is based upon these two elementary processes; and yet, if we were classifying systems, we should place him rather with the voluntarists than with the sensationalists.[47] Could there be stronger evidence for the point that I am urging?

In fine, then, experimental psychology tries to save what is psychological from associationism on the one hand and from physiological sensationalism on the other. Associationism it transforms and reinterprets from beginning to end. It accepts from physiology the view that sensations are the outcome of analysis, while it rejects or modifies the concrete form in which the view is presented, the naïve doctrine of psychical cells and organs and centres. It saves what it can, and adds only where it must; and for this obedience to the law of parsimony it pays a price, the price of that mistaken and undeserved criticism which confuses the new with the old. But, on the whole, it finds its account in the saving. And if you will avoid the confusion, and are prepared to agree that the position to-day is, in general, as I have described it, then I am ready on my side to plead guilty to a 'sensationalistic' bias.

LECTURE II

'REFERENCE TO OBJECT' AS THE
CRITERION OF MIND

LECTURE II

I MAINTAINED, in the preceding Lecture, that it is possible to ideate a meaning,—that the meaning, say, of the word 'animal' may be given, psychologically, as a visual image which appears before the mind's eye when the word is presented. This doctrine, now, is open to an obvious objection. 'Your word and your visual image,' a critic might say, 'are simply two ideas, two items of experience regarded, to use your own phrase, under the form of existence. But two existences do not make a meaning. You have only pushed the problem of meaning a step further back, from presented word to imaged animal; you have still to show how the image itself can mean. As a matter of fact, meaning consists in reference, reference to the object of thought or of idea; and this reference, as an author whom you cited very rightly said, can be known, but certainly cannot be imaged.'

But, indeed, I need not quote an imaginary critic; I can take the objection, bodily, from a recent article. Let me read a few sentences.

"The fundamental problem of meaning [is] the relation of sign to thing signified, the 'objective reference'
of the sign.   There are passages in Professor James'
Psychology in which he says explicitly that the objective reference of the sign *consists* in its psychic fringe.
. . .   [But] so long as the fringe is merely a psychical
fact or occurrence, it seems nonsense to say that it *is* the
meaning of another psychical occurrence.   It amounts
to saying that the meaning of a sign is to be found in
other signs.   But where, then, is the 'thing signified?' "[1]

I have no wish to slur this objection. I believe, in spite of it, that two ideas do, under
certain circumstances, make a meaning; and I
shall try, later on, to specify the circumstances.
In the meantime, however, it seems necessary to
consider this question of 'objective reference.'
And I think we cannot do better than go direct
to those psychologists who make reference to an
object the criterion of mind, the character that
distinguishes the mental from the physical, and
whose classification of mental phenomena depends accordingly upon the various forms that
objective reference may take.

I

I begin with Brentano. If you turn to the
table of contents of the *Psychologie vom empirischen Standpunkte,* you will find a section entitled "Characteristisch für die psychischen

Phänomene ist die Beziehung auf ein Object,"
—characteristic of psychical phenomena is their
reference to an object. The phrase is ambiguous,
and 'reference to an object' does not mean
what, at first thought, you would suppose it to
mean. Read, for instance, Brentano's summary
of the most notable essays towards a classification of mental phenomena that have been made
in the history of psychology. They are four in
number: three of them we owe to Aristotle, the
fourth to Spencer and Bain. The last-mentioned
authorities divide mental phenomena into two
great groups, as primitive and derivative. The
Aristotelian classifications distinguish, first, psychoses that are and psychoses that are not connected with bodily processes; and secondly,
psychoses that are shared by man with the animals, and psychoses that are peculiar to man.
The remaining principle of classification, "which
at all times has found wide-spread application,"
distinguishes mental phenomena by differences
in the mode of their intentional inexistence.[2]
Since it is this fourth principle that Brentano
himself accepts, we shall find in it the meaning
of that 'reference to an object' which for him
characterises mental phenomena at large. What,
then, is this 'intentional inexistence' ?

"Every psychical phenomenon," Brentano

says, "is characterised by what the scholastics
of the Middle Age have termed the intentional
. . . inexistence of an object, and what we
should term . . . reference to a content,
direction upon an object ('object' not meaning
here a 'reality'), or immanent objectivity. All
alike contain within them something as their
object, although they do not all contain the object in the same way. In idea something is
ideated, in judgment something is accepted or
rejected, in love something is loved, in hate hated,
in desire desired, and so on. This intentional
inexistence is the exclusive property of psychical phenomena. No physical phenomenon
shows anything like it. And we may accordingly define psychical phenomena by saying that
they are phenomena which intentionally contain
an object."[3] In other words, the 'object' to
which a mental phenomenon refers is not an
object in the outside world, a physical object in
our sense,—though Brentano would make it a
physical phenomenon,—but rather what we
should term a mental content. Brentano splits
up idea, judgment, interest, into act and content: the act is psychical, the content physical.
"I understand by idea not that which is ideated
[the content of the idea], but the act of ideation.
Thus, the hearing of a tone, the seeing of a

coloured object, the sensing of warm or cold,
[these are psychical phenomena; whereas] a
colour ... that I see, a chord that I hear, warmth,
cold, odour that I sense, these are examples of
physical phenomena."[4] We shall therefore do
well to avoid so far as possible, the use of the
word 'object,' and to speak of the psychical
phenomenon as evincing the distinction of act
and content.

What shall we say to a view of this kind?
Well, our first question may very properly be
the question of the universality of the alleged
criterion. All psychical phenomena, says Brentano, show this immanent objectivity. Now listen
to Hamilton. "In the phenomena of cognition,
consciousness distinguishes an object from the
subject knowing. This object may be of two
kinds:—it may either be the quality of something
different from the ego [object-object]; or it
may be a modification of the ego or subject
itself [subject-object] . . . This objectification is the quality which constitutes the essential
peculiarity of Cognition. In the phenomena of
Feeling, . . . on the contrary, consciousness does
not place the mental modification or state before
itself; it does not contemplate it apart,—as separate from itself,—but is, as it were fused into
one. The peculiarity of Feeling, therefore, is

that there is nothing but what is subjectively
subjective; there is no . . . objectification of any
mode of self."[5] In Feeling, then, in Pleasure
and Pain or, as we should say, in pleasantness
and unpleasantness, we have, according to Hamilton, psychical phenomena that are not analysable into act and content. If the exception stands,
Brentano's criterion is invalid.

Brentano replies,[6] first, that certain feelings
do, unmistakably, refer to a content, and that
language indicates this reference. I am glad
about something, I am pleased at something, I
am sorry for something. Joy and sorrow, like
affirmation and negation, love and hate, desire
and aversion, follow in the train of an idea and
refer to the content of that idea. But secondly,
even where the reference is not immediately evident, as in the experience of a cut or a burn,
there is still something more than mere pain (that
is, unpleasantness) in consciousness. We say:
I have burned my hand, I have cut my finger;
spatial localisation is involved, the idea of a
definite locality. Indeed, there is more than
that. Just as act and content are implied whenever I say: I see a colour, I hear a tone, so precisely are act and content implied when I say: I
feel pain, or I feel pleasure. The cut or burn
or tickle is given as content, as a physical phe-

nomenon, and the concomitant feeling, the psychical phenomenon, can be distinguished from it
by any but the most superficial observer. Feeling, then, always has a content.

It is, however, true, thirdly, that the content
to which a feeling refers need not be a physical
phenomenon. When I listen to a consonant
chord, the pleasure that I feel is not so much a
pleasure in the tones as a pleasure in hearing.
"Indeed, one might perhaps say, and be right in
saying, that the pleasure in a certain sense really
refers to itself, so that Hamilton is more or less
accurately describing what happens when he declares that, in feeling, consciousness is fused into
one." This is a rather puzzling statement; but
we get light upon it if we turn to Brentano's
psychology of cognition. Consider what is
meant, in Brentano's system, by a pleasure in
hearing. It is act of act: a psychical phenomenon takes, as its content, not a physical but another psychical phenomenon. Can, then, an act
be the content of another act? Yes: Brentano
saves himself from the infinite regress of psychical phenomena by the hypothesis that, for
example, the idea of a tone (act and content),
and the idea of that idea (act and act), and the
idea of the idea of that idea (act and act and
act), and so on, are given together in an *eigen-*

thümliche Verwebung, a peculiar interweaving,
—Hamilton's fusion: the single act of ideation
has as its content both the physical phenomenon
of tone and itself, the act of ideation, once or
oftener repeated.[7]   So pleasure may be pleasure's own content; and, if so, feeling will always
be a phenomenon of the subjective-objective, and
not of the subjectively subjective sort.   Besides,
—here Brentano again resumes the aggressive,—
the term 'subjectively subjective' is, after all,
self-contradictory; for if you have no object,
then you have no right to speak of a subject.
And when Hamilton affirms that, in feeling,
consciousness is fused into one, he is really bear-
ing testimony against his own position.   To get
a fusion, you must have at least two things to
fuse; and the two things are, naturally, Brentano's act and content.

Hamilton's objection has been met; but I
question if it has been satisfactorily met.   Suppose that an affective process may stand alone
in consciousness, without basis or accompaniment
of sensation.   Külpe believes that such a state
of things is possible: "we have feelings which
are not accompanied by or attached to definite
sensations, or which arise where the nervous conditions of sensation are debarred from the
exercise of their ordinary influence on con-

sciousness."[8] Ladd asserts that "the feelings may assume either one of the three possible time-relations towards the sensations and ideas by which we classify them; they may fuse with them in the 'now' of the same conscious state, or they may lead or follow them."[9] Wundt also believes that the affective process may enter consciousness alone, as the herald of the sensory process with which it is connected.[10] Suppose, then, that this is the case. Is there any reason for saying that the isolated pleasantness is the pleasantness of a pleasantness, or the isolated unpleasantness the unpleasantness of an unpleasantness? Surely there is none,—unless it be that you have to save a theory. Surely, it is the theory that reads the fusion and the interweaving into what appears, introspectively, as an unanalysable experience. I am not defending Hamilton's terminology, you see; I think, indeed, that the less we hear in psychology of subject and object, the better for us and for the science. But I argue that, if the separate occurrence of affective processes is a fact of observation, as Külpe and Ladd and Wundt testify that it is, then a valid exception has been found to Brentano's definition of the psychical. We are in presence of a psychical phenomenon that is, so to say, all act, and has no content.

However, I am forced to go farther. I do not discover, in my own case, that affective processes can stand alone in consciousness.[11] And as there are psychologists who agree with me, I feel constrained to leave the question open, and to consider Brentano's position on its merits. My fundamental objection to it may at this point be stated very briefly as follows: I think that a psychological fact, a datum of observation, has been cast, by reflection, into logical form; and I think that, here as everywhere, the interjection of logic has been detrimental to psychology. I come back to this matter later on. In the meantime I notice that Brentano himself, who, as you will remember, declares that the principle of immanent objectivity "has at all times found widespread application" in attempts at classification,—I am not now discussing whether this statement is right or wrong,—Brentano himself shows that it has led to very different results in different hands.[12] Aristotle was satisfied to distinguish thought and desire; the moderns have adopted the threefold division into idea, feeling and appetition; Brentano throws feeling and desire into the single category of interest, and recognises judgment as an ultimate form of psychosis alongside of idea. Changes of this sort seem dictated rather by convenience of logi-

cal arrangement than by direct reference to experience. It is true that Brentano appeals, even
more confidently than I am inclined to do, to
the 'immediate evidence of introspection' and
the 'judgment of the impartial observer.'[13] This
is the way of all psychologists when they are in
straits for an argument, and you must not lay
too great stress upon either side of the contention:
the experimental technique for the study of judgment, in particular, has not yet been perfected.
But I call your attention to two further points.
The first is, that Brentano has not yet published his second volume. Since the volume that
we have dates from 1874, it is only fair to suppose that its author found it difficult to complete
his system on the principles adopted at its incep-
tion. The second is, that Brentano's arguments
in favor of his criterion are couched in terms
which themselves imply that criterion. "Let us
suppose," he says, "that hearing has no other
content than itself. Still, no one could make the
same assumption with regard to other psychical
acts, such as the acts of recollection and expectation,—the recollection of a past or the expectation of a future hearing,—without committing
himself to the most obvious absurdity."[14] The
phrase 'hearing has no other content than itself' is intended to represent the views of those

who, like James Mill,* draw no distinction of
act and content. I do not think, however, that
this position is fairly represented by the statement that 'hearing has no other content than
itself'; Mill's words have been translated into the
language of a foreign theory; and it is only
through the translation that Brentano's parallel
of present hearing with the recollection of a past
and the expectation of a future hearing becomes
relevant. "In themselves," remarks John Mill,
"[memories and expectations] . . . are present
feelings, states of present consciousness, and in
that respect not distinguished from sensations."[15]
Precisely! If you take a memory-consciousness
and an expectation-consciousness as they are
given existentially to psychology, you find no
more reason to distinguish act and content in
them than you find in the case of sensation.†—

All that I have said, so far, may be summed

---

* Mill takes as illustration the prick of a pin. "Now, when,
having the sensation, I say I feel the sensation, I only use a
tautological expression: the sensation is not one thing, the feeling
another; the sensation is the feeling. . . . The same explanation
will easily be seen to apply to Ideas. . . . To have an idea, and
[to have] the feeling of that idea, are not two things; they are
one and the same thing." That is explicit: and, in his section on
Hearing, Mill is careful to point out the ambiguity of the term,
and insists that hearing, as 'the feeling I have by the ear,' is
'the sensation called a sound.'

† It is true that John Mill at once loses himself in the epistemological difficulty of "a series of feelings which is aware of
itself as past and future"; I have said that this confusion of

up in a few words. I take the act-and-content
psychology to be a psychology not of observation
but of reflection. I note that it has led, in different hands, to very different classificatory systems.
I think that Brentano found a difficulty in car-
rying it over from the general to the particular.
And I regard his criticism of the opposing standpoint as unfair, because it implies throughout
the very distinction which is in dispute. It would
be satisfactory, now, if we could find a psychology which, without entering upon controversial
ground, set forth the principles and the facts
of the science in accordance with Brentano's
criterion; the issue would then be narrowed down
to that of observation and reflection, and we
could compare the exposition, as a whole, with
that which we have, for instance, in Külpe's
Outlines or in Ebbinghaus' *Grundzüge.*

Such a work we find, in fact, in Witasek's
Grundlinien der Psychologie, published last year,

psychology with philosophy is characteristic of the English school.
But that does not affect the correctness of the psychological position from which he starts. On the other hand, I am not sure that
his present co-partner in the confusion, Brentano, is not open to
the further charge of psychological confusion, of confusion within
the limits of his own definition of the psychical. I am not sure
that Brentano's parallel of act of memory and act of expectation
with act of idea can be admitted, even by a psychologist who
accepts the act-and-content criterion; both the nature of the act
itself and the relation which it sustains to content appear to be
widely different in the two cases.

—a compact and thoughtful little book, of which
I should be glad to say pleasant things; but with
which I am here concerned only under a single
aspect, and from whose teaching in that especial
regard I dissent. Witasek does not, as Brentano
does, make immanent objectivity the criterion
of mind; but he asserts that all the fundamental psychical formations, the *psychischen
Grundgebilde*, show, "at least in a certain sense,"
the distinction of act and content. He illustrates
the distinction by reference to idea. There is a
certain part of the constitution of an idea (*Teil
der Beschaffenheiten einer Vorstellung*) by
means of which it brings a determinate object to
consciousness; this is its content. There is also
a certain respect in which an idea resembles all
other ideas but differs from formations, like
feeling and judgment, that are not ideas; a
respect in which, further, one idea differs from
another, idea of perception from idea of imagination. This second part or aspect of the idea is
its act. Content and act are inseparably connected in the idea, and both alike are psychical;
both, therefore, are to be distinguished from the
object of idea, which is usually physical.[16]

My first criticism upon this introductory passage—in what follows I shall combine criticism
with exposition of Witasek's system—is that it

makes the idea the typical, indeed the only full
and complete, mental process.[17]   The fundamental psychical formations are, we are told, of
two kinds, intellectual and emotional.   The intellectual divide again into ideas and thoughts,
the emotional into feelings and desires.[18]   Now
at the beginning of the book, the psychical fact,
the subject-matter of psychology, is defined by
reference to idea, and the other kinds of psychical formation are listed, so to say, in an appendix.[19]   When the distinction of act and content
is first drawn, we are left 'doubtful' whether the
content of feeling, wish, etc., is directly or in-
directly given: given, that is, in the same way
as content of idea is given with act of idea, or
given only secondarily, as something that is already content of idea.[20]   But when we reach the
special psychology of feeling and judgment, the
doubt has disappeared.   "No content is necessarily and by its very nature bound up with the act
of feeling, as content of idea is bound up with
act of idea; . . . the act of feeling is a psychical
formation which brings into consciousness no
new content of its own."[21]   Feeling-content is,
always, ready-made ideational content: "there
are no contents, accompanied by feelings, that
cannot be classified outright as contents of idea."
The same thing holds of judgment.   "In judg-

ment, as in idea, we must distinguish the two moments of act and content; but while the act, which supervenes upon the ideas comprised in the judgment, is something novel and peculiar, the content of judgment is identical with the content of these ideas." Here, it seems to me, we have psychology committed to a sensationalism or an intellectualism that is far more dangerous, because far more closely connected with theory of knowledge, than the laboratory sensationalism of which I spoke in the last Lecture. The idea, let me repeat, is the sole mental process that fulfils the definition of psychical fact; thought and feeling and desire can be brought under the definition only by a change in the meaning of 'content'; intrinsically they are all act, and the content upon which their act is directed is content that has already been brought to consciousness by act of idea. I submit that, other things equal, that psychology will be preferable which refuses thus to prejudice the issue in favour of idea, and which places all mental formations, as psychical facts, upon the same level.

My second criticism is this. If, in every type of conscious process, you distinguish act and content, you have to duplicate your psychology; everything must be treated twice over, from the point of view of act and from the point of view

of content. There is, of course, a certain saying, if all content is ultimately content of idea;
but even so you have to treat of the relation of
the other types of act to this one type of content.
Things thus become very complicated. Why
not, you will say, if the psychical facts themselves
are complicated? Well, I grant that objection;
my criticism lies farther on. It is that the dupli-
cation of treatment leads both to over-articula-
tion and to neglect of analysis. You get too
many headings, and you are too apt to assume
that the processes covered by the headings are
psychologically irreducible. Let me illustrate
by reference to Witasek's psychology of judgment. The act of judgment has, he says, two
characteristic and essential moments: first, the
moment of belief, supposition, conviction, and
secondly the moment of affirmation and negation. But there is a further complication. The
contact (*Berührung*) of ideational content with
the moment of affirmation-negation gives rise
to a new quasi-content, the fact which the judgment affirms or denies, the objective of the judgment. In order, then, to get a psychology of
judgment, we have to distinguish act, content
and object of idea, and twofold act and quasi-
content of judgment. The objective of judgment, like the object of idea, is not strictly

subject-matter for psychology; it is, however, psychologically useful as indicating the way in which the act of judgment 'approaches and connects with' the ideational content of judgment; we are able, for instance, by means of it, to psychologise the difference between the existential and the categorical judgment of the text-books of logic.

Both moments in the act of judgment vary in this matter of contact with contents. There are, further, a qualitative differentiation within the moment of affirmation-negation, and an intensive differentiation within that of conviction. Affirmation and negation are themselves qualitative opposites, connected by qualitative transitional forms, probabilities, which under favourable circumstances are numerically determinable. The mention of probabilities leads us, however, to a third moment or attribute of certain acts of judgment: the attribute of evidence. This may be evidence of certainty, correlated with affirmation and negation, the direct yes and no, or evidence of probability, correlative with some qualitative intermediary between affirmation and negation. I understand that the two probabilities are distinct: that you may have, in the act of judgment, both the affirmation of probability, so to say, and the evidence of probability.

Finally, probability itself—one is reminded of
the White Knight's Song in *Through the Looking Glass!*—is the moment of the objective which
the judgment of probability apprehends.—And
we have still to consider the moment of conviction, which belongs with that of affirmation-negation to the act of judgment. This moment, as
I have just said, is intensively, not qualitatively,
variable; it admits simply of degrees of assurance, from maximal assurance or positive conviction down to zero assurance or to suspense of
judgment. The intensive scale of degrees of
assurance is by no means to be confused with
the qualitative *continuum* of probabilities.—

You will naturally suppose that this account
of Witasek's psychology of judgment is a mere
outline, abstracted from a long chapter in which
the subject is worked out in detail and abundantly illustrated. Not at all! I have given you
the contents of a little less than eight pages.[23] I
think that those pages suffer from over-articu-
lation. I think, also, that their author is too
ready with his acceptance of psychological ultimates. There are the variable modes of approach
of act to contents; there is the qualitatively variable moment of affirmation-negation; there is
the intensively variable moment of conviction;
there is the variable attribute of evidence: there

are all these things, and they are all ultimate
and irreducible. No! I come back to my original
point: this is a psychology of reflection. You
must read for yourselves; especially, you must
assure yourselves that the treatment of judgment is not exceptional, but typical of the book;
you must estimate the system as a whole, and
compare it as a whole with other systems. In my
opinion, it is the artificial product of a wrong
initial attitude; logical construction has fore-
stalled introspective examination.[24]

I said just now, however, when I was treating
of Brentano, that it is a psychological fact, a
datum of observation, that has been thus cast
into logical form. And while I cannot accept
the distinction of act and content, I believe that
the distinction rests upon a truly psychological
foundation, that the logic is the logic of psychology. There are, in a certain sense, a hearing,
a feeling, a thinking, which are distinguishable
from the tone and the pleasure and the thought.
Only, the distinction comes to me, not as that of
act and content, but as that of temporal course
and qualitative specificity of a single process. I
entered a plea, in the last Lecture, for a more
general recognition of the process-character of
mind; and I suggest here that this character is
the psychological key to the problem that Bren-

tano and Witasek seek to solve in terms of act
and content.   The way in which a process runs
its course,—that is its 'act,' that is what constitutes it sensing or feeling or thinking; the
quality which is thus in passage,—that is its 'content,' that is what constitutes it tone or pleasure.
The durational and the qualitative aspects of
mental experience (I use the term 'qualitative'
in the widest possible sense) are discriminable as
aspects, though they are inseparable in fact; and
the psychology of act and content does good
psychological service if we take it to insist that
the discrimination is essential to a complete analysis.   Experimental psychology, I should readily
admit, has not hitherto done its duty by duration.   Nevertheless, we have in the idea of 'process' an instrument of analysis that is adequate
to its task, and that relieves us from the fatal
necessity of asking help from logic.[25]

II

We set out to discuss the views of those psychologists who make objective reference the
criterion of mind, the character that distinguishes
the psychical from the physical.   So far, we have
dealt only with one form of this objective reference,—with immanent objectivity, or the reference of act to content.   We have now to

consider another form, which we may perhaps designate transitive objectivity. "Human consciousness," says Stout, "is normally concerned with some object or other. . . . There are three ways in which our consciousness is related to its object, . . . three ultimate modes of being conscious of an object: knowing, feeling and striving. . . . The word *object* must not be taken to mean merely material object, but whatever we can in any way be aware or cognisant of. . . . The object itself can never be identified with the present modifications of the individual consciousness by which it is cognised."[26] "Brentano's 'object' is . . . an appearance in consciousness . . . [But] the object as we mean and intend it, cannot be a modification of our own consciousness at the time we mean and intend it."[27] Witasek, too,—you will remember that he does not make the distinction of act and content a criterion of mind, though the distinction is drawn throughout his psychological system,—writes to the same effect as follows: "My ideation, my thinking, my feeling and my willing are always in their own peculiar way 'aimed' at something; I ideate *something,* a something that is not ideation, perhaps a book; my thinking apprehends things that are themselves not thinking, that do not belong to mind at all. . . . The same thing holds of feeling and willing."[28] "The perceived is something different from the perception. The former is usually something physical, the latter is always psychical. The former is then subject-matter for the sciences of external nature, physics, chemistry, etc.; the latter belongs to psychology."[29]

There is a real and important difference between this view and that of Brentano, although the two views cross and overlap in a rather puzzling way. Brentano makes the act of idea refer to the content of idea; and he regards the content of idea as a physical phenomenon, to be studied in its laws of coexistence and succession by the methods of natural science. Stout and Witasek regard the whole idea, Brentano's act and content both, as psychical phenomenon, and make this total idea refer to some extra-mental object. Witasek, however, keeps the three terms distinct: act of idea, content of idea, object of idea, all play their separate parts in his system. Stout, if I understand him aright,—and Stout is one of the men whose visual patterns I find it almost impossible to trace, although I get along very well with Brentano and Witasek; so that I am never quite sure that I have fully grasped his meaning,—Stout seems, in general, to run content and act together, to consider content as simply a specific determination of act; so that, for instance, in a visual perception of red we have to distinguish, not the act of perceiving, the content red, and the red object, but rather a redly determined or redly modified perceiving, and the red object.[30]   However this may be, the difference between Brentano, on the one hand, and Stout and Witasek, on the other, is, as I have said, real and important.

What, then, shall be our attitude to this extra-mental reference, and its claims as criterion of mind and as principle of mental classification? Well, we might dismiss it at once, solely on the ground of the adjective 'extra-mental.' "The concept of transcendence," Bühler writes, "has no sort of application in psychology. Be the object what it may, its determinations cannot be presented or given to us, cannot have significance for us, unless we are conscious of them. All the objective determinations of which I know are known in or by modifications of my consciousness; that is a self-evident proposition. And it is only with these modifications that psychology is concerned. . . The concept of something that transcends itself is just as contradictory in the sphere of psychical reality as it is everywhere else. Hence the question of transcendence is not, as Stout and Hoernlé think, a central prob-

lem of the psychology of thought: on the contrary, it is not a psychological problem at all."[31]
I am afraid that Stout and Hoernlé will not be
so easily convinced. But it is enough for my
purpose to quote a sentence from Witasek: "This
[transitive] reference would be puzzling, nay
more, it would be inconceivable," he says, "were
we not so thoroughly familiar with it from our
inner experience."[32] But 'inner experience' is,
I suppose, identical with 'modification of consciousness,' in Bühler's sense. The objection is
too summarily stated; it must be recast, and more
carefully phrased, if it is to be effective.

I shall not attempt its restatement here; nor
shall I do more than mention, in passing, the
objection that the rule of transitive reference
has obvious exceptions. We saw that this objection was raised, also, against Brentano's distinction of act and content. It may be raised,
far more cogently, against the distinction of
idea and object of idea. The feelings, for example, at once suggest themselves, and with a
greater insistence than before. But, besides the
feelings, we may instance the organic sensations:[33] what is the 'object' of mind in the
sensation of hunger?—we may instance Bain's
passive sensibility,[34] and Stout's sentience, or
mere sensation, or anoetic consciousness;[35] we

5

may instance those faintest sensations which, as
we know from Külpe's experiments, are as
likely to be subjectified as to be objectified;[36]
we may, perhaps, instance the 'passive contents'
found by Messer in his experiments by the
method of the associative reaction, where the
stimulus-words called up ideas that, intrinsically,
were well adapted to touch off the response, but
that, as a matter of fact, lacked all motor tendency, so that it simply did not occur to the observer to utilise them for associative purposes.[37]
In all these cases, it might be argued that the
transitive reference is absent.

Nevertheless, I think that there is another and
a bolder line for the objector to take. You will
remember that Brentano made the distinction
of act and content a peculiarity of the psychical
phenomenon; "no physical phenomenon shows
anything like it."[38] Witasek is just as emphatic
with regard to transitive reference. "It is strictly
limited to the psychical domain; search the
physical world, the world of material things, as
closely as you will, there is no trace of it to be
discovered; you find spatial contiguity, spatial
inclusion, relative movement, all sorts of relations, but this inner state of reference to and
direction upon, this pointing of one thing to
another, has no place in the scheme. Physical

things stand separate and self-contained; none points beyond itself in that peculiar sense which is made known to us by ideation, by physical phenomena at large."[39] Dogmatic statements of this sort are apt to stimulate to the very effort that they declare to be impossible. Suppose that we do make search, more or less careful, in the world of material things, and see if we cannot find a pointing, more or less analogous to the pointing of idea to its object!

When I first proposed this task to myself, my thought ran at once to cases in which the presence of one material phenomenon indicates the presence of another. A column of smoke indicates the existence of a camp-fire; a drop of the barometer indicates a change in the weather. But it is soon seen that instances of this kind will not serve our purpose. The pointing-relation which we are seeking to parallel may, as Witasek says, be *in* consciousness, but it is certainly not *for* consciousness. It is, you will remember, itself the criterion of consciousness, the character that marks off the psychical from the physical. It is intrinsic to mental process; and its analogue must be similarly intrinsic to physical process. Smoke, now, is a sign or symptom of fire; but it is symptomatic only to me, to the mind of the observer. We must look further.

I thought, in the next place, of the doctrine of orthogenesis, defined, in our convenient *Dictionary,* as "evolution which is definitely directed or determinate by reason of the nature or principle of life itself."[40]   Eimer, the protagonist of this doctrine, declares that "organisms develop in definite directions . . . through purely physiological causes."   "The causes of definitely directed evolution are contained . . . in the effects produced by outward circumstances and influences such as climate and nutrition upon the constitution of a given organism. . . . Development can take place in only a few directions because the constitution, the material composition of the body, necessarily determines such directions and prevents indiscriminate modification."   "The variations in living beings follow in perfect conformity to law a few definite directions."[41]   Eimer's special views are not popular with biologists, since they imply some sort of vitalism, and also the inheritance of acquired characters.   But then, if you object to either or both of these implications, you may substitute for orthogenesis the doctrine of orthoplasy, of "determinate or definitely directed evolution under the laws of natural and organic selection."   "Orthoplasy,"—I am again quoting the *Dictionary,"*[42]—"emphasizes natural selection working upon variations in many cases screened and fostered by the presence of individual modifications." It gives you the same result as orthogenesis, without committing you to Eimer's interpretations.

Well! but a 'definitely directed' evolution, working itself out in terms of mechanical cause and effect: does not that furnish an instance of the pointing-relation? Does not every term in the evolving series point forward to the next following term in a perfectly definite and unequivocal way? I see no escape from that conclusion. And I think that we must go even farther. Does not the very notion of an evolution imply this relation of forward pointing? And since evolution is not confined to the organic world, but governs the inorganic as well, are we not forced to say that the whole course of nature, the entire realm of mechanical causation, manifests the same relation? If we accept the principle of evolution at all, I see no escape from this wider conclusion.

So we arrive at the position that a pointing-towards, a direction-upon, a reference-to, is intrinsic to all natural phenomena. There remains the question whether this particular mode of pointing is analogous to the pointing of psychical phenomenon to its object. And here objection seems in place. The pointing of term to term in the evolutionary series represents, so to say, a linking together of different things, a passage away from one thing and up to another; and, in so far, physical things still "stand separate and self-contained," as they do in Witasek's pages. Granted that the pointing is intrinsic to natural phenomena: nevertheless, the word 'intrinsic' has shifted its meaning. The pointing is intrinsic to the behaviour of things, of causes and effects; but it is intrinsic to the very nature or essence or constitution of mind. Our analogy is faulty, because it offers what is simply an external character in lieu of a constitutive factor. The relation of mind to object is more than a mere pointing, a *Hinweisen;* it is also an *inneres Bezogensein,* a relation of necessary implication.[43]

I confess that I cannot meet this objection. Even, however, if we were obliged to stop here, I think it would have been worth while to remind you that the pointing-relation—to take that term in its widest sense—is not uniquely an affair of mind; that it has an analogue in the external world, which appears wherever the law of evolution runs. I might have added that, since there undoubtedly is a difference between the physical and the psychical, the analogy would naturally be expected to show imperfection. But let me

guide you a step further still. The pointing-
relation that inheres in mind is a relation, we
said, of necessary implication. Now think of
an organism, of the solar system or of the living
animal. Did not the constitution of the solar
system point to and imply the existence of
Neptune; and was not Neptune sought and
found in consequence? Does not the occurrence
of some fossil tooth or bone point to and imply
the existence of a total animal of a certain size
and shape; and do we not reconstruct the fauna
of the prehistoric world accordingly? I am
speaking, always, of intrinsic pointing and intrinsic implication; I am not concerned with
the consciousness of the astronomer or of the
palæontologist, though it is difficult to phrase
the illustrations without giving that suggestion.
The argument is that the constituent parts of
any organised whole, whether the whole be the
entire universe of stars or the individual living
creature, point to and imply one another as such,
as parts of a whole; so that we may substitute for
the analogy of serial linkage, which we just now
drew from the course of evolution, the better and
closer analogy of physical organisation. I have
no liking for vitalism, and I have a definite dislike of teleology;[44] I am thinking solely of a
world in time, a mechanistic world that is ade-

quately described in terms of cause and effect;
my science is altogether orthodox. But it seems
to me that the very fact of natural law, of such
a law as the conservation of energy, means
organisation; and that, wherever you have organisation, you have also this relation of pointing-
with-implication. And if that relation is not
identical with the transitive reference of idea to
object, is it not, at any rate, a near kinsman?

The analogy may, indeed, be pressed in some
detail. Every constituent part of an organism
points to and implies all the other parts. In the
same way, the ideational process which is the
vehicle of conceptual meaning is involved in a
network of reproductive tendencies; it points to
and implies all the special ideas that fall under
the concept in question. The transitive reference
of mind is, therefore, not necessarily a reference
of one to one but may be a reference of one to
many. And conversely, one and the same object
may be signified by many different mental
processes: precisely as the existence of an undis-
covered planet, of a certain mass and orbital
path, may be indicated by various planetary
irregularities, or a heart of a certain type may be
variously indicated by a number of fossil remains.
I have no desire to push these parallels too far;
but they show—do they not?—that our analogy

from physical organisation is more than external.

Nevertheless, I fear that many of you have found this entire discussion exceedingly crude. You have been accustomed to view the transitive reference of mind from a philosophical standpoint, the standpoint of a theory of knowledge; and my quest for its physical counterpart has seemed to you to miss the real issue, to shoot beside the mark. I must insist, however, that this transitive reference is offered by psychologists, in works upon psychology, as the psychological criterion of mind and as a principle of psychological classification. And psychology moves upon the plane of natural science, and not upon the plane of philosophy. Hence it is upon the scientific level that the criterion must be tested. If philosophy finds the transitive reference of mind unique, psychology as science is not bound by that decision,—any more than, if the relation appeared as unique in our 'inner experience,' this verdict of introspection would be binding upon philosophy. Close as the connection between psychology and epistemology may be, it is, after all, the connection of a special science with a general philosophical discipline.

On the other hand, I must not be unfair to the psychologists. The passage which I quoted, some time ago, from Witasek,—the passage in which he declares that transitive reference is "strictly limited to the psychical domain,"—continues as follows. "Here is the most tangible, the most characteristic difference between the two fields [of physical and psychical], though we cannot either say that it is what constitutes their essential diversity (*Wesensverschiedenheit*); it, too, is merely an index of this diversity, which itself cannot be expressed except by the antithesis of material and mental."[45] If, as I hope, the term 'essential diversity' does not mean ultimate, metaphysical diversity, but simply diversity in first-hand experience, Witasek here shows that he would be ready, were proof forthcoming, to adopt any other criterion of mind which should come nearer than that of transitive reference to empirical reality.

In the first part of this Lecture I argued that the psychology of act and content is a psychology of reflection, and that the psychology of process, which translates that distinction into terms of temporal course and qualitative specificity, comes to closer quarters with the subject-matter of the science. In the second part I have argued that transitive reference cannot be made the criterion of mind, since it appears—no doubt with minor differences—in every form of organisation. It seemed more important to urge this consideration

than to repeat, *mutatis mutandis,* what I had
already said against the doctrine of immanent
objectivity. In fact, however, I believe that the
introduction of an 'object' leads to more serious
consequences, is fraught with greater peril to
scientific psychology, than the setting off of a
'content.' It brings us into flat contradiction
with the results of observation, since many of
our mental processes are in truth objectless. And
it must do this, for the reason that its underlying
assumption is mistaken: it assumes or implies
that mind is organisation; it thus confuses mental process with psychophysical process, mind
with organism, psychology with biology. Not
mind but man, embodied mind and ensouled
body, is the subject of which we may predicate a
transitive reference;[46] if we are dealing in
abstraction with mind, then our proper business
as psychologists is simply to describe and to explain mind in existential terms. It is matter for
congratulation that the experimental study of
the thought processes, now well begun, has made
a systematically controlled introspection the final
court of appeal.

LECTURE III

METHODS AND RESULTS: THE *BEWUSSTSEINSLAGE*

LECTURE III

METHODS AND RESULTS: THE
BEWUSSTSEINSLAGE

THOSE of you who follow the progress of experimental psychology will remember the flutter aroused, some two years ago, by the publication of Wundt's critical essay on *Ausfrageexperimente,* on what we may call experiments by the method of examination. "These experiments," we were told, "are not experiments at all in the sense of a scientific methodology; they are counterfeit experiments, that seem methodical simply because they are ordinarily performed in a psychological laboratory and involve the coöperation of two persons, who purport to be experimenter and observer. In reality, they are as unmethodical as possible; they possess none of the special features by which we distinguish the introspections of experimental psychology from the casual introspections of everyday life."[1] Yet I was expressing satisfaction, at the end of the last Lecture, that the experimental psychology of thought had appealed, openly and with confidence, to a systematically controlled introspection. Was not, then, that self-congratulation a little premature?

To answer this question, we must make a critical study of the methods which have actually been employed. I cannot go into detail; but I can say enough to give you a general idea of the way in which the experiments have been conducted.

I

The methods followed by the two first investigators, by Marbe in his *Experimental Investigation of the Psychology of Judgment* (1901) and by Binet in his *Experimental Study of Intellection* (1903), are extremely simple. Both men lay great emphasis upon introspection. We want to find out, Marbe says, "what experiences must supervene upon a conscious process in order to raise it to the rank of a judgment. So . . . we place the observer under conditions in which he may experience the most diverse kinds of mental process in their passage to judgments (*die verschiedensten zu Urteilen werdenden Bewusstseinsvorgänge*), and then ask him to report what concomitant experiences supervened upon those processes, and endowed them with the character of judgment."[2]   I quote Marbe's own account of his first experiment.

"In the first experiment, I placed before the observer . . . two objects of the same size and shape but of different weight, and instructed him to lift them in turn to the same height with the same hand, and then to invert the one that he found the heavier. The act of inverting the weight was evidently right if the objectively heavier, and wrong if the objectively lighter weight was chosen. It was therefore, so far as it came to the observer's consciousness, a judgment."   Marbe has provisionally defined the judgment as a conscious process to which the predicate right or wrong (*richtig* or *falsch*) may be significantly applied.[3] "As soon as the observer had inverted the weight which he took to be the heavier, he was required to report the conscious processes that he had experienced after lifting the second weight. He was instructed not to confine himself to the experiences which ran their course coincidentally with the perceptions that took on the character of judgment, since it might possibly be of interest to know what conscious processes introduced the act of judgment. The experiment was performed three times with each observer, one or both of the weights being changed in the repeated trials."[4]

This procedure is typical of the whole enquiry, although Marbe varied his experiments in many ways. The observer might be asked, for instance, to listen to the tone of a tuning-fork, and then to sing the same tone as accurately as

6

he could; or to add together a pair of numbers called out to him by the experimenter; or to reply to specific questions regarding articles of daily use, well-known facts of history, and so forth. He might respond by a gesture, or by a Yes or No, or he might simply answer to himself, mentally, without expression. In every case, he was required, at the end of the experiment, to give a full introspective account of his experience.[5]

Binet's work is mainly taken up with an analysis of the intellectual processes of his two little girls, aged respectively fourteen and a half and thirteen years.[6] "It has been my aim," he writes, "to give a wider scope to introspection, and to carry investigation into the higher mental phenomena, such as memory, attention, imagination, the course of ideas. . . . All the experiments that I have made upon ideation have called for no more elaborate apparatus than a pen, a supply of paper, and a great deal of patience; they have been made outside of the laboratory."[7] The experiments are of the kind known as mental tests. Thus, the observer, seated with pen and paper before her, receives the instruction: Write down twenty words. The time required for the completion of this task is noted, privately, by the experimenter. When the words are written, the experimenter takes the paper, and comments as follows:

"I am going to ask you a question about these words that you have written. You know that you may write a word quite mechanically, without thinking of anything; or you may write the word and think of the thing it stands for, but without thinking of any particular thing,—you just think of something, a table, perhaps; or again you may write the word and think of some particular thing, like our table in the dining-room. Now as I read off these words that you have written, you will tell me exactly which of these three classes it belongs to: whether you wrote it without thinking of anything, or whether you just thought of something, or whether you thought of some particular thing."[8]

The words are then read off, one by one; the observer explains the meaning which she attached to them, and how they were suggested to her; and the report is taken down in full, narrative and question and answer, by the experimenter.

This procedure, again, is typical of the whole enquiry, though a great variety of tests was employed. Thus, words were read or shown by the experimenter, and the observer reported how she understood them, what idea they aroused in her; sentences were written down by the observer at command, or sentences begun by the experimenter were completed by the observer; compositions were written upon assigned subjects;

recollections were called up; objects and events were described. The experiments upon attention included the cancellation test, tests upon direct memory of series of figures, tests of the time of simple reaction. Finally, a series of tests was devoted to memory,—memory of isolated words, of poetry, of objects, of narrative prose, of pictures, of spatial magnitudes, of time intervals. And the results, viewed always in the light of the introspective records, are made the basis of a differential characterisation of the two youthful observers,—furnish, so to say, psychological portraits of two types of intellection.[9]

Different as these French and German methods are, they both strike the note of experimental simplicity; instruments have practically disappeared, and the outcome depends altogether upon the tact of the experimenter and the introspective capacity of the observer. Marbe worked with professors and instructors and graduate students whose ability and integrity are above question; Binet, who himself displays keen psychological insight in the application and interpretation of his tests, pays a deserved tribute to the psychological qualifications of Marguerite and Armande.[10] Now, however, the instruments, for a time, come back again. The German studies of the next three years—Watt's *Experimental Contributions to a Theory of Thought* (1904), Ach's *Volition and Thought* (1905), and Messer's *Experimental Investigation of the Psychology of Thought* (1906)—employ the Hipp chronoscope and its most modern accessories.

Watt worked by the method of the associative reaction. Familiar substantives, printed black on white, were shown to the observer, who replied by uttering an associated word. The associations were of the sort termed, technically, the 'partially constrained': the observer was required, in six different series, to associate to the visual word a superordinate, coördinate, or subordinate idea, or a whole, a part, or another part of a common whole. Watt is able to utilise the times of reaction in various ways; but he also pays special attention to the introspections. "After every experiment the observer reported the whole contents of his experience, and made any remarks upon it that he pleased. The report was at once written down in full by the experimenter, and was occasionally extended by appropriate questioning."[11] Moreover, at the conclusion of the principal experiments,

"Series were taken with all the observers, in which they were instructed to make a particular stage of the course of reaction the object of an especially careful observation. It seemed best to mark off four of these stages: the preparation for the experiment, the appearance of the stimulus-word, the search for a reaction-word (if such search occurred), and lastly the cropping-up of the reaction-word. . . . The method was eminently successful. The restriction to a single phase of the complicated process of reaction enabled the observers to introspect more carefully and with better result."[12]

It is upon these introspections that Watt bases the theory of thought with which his dissertation concludes.

Ach is concerned, primarily, with the analysis of voluntary action, and treats of the psychology of thought only in so far as it is involved in that analysis. We must, however, take account of him, first, because his incidental contribution to our subject is important, and secondly because he names and fully discusses the method of 'systematic experimental introspection.'[13] Ach distinguishes, in every psychological experiment, a fore, mid and after period. The fore period covers the time from signal to stimulus. The mid or principal period is occupied by the experience upon which the experiment is expressly directed. The after period is a time of indefinite duration, but certainly lasting several minutes, which follows immediately after the conclusion of the experiment. The method of

systematic experimental introspection requires
that the events of the fore and mid periods be
introspectively examined, as a whole, during the
persistence of the perseverative tendencies in the
after period.[14]   Introspective observation is thus
confined to what a psychologist of the 'image-
mongering' type[15] would be apt to term, with
Fechner, the memory after-images of his experience.[16]   Moreover, if the introspective report is
to be complete and unequivocal, the experimenter
must come to the help of the observer; there must
be free exchange of question and answer; so that,
as Ach remarks, "in this method of systematic
experimental introspection, the experimenter
plays a more prominent part than in any other
psychological method."[17]   Ach himself employs
the method in a series of experiments upon
simple and compound reactions,—and he could
hardly have chosen a more promising field.   For
although Külpe said as long ago as 1893 that
"reactions are nothing else than exact types of
. . . voluntary action, . . . so that their mere
duration is but a small part of their psychological
significance,"[18] and although Wundt has repeat-
edly endorsed this statement,[19] no one before
Ach had made any serious attempt to build up a
psychology of volition upon the introspective
data which the reaction experiment affords.

Messer's work may be regarded as a continuation and extension of Watt's. He begins with experiments on 'free' association,—a word is shown, and the observer, having read and understood it, replies by uttering the first word that occurs to him.[20] The following series distinguish between association of ideas and association of objects: thus, the word being shown, the observer is required to name, in one set of experiments, a coördinate object, in another, a coördinate idea; or in one set to name a character of the idea expressed by the word, and in another to recall and to characterise a particular object that falls within the range of its meaning.* Further series set more complex tasks to the observer. Thus, two names are shown—names of philosophers, artists, statesmen—and the observer is instructed, first, to compare them objectively, to pass judgment upon their relative merits, and secondly to say which of the two he himself agrees with or

---

* Instances of coördinate objects are duck-swan, hand-foot; the associated object (swan, foot) belongs with the object denoted by the stimulus-word (duck, hand) to a whole (a pond, the observer's body). Instances of coördinate ideas are cellar-vault, piano-violin; the associated idea (vault, violin) belongs with the idea expressed by the stimulus-word (cellar, piano) to the same general idea or *Oberbegriff* (underground chamber, musical instrument). Instances of idea and character are country-fertile, shop-full; of idea and character of some particular object, river-wide, shop-pretty (externalised visual idea of a particular river, of a particular florist's shop).

prefers. Or again, objects, or pictures, or printed sentences of philosophical import are laid before him, and he makes a remark about them, or gives his opinion of them. In experiments of this latter sort the chronoscope is replaced by a stop-watch, which is started when the object or sentence is exposed and stopped as soon as the observer begins to speak.[21]—It is clear, I think, that Messer's problem grew as his work progressed. Watt and Ach seem to have begun with their programme pretty clearly in mind, and to have followed it out pretty much as they had planned; Messer seems to be led from experiment to experiment by the suggestion of his own results.[22] The consequence is that his pages are by no means easy reading; one is conscious of a certain lack of logical coherence as one passes from section to section; while, on the other hand, as a mine of introspective information, his paper is perhaps the most valuable of those issued from the Würzburg laboratory. For after every experiment of every series—there were fourteen series in all—the observer "reports the whole contents of his experience from the appearance of the stimulus-word to the moment of reaction."* When occasion arises, questions are put

* Messer's paper fills 224 pages of the *Archiv f. d. ges. Psychologie,* and at least a half of these are in fine print. There

by the experimenter: Messer, however, unlike
Ach, makes but sparing use of this means of
obtaining information.[23]

We come now to the *Ausfragemethode* proper,
to that method of examination which Wundt
condemns as a mere travesty of the experimental
procedure. In 1907 Bühler published the first
installment of his *Psychology of the Thought-
Processes: Facts and Problems,*—the article
Ueber Gedanken, On Thoughts. His problem
is very general: What do we experience when we
are thinking? To solve it, he says, the prime
necessity is, to make your observers think. And
to make them think, he reads to them some
aphorism of Nietzsche, some couplet from
Rückert, or puts some question suited to their
temper and attainments. The question is always
answerable by Yes or No: Was the Pythagorean
proposition known in the Middle Ages? Can
our thought apprehend the nature of thought?
Does Monism really involve the negation of per-
sonality? The aphorisms are thrown into ques-
tion-form by a preliminary: Do you understand?

can be no doubt that the method of 'systematic experimental
introspection,' whatever its advantages, runs to bulk. If it comes
into general use, and still more if, as Ach proposes, the conversations between experimenter and observer, the introspective inter-
views, are taken down by the phonograph and stored for future
reference, we shall be forced to employ a staff of 'introspective
computers' to render our materials manageable.

Do you agree with this?—For example: Is this true? 'To give every man his own were to will justice and to achieve chaos'; Do you grasp this? 'Thinking is so extraordinarily difficult that many a man had rather pass judgment.' The harmless necessary stop-watch is started as the stimulus begins, and arrested as the observer replies by Yes or No. When the answer has been given, the observer undertakes a description, as accurate as possible, of his experience during the experimental period.[24] Bühler, like his predecessors, lays great stress upon the attitude of the experimenter and the introspective calibre of the observer. The experimenter must be in full sympathy with his observers; he must think, by empathy, as they think, understand as they understand, speak in their language. And the observers themselves must be picked men, *sujets d'élection:* Bühler had seven at his disposal, but relies exclusively upon the reports of the two most experienced, Külpe and Dürr,[25]— I give a single instance of question and report.

Can our thought apprehend the nature of thought?— Observer K. 'Yes.' 6 sec.—The question struck me comically at first; I thought it must be a trick question. Then Hegel's objection to Kant suddenly òccurred to me, and then I said, decidedly: Yes. The thought of Hegel's objection was fairly full; I knew at the moment precisely what the whole thing was about; there were no words in it, though, and there were no ideas either. Only the word 'Hegel' came up afterwards, in auditory-motor form.[26]

I should mention here that Woodworth, in 1906, had already used a method of question and answer, although apparently in cruder form. The observer was required to answer such questions as: Which is the more delightful, the smell of a rose or its appearance? Who was the greatest patriot of Hungary? What is the difference between similarity and congruity? Should a man be allowed to marry his widow's sister?* As soon as the answer was given, or sometimes before, the experimenter broke in, and demanded a description of the process of seeking and finding the solution of the problem. "The introspection may be made more reliable by calling for answers to very definite questions, as: Any visual picture? Any words heard? Any feeling of bodily movement?" For example:

What substances are more costly than gold?—Diamonds.—I had no visual image of the diamond; the thought of diamonds was there before the sound of the word. You don't think of the words you are going to say before you say them. It is the same way in conversation: you know what you want to say, but the

* I may be obtuse: but I confess that I can find in this question no food for thought.

words come so quickly that you don't have a chance to think of them before you say them.[27]

If this is not Bühler's method, it is at any rate a link which connects his work, at the one extreme, with that of Marbe and Orth, at the other. Orth I have not before mentioned; he performed, in 1903, some experiments that will presently occupy our attention.*

In a later publication (1908), Bühler describes experiments on thought-memory, which are based upon a method akin to Müller and Pilzecker's *Treffermethode,* or method of right associates. A series of twenty paired titles, as we may call them, is read to the observer:—the point of Archimedes, the egg of Columbus; destruction of the Phœnician sea-power, fate of the Spanish Armada; and so on—with the instruction that the two topics are to be connected in thought. Then the first members of the pairs are repeated, in a different order, and the observer seeks to recall their thought-associates. The procedure is modified in various ways. Thus, a list of half-sentences is read, in a certain order; the observer listens and understands. Then the list of complementary half-sentences is read, in another order, and the observer is asked to complete each one, as it comes, by reproducing the appropriate

* P. 102.

term of the first list. Or a series of brief, pro-
verbial expressions is read without other instruction than that the observer is to listen and
understand. Then a second series is read, with
the instruction that he is to recall an expression
of similar tenor from the first series. For instance: 'When the calf is stolen, the farmer
mends the cow-house' is paralleled, in the second
series, by: 'When the wine is running in the
cellar, everybody goes to look after the cask.'
Or, finally, a list of thoughts, more or less aphor-
istic in form, is read and understood; then a
catch-word is given, and the observer tries to
recall the complete thought. In all these experiments, full introspective reports are taken.[28]

So far, then, there has been nothing new in
the technique of this work upon thought. We
have the familiar method of mental tests; we
have the method of reaction, reduced in Marbe
and Orth, Woodworth and Bühler to its lowest
technical terms, but still recognisable for what
it essentially is;[29] and we have the memory
methods. The two methods that remain to be
considered, methods described in 1908 by Störring and Woodworth, are still of the reaction-
type. Störring showed his observers a card,
upon which were printed the premisses of a syllogism. The observers were instructed not to

hurry, but to draw the conclusion from the
premisses with the consciousness of absolute certainty. The time from the exposure of the card
to the first utterance of the observer was mea-
sured by a stop-watch. The syllogisms ranged
in difficulty from 'U is left of L, F is left of U,
therefore . . . ' to 'No k belongs to the genus s;
all f belong to the genus k; therefore . . . '[30]
Woodworth employed, not the syllogism, but
the rule-of-three. He asked such questions as:
London is to England as Paris is to — ? The
hand is to the fist as a nation is to — ? The
observers supplied the missing term, and reported, as Störring's observers did also, upon
their experience during the solution of the
problem.[31]—

I fear that this account of methods has been
tedious; I have given it, in order that you might
have some ground upon which to base your judgment of results. My own opinion, which I must
here state briefly and dogmatically, is as follows.
I think that Marbe and Binet made a good beginning: though I must add that, when I read
Marbe, I took his procedure to represent rather
the temporary poverty of the Würzburg laboratory than any act of free choice; and that, when
I read Binet, it never occurred to me to regard
his conclusions as final, or in fact as anything

more than problems set to future analysis. I think, further, that the investigations of Watt and Ach constitute the logical continuation of the inquiry thus begun, and that in 1905 the outlook for an experimental psychology of thought was distinctly promising. The time had come for putting the subject into commission. Unfortunately, Messer attempted to cover the whole ground, and his task was too great for him. Still more unfortunately, Bühler gave a turn to the inquiry which, in my judgment, has served to retard rather than to advance the progress of our knowledge.

Do I not then believe, after all, in a method of systematically controlled introspection? Very emphatically I do: with all my heart, with all my mind, and with all my strength. My belief in introspection is old enough to have attained its majority; for it was in 1888, when for the first time I was reading James Mill's *Analysis,* that the conviction flashed upon me—'You can test all this for yourself!'—and I have never lost it since. But the question here is, not whether we believe at large in a method of experimental introspection, but whether the special methods followed by Messer and Bühler are adequate to their task. I remarked just now that Messer's paper is a mine of introspective information. So it is: but on a number of not very closely articulated problems. Messer, if I read him aright,—and I hope that I am not doing him injustice,—failed to get his bearings in the wide field that he had undertaken to survey; he worked piecemeal. The observations that he took in this way are valuable, both positively and negatively, by what they say and what they omit; and their value is largely due to the separateness, the discreteness, of the problems attacked; you may almost say, if you will, that Messer's work is valuable because he was forced, against his intention, to see many issues where Watt and Ach had seen but one. Nevertheless, all the work must be done over again. It is, of course, easy to be wise after the event; and we must remember that, just as Ach wrote too early to take account of Watt, so Messer wrote too early to take account of Ach.[32] But we who come later can see very clearly that, with Watt and Ach, the time for a single-handed grappling with the psychology of thought had passed. Part-problems were now the order of the day: part-problems, attacked by every refinement of technique that laboratory experience could suggest; part-problems, with rigorous technical control of the introspections. We get, instead,— with Messer, a series of studies more or less

7

discrete, broken aspects of the whole offered for clear vision of a part; with Bühler, a revolutionary attempt to rewrite the psychology of thought from the beginning. And while Watt and Ach could use their chronoscope times to good systematic purpose, Messer is content at first merely to mention them and later to drop them altogether, and Bühler so shapes his method that anything like an experiment in the ordinary sense of the term, any regulation or regular variation of conditions, is impossible.

II

To criticise further at this point would be to anticipate. I pass to a consideration of the principal results of these experimental investigations of the thought processes; and I begin with the discovery of the *Bewusstseinslage*.

You will remember that Stout, in his *Analytic Psychology* (1896), maintained the occurrence in consciousness of 'imageless thought.' "There is no absurdity," he says, "in supposing a mode of presentational consciousness which is not composed of visual, auditory, tactual and other experiences derived from and in some degree resembling in quality the sensations of the special senses; and there is no absurdity in supposing such modes of consciousness to possess a representative value or significance for thought."[33] In controverting this position, James Angell gives some illustrations of imagery from his own experience.

"When the process is that of apprehending a sentence, I find in my own case the imagery involved is frequently constituted by a matrix of vague, shifting, auditory word images, in which some significant word is likely to be most prominent, and which is accompanied by a tingling sense of irradiating meaning, which, if the sentence comes to a full stop, is likely to work itself out in associated images of a fairly definite type."

"In those cases where we hang upon the dying sound of the word or its fading visual characteristics, without clear-cut imagery dissevered from the perceptual process itself, there is often present . . . a definite (quasi-affective) attitude of familiarity with the word, and a feeling of placid conviction that at any moment the explicit associates which give it meaning could, if necessary, be summoned before us."[34]

These accounts, I say, are offered as illustrations of the imagery which in a particular mind serves as the psychological vehicle of thought. Stout, however, replies that the 'tingling sense of irradiating meaning' and the 'placid conviction' that the associates can be explicated are precisely the sort of thing that he wishes to emphasise in his doctrine of imageless apprehension. He even rubs it in: " 'Irradiation,' " he says, "is a particularly good word."[35] Well! my own point is that these experiences are also precisely the sort of thing that the German investigators designate as *Bewusstseinslage,* an almost untranslatable term, meaning something like posture or attitude of consciousness.

The word *Bewusstseinslage* was first employed, at Marbe's suggestion (1901), by Mayer and Orth, who had undertaken a qualitative study of association by the word method. These investigators found that the association might be direct, from word to word, or indirect, by way of interpolated processes. And they divide the interpolated processes into three classes: ideas, volitions, and *Bewusstseinslagen.* In their own words:

"Besides ideas and volitions, we must mention a third group of facts of consciousness, which has not received sufficient emphasis in current psychology, but whose existence has been impressed upon us again and again in the course of our experiments. The observers very often reported that their experience consisted of certain conscious processes which obviously refused description either as determinate ideas or as volitions. Thus, Mayer observed that the hearing of the word *Versmaass* [metre] was followed by a peculiar conscious process, not characterisable in detail, to which the spoken word *trochee* was associated. In other cases the observer was able to furnish some description of these facts of consciousness. Orth, for instance, observed that the word *mustard*

touched off a peculiar process which he thought might
be characterised as the 'suggestion of a familiar form
of expression.' Then came the associated word *grain*. In
all such cases the observer was unable to find in consciousness the least trace of the ideas which he afterwards
employed in his report to describe the facts of experience.   All these conscious processes we shall include,
despite their evident and often total differences of
quality, under the single name of conscious attitudes.
The introspective records show that the conscious attitudes were sometimes affectively toned, sometimes completely indifferent."[36]

Marbe's own experimental study of judgment
(1901) helps us in two ways to a further understanding of the conscious attitudes.   It gives
us, first, a long list of indicative terms.   In a few
cases the observers can say nothing more of their
attitudes than that they are peculiar, or indefinite, or indescribable; but for the most part they
are able to characterise them in a more positive
way.   And it gives us, secondly, hints of the behaviour of the attitudes in the general flow of
consciousness, hints of their relation to other and
better known conscious processes.

The attitude most frequently reported is that
of doubt, with the cognate forms of uneasiness,
difficulty, uncertainty, effort, hesitation, vacillation, incapacity, ignorance, and the opposite experiences of certainty, assent, conviction that a

judgment passed is right or wrong. To the old-fashioned psychologist all these terms have an emotive ring, and it is worth noting that the same observers refer to surprise, wonder, astonishment, expectation and curiosity as emotions. But there is another group of attitudes that do not carry the emotive suggestion. These are described, in confessedly roundabout phrase, as remembrance of instructions, remembrance that one is to answer in sentences, recollection of the topic of past conversations, realisation that nonsense-combinations have been presented earlier in the experimental series, realisation that sense or nonsense is coming, realisation that a certain division will leave no remainder. Here we are in the sphere of intellection. And the general behaviour of the attitude appears to consign it to that sphere. For it may be affectively toned or it may be affectively indifferent; it may be touched off, associatively, by an idea, and it may form part of an ordinary associative complex; it may be attended to, and it may be forgotten. In a word, it behaves just as ideas behave.[37]

Orth, in his *Gefühl und Bewusstseinslage* (1903),—the study to which I referred a little while ago,*—brings the conscious attitudes into relation with James' fringes, with Höffding's

* P. 93.

quality of familiarity,[38] and with many of Wundt's feelings. When, for instance, Wundt declares that feeling is the pioneer of knowledge, or that a novel thought may come to consciousness first of all in the form of a feeling,[39] he is, in Orth's opinion, referring in fact not to feeling proper but to conscious attitude. For the rest, Orth asserts that these attitudes, however widely they may differ in other respects, have in common the character of obscurity and intangibleness; they cannot be further analysed. When we name them, or seek to describe them, we are simply translating, substituting known for unknown; in actual experience, the attitudes are peculiar modifications of consciousness, which cannot be identified with sensation or idea or feeling. Many of them consist in a sort of direct apprehension; but in any case, and altogether apart from this function, they appear to be more closely related to cognition, and thus to sensation, than to feeling.[40]

We come next to Ach (1905), who gives us both a classification and a theory. In the experimental after-period, the period of introspection, Ach's observers often reported that a complex conscious content was simultaneously present as knowledge,—as a *Wissen*,[41] or what

James calls a knowledge-about as distinguished from a knowledge of acquaintance.

"At the end of the experiment, that is, at the beginning of the after-period, the observer frequently has a peculiar consciousness of what he has just before experienced. It is as if the whole experience were given at once, but without a specific differentiation of the contents. The entire process, according to the report of one observer, is as if given in a nutshell."[42]

This imageless presentation of a total knowledge-content is termed by Ach *Bewusstheit*, awareness. And awareness is of two principal kinds: awareness of meaning, and awareness of relation. Awareness of meaning is always accompanied or preceded by some sensation or image, which "constitutes the imaginal representation in consciousness of the content imagelessly present as knowledge," and thus stands as symbol of the meaning-content.[43] Suppose, for instance, that I am reading a paragraph, quickly but understandingly, and that I come to the word 'bell.' Under other circumstances, if the word had a special significance or if it stood alone, I might take its meaning imaginally; a group of apperceiving ideas—the idea of its sound, the visual image of a bell—might spring up and assimilate it. As it is, the apperceiving masses are not realised; the meaning of the term is present simply as an awareness. The visual word-form 'bell' rouses a number of associated ideas to a state of preparedness, gets them ready, so to say, to make their appearance in consciousness; or, to speak in physiological terms, stirs up a number of reproductive tendencies. The associated ideas need not actually appear; the reproductive tendencies need not discharge their full function; the half-arousal, the subexcitation suffices to set up a determinate, unequivocal reference, which manifests itself in consciousness as knowledge or meaning.[44] That is Ach's theory. We are looking, if you like, at a sailor standing alone by the helm of his vessel. But that innocent-looking steersman is a pirate; he is in league with a numerous crew who are crouching, repressed but alert, behind the bulwarks; his association with them constitutes him a pirate; they give him his meaning. Now, perhaps, an impatient head shows over the side. Likely enough! but its appearance does not change the meaning of the figure in the stern; our friend is no more a pirate than he was before; his *Begriff* is the same, only that it has acquired an explicit *Merkmal*.

Since awareness has degrees of intensity, and these degrees must have their psychophysical substrate, Ach defines *Bewusstheit* as a progres-

sive function of this subexcitatory state of the
reproductive tendencies.[45] He makes no attempt
to work out a complete classification, but calls
attention at once to two transitional forms between awareness of meaning and awareness of
relation.   The first is the awareness of determination, our immediate knowledge that the present
flow of mental processes is or is not directed by
some preconceived purpose, or some foregone
suggestion or instruction.[46] The second, which
is in reality a special case of determination, is
the awareness of tendency, a general knowledge
that the course of consciousness is determined,
without specific representation of its direction
or goal; such awareness as we have when we say
'It is on the tip of my tongue,' or 'I know there's
something that I haven't done.'[47]   The awareness of relation itself Ach identifies with Marbe's
Bewusstseinslage.   It is true, of course, that
reference or relation is also involved in the awareness of meaning; the arousal of the reproductive
tendencies implies that the sensation or idea is
given to consciousness in a network of relations.
But the reference here is forward, to a fact of
the future, to the ideas which are making ready
to cross the conscious limen; in the awareness of
relation the reference is backward, to some content of a previous consciousness.   Instances may

be found in surprise, perplexity, doubt, and in the opposite states of satisfaction, certainty, relief,—names that are already familiar to us from Marbe's list of conscious attitudes. In all these cases, Ach says, we are *eingestellt,* predisposed or adjusted, to receive a certain impression. An impression comes, and either fulfils or interferes with this predisposition; but, whatever its character, it is spontaneously referred to some fact of our past experience.[48]

I wish that Ach had discussed, even schematically, the psychophysics of the *Bewusstseinslage,* of this awareness of relation. He does not: and I can only guess that he would regard the indeterminate play of reproductive tendencies as the ideal limit towards the one extreme, the extreme of 'meaning,' and the single function of what he calls the determining tendencies[49] as the ideal limit towards the other extreme, the extreme of 'relation,'—while in fact every case of either type of awareness will require the coöperation, in varying measure and in various complication with other psychophysical factors, of both sets of tendencies. However this may be, his theory of meaning is explicit, and he tells us that 'meaning' grades off into 'relation' through intermediate forms.

Messer (1906), like Ach, offers us both a

classification and a theory, though his classification is more and his theory is less detailed. He distinguishes a group of intellectual and a group of emotional attitudes; the former are matters of understanding, pure and simple, the latter are complicated by affective and volitional moments.[50] So far, we are on psychological ground. When, however, he comes to distinguish the sub-classes under these two main headings, Messer forsakes psychology for logic. Anything and everything that can be made the topic of thought may appear, he says, in the form of a conscious attitude; hence, if we classify by topic, we obtain an 'extraordinary variety' of attitudes; hence, again, a full survey is impossible,—we can only fall back on logic, upon fundamental and formal distinctions.[51] Logic, it is true, is not psychology; logic, indeed, abstracts from the very things that psychology investigates, "ob und wie [ein Denk]inhalt in einem menschlichen Bewusstsein repräsentiert ist"; nevertheless, a logical classification may be of great assistance to psychology, may even help toward that goal of psychological ambition, a psychology of the categories.[52]

'But why go to topic at all?' the psychological reader may exclaim; 'why not try a psychological classification?' Well, there the psychological reader, as we shall see in the next Lecture, has his finger on a very sore point of method. Messer is making the best of a bad job; he appeals to logic because he has nothing else to appeal to. And so he classifies his intellectual attitudes as those of reality, of spatial properties and relations, of temporal properties and relations, of causal connection, of teleological connection, and of logical relation (identity and difference, whole and part, etc.). Similarly, the emotional attitudes are those which have as their content the relation between the subject and the object of thought (familiarity, value); those which contain, further, an objective relation to the task set by the experimenter to the observer (appropriateness, relevancy, correctness); and those in which this supervening relation to the task in hand shows merely as a subjective state (question, reflection, doubt, assurance, ease, perplexity, etc.).[53]

All this does not greatly help us. It is, however, worth while to note that Messer's intellectual attitudes correspond to Ach's awareness of meaning, and Messer's emotional attitudes to Ach's awareness of relation, and thus to the original *Bewusstseinslagen* of Marbe and Orth. Indeed, the correspondence is, for psychological purposes, almost too exact; it suggests a common

logical principle rather than a common outcome
of introspection. For that matter, Messer ob-
literates the psychological difference almost as
soon as he has described it. The emotional
attitudes, he explains, are those in which an
affective moment of pleasantness-unpleasantness
is usually reported by the observer, or in which
we may trace the influence of 'will,' in the sense
of a causal activity on the part of the psychophysical subject. But feeling and will are merely
concomitants of the attitude. Attitude itself is
always intellectual. We may, perhaps, call it
'thought' when the complete explication of its
topic or content requires one or more sentences,
and we may call it 'meaning' when it carries the
content of single words or phrases; we may thus
dispense altogether with what was, from the beginning, merely a provisional term.[54]

So we find in Messer a classification borrowed
and adapted from logic; a classification based
on the presence or absence of affective and volitional concomitants; and a classification in terms
of the relative simplicity or complexity of the
content or topic of thought. His theory of attitude is summed up in a single sentence. "[I
assume] that the real psychical processes which
underlie an explicitly formulated thought may
run their course in all sorts of abbreviated forms,

telescoping into one another, making various demands upon the store of psychophysical energy."[55]   For 'real psychical processes' we may here substitute 'cerebral disposition.' Messer's theory then becomes practically identical with Ach's. "The unconscious real processes that underlie understanding"—Ach's reproductive and determining tendencies—"occur in various degrees of intensity, according to circumstances, . . . and consequently throw more or less light (*einen verschiedenen Reflex*) into consciousness, are consciously represented in different degrees of clearness, from distinct verbal ideas down to unanalysable attitudes."[56]   Ach had pointed out that our awareness of meaning always involves a process of what he terms associative abstraction; the associative relations that manifest themselves in consciousness as meaning are those of the greatest regularity, of most frequent occurrence; accidental and occasional associates are aroused but little, if at all, in the stirring up of the reproductive tendencies.[57]   Messer—and this is one of the most valuable features of his work—supplements Ach by pointing to transitional forms, by showing the various stages of *Entfaltung,* of development or elaboration, that a thought-process may pass through in consciousness.   Thus a visual idea (we are dealing with visual ideas considered as vehicles of logical meaning) may begin as a mere 'feeling of visual direction,' vague and inchoate to the last degree, and may grow during the experiment to a picture of almost hallucinatory clearness;[58] and the meaning of a word has a continuous scale of representations in consciousness, from the zero-point of inseparable fusion with look or sound of the word itself up to distinct realisation as a group of visual and verbal associates.[59] Attitude, the background of meaning or reference against which a mental process is seen, may be just a glow or halo of indiscriminable consciousness, or may be as articulate as the background of cherubic faces upon which Raphael painted his great Madonna.

Messer's series of transitional forms are, however, logical rather than psychological; the members of the series are, as a rule, selected from the mass of introspective material and arranged in order by the writer. It is, plainly, very desirable that the transition should be observed within a single mind. That, it seems to me, is one of the part-problems most obviously suggested by the work of Watt and Ach, —a systematic study of the genesis of conscious attitude from explicit imagery.[60]

Here, then, we may for the present leave the

Bewusstseinslage. Watt and Bühler employ the
term, but in such intimate connection with a
theory of thought that we must postpone their
discussion to the next Lecture. Binet, too, gives
illustrations of imageless thought that must undoubtedly be classed with the conscious attitudes.
The word 'to-morrow,' for instance, aroused in
one of his observers a 'thought' which she defines
as "something that you can translate by words
and feelings; something vague; it is too difficult
to describe":[61] evidently, a *Bewusstseinslage* of
meaning. But I have given you enough, both of
instances and of theory; you know what the
facts are, and you know the attempts that have
been made to explain them. We pass, therefore,
to the consideration of thought itself.

LECTURE IV

METHODS AND RESULTS: THE
THOUGHT-ELEMENT

LECTURE IV

DESCARTES, as we all know, laid some stress, in his philosophy, upon the fact of thinking. And the Cartesian psychology distinguishes between thinking in images and pure thinking, between imagination as the faculty of the picturable and pure intellection as the faculty of the unpicturable.[1] The modern notion of an 'imageless thought,' as we find it in Stout and Binet, evidently harks back to this doctrine, while the concepts of 'awareness' and 'attitude,' as used and explained by Ach and Messer, offer a compromise between the intellectualism of Descartes and the sensationalism of Locke,—or, as we might here say, the sensationalism of Aristotle.[2] We have now to ask whether the theory of 'imageless thought' is borne out by the results of experiment, is attested by a controlled introspection.

Marbe (1901) offers a provisional definition of judgment as a conscious process to which the predicate right or wrong may be significantly applied, and tries to find out what experiences

117

must supervene upon conscious processes in order to make this predicate applicable, to raise them to the rank of judgments.[3] He reports no less than eight series of experiments, carried out by various modifications of the method which I have already described; and his results are flatly and unexceptionally negative. The observers discover, much to their own astonishment, that "there are no psychological conditions of judgment, whatever the experiences may be that in the particular case pass over into judgment (*zum Urteil werden*)."[4] And what holds of the primary experience of judgment holds also of the understanding of judgments already formulated:

"The understanding of judgments, read or perceived, does not depend upon psychological facts, that are bound up with the reading or perception of the judgments. In like manner, the read or perceived judgments are not bound up with different experiences, according as we are able or unable to appraise them; nor are they connected with different conscious processes according as we pronounce them, in the particular case, to be right or wrong."[5]

Marbe is led by these results to modify his definition of judgment. "All experiences may become judgments, if it lies in the purpose (*Absicht*) of the experiencing subject that they shall accord, either directly or in meaning, with other

objects."[6]   Only, as the experiments prove, the
purpose of the subject need not be conscious.
You say to a painter: "That's much too dark!"
—and he, with some impatience at your simplicity, replies: "Of course it is; I made it
too dark on purpose"; but he had no explicit
purpose in his mind as he painted. In this sense,
judgments may be regarded as purposed experiences; the end, in whose interest the experiences are evoked, is their accordance, direct or
through meaning, with the objects to which they
refer.[7]   As for the understanding of a judgment, that is simply our knowledge of these
objects that, in the purpose of the judging subject, are to accord with the judgment or with its
meaning.[8]   Or, since knowledge is never given
in consciousness (*ein Wissen ist niemals im Bewusstsein gegeben*),[9]—remember that Ach and
Bühler are still below the horizon!—our understanding of a judgment is simply our capacity
of experiencing certain other judgments; a capacity which depends, like musical ability, upon
physiological dispositions, and which comes
to consciousness only in its particular manifestations.[10]

There is, then, so far as appears in these
experiments, no psychological judgment-process,
nothing that in direct experience marks a judg-

ment as judgment. If we call the observers'
consciousness a judgment-consciousness, we do
so for extra-psychological reasons, because we
take it to be guided and directed by an unconscious, dispositional 'purpose.' Marbe declares
expressly that no hint of the purpose shows in
the observers' own reports.[11]

This negative result of Marbe's investigation
is pronounced by Watt to be "extraordinarily
important. For it constitutes an unanswerable
argument against any theory which maintains
that, in order to judgment, this, that or the other
conscious experience is or must be psychologically realised."[12] Marbe, however, confined himself to an introspective examination of the
contents of consciousness in the interval between
stimulus and reaction. Watt takes into account,
further, the period immediately preceding the
stimulus, the period of preparation for the reaction; and what he there finds turns out, also,
to be extraordinarily important. "Marbe," he
says, "has no psychological criterion of a judgment; I have one, and one only,—the task or
problem (*Aufgabe*)."[13] "What transforms into
judgments the mere sequence of experiences that
we discover when we analyse the processes of
judgment, and what distinguishes a judgment
from a mere sequence of experiences, is the

problem."[14] Watt's observers, you will remember, were instructed beforehand that they were to associate part to whole, or subordinate to superordinate idea; in every experimental series a determinate task or problem was set them; and it is the influence of the problem that raises the associative consciousness to the rank of judgment, so that, as Watt puts it, "all my experiments were judgments."[15] Marbe's observers were also engaged upon tasks or problems. But the nature of these tasks was extremely simple. Moreover, the instruction given by the experimenter restricted their field of observation, as I said just now, to the mid experimental period. For one or both of these reasons, the *Aufgabe*, as psychological criterion of judgment, failed to make itself apparent.

That is straightforward enough. But one wishes that Marbe had taken account of cases in which a purpose *is* present in consciousness,—that he had arranged experiments in which a purpose should be overtly realised by the observers. The existence of purpose, he says, is essential to judgment; and he adds only that an *Absichtlichkeit* "need not be demonstrable in consciousness,"[16] and that in fact no reference is made to purpose in the introspective reports before him. Watt finds that the *Aufgabe* may come to consciousness immediately after the exposure of the stimulus-word, though normally it does not.[17]   It is useless to speculate on what Marbe might have found, had he carried his experiments a little further; but it is surprising, and somewhat puzzling, that he does not make conscious purpose, where it occurs, a psychological criterion of the judgment.

Watt, on his side defines "a judgment or an act of thought as a sequence of experiences whose procession from its first term, the stimulus, has been determined by a psychological factor [that is, by the problem]. As conscious experience, this psychological factor is itself past and gone, but it still persists as an appreciable influence."[18]   I do not, however, understand this to mean that the *Aufgabe* must be antecedently conscious on every occasion when it is effective. Let me read another passage:

"A preparation that is common to all problems alike," says Watt, "consists in a certain adjustment of the body. The observer directs his gaze, more or less attentively, and in a state of expectation that is accompanied by strain sensations of more or less vivacity, upon the screen that conceals the stimulus-word. Now he will say the name of the problem two or three times over to himself: subordinate idea, superordinate idea, find a part, etc.; perhaps he will think of two or three instances. This process is fairly clear in consciousness at the beginning of the series, and especially on the change to a new problem; but it weakens with time, so that in the second or third experiment the name of the problem is said once only, and finally internal speech lapses altogether and the conscious tension almost wholly disappears. All that remain, therefore, is the adjustment of the body—the fixation of the screen, the approach of the lips to the voice-key, etc.—and a state of faint expectancy. This is the course of events when the problem is easy and the observer has grown used to the experimental procedure."[19]

It seems, then, that the problem must have been fully conscious, as specific problem, at some past time, if the present experience of the observer is to be a judgment; but that it may, with repetition, tend more and more to disappear; so that finally nothing is left of its specific determination, and judgment is touched off mechanically, automatically, so to say reflexly, by the experimental surroundings. It seems that we have, in the sphere of thought, precisely what we find in the sphere of action. The skilled pianist had, once upon a time, to learn his notes; now he sits down to the instrument, and plays mechanically, automatically, so to say reflexly, in a certain key and at a certain tempo.

Messer makes the point more explicit. Instead of waiting till the association has been effected, he now and again interrupts an experiment at the end of the fore period, and asks the observer to describe the contents of consciousness. Sometimes the problem is clearly there; sometimes, however, the report runs: "Problem not in consciousness; I simply thought, It's taking a long time," or "No repetition of problem, only attention to the apparatus."[20] Messer applies this result as follows:

"We may say in general that many of the 'problems' that give direction to human activity have this character of the obvious, and in so far of the unconscious, and that philosophical reflection and self-examination are needed to raise them into the clear light of consciousness.

"Among these 'problems' that are wholly matters of course to us, and for which we are so to say continually predisposed, we may without any question place the problem of the cognition of real things, that is, of giving such a form to our perception, thought and speech that they are adequate to real things, whether we are concerned with the persistence, properties, states, changes, relations or value of the real. Just because this predisposition is altogether accustomed and obvious, it will not of itself and unaided come to consciousness as what it is."[21]

"This relief of consciousness," he goes on, "the gradual mechanising by practice of processes that at first demanded effort of attention and consideration from various points of view, is one of the most firmly established results of psychology."[22]

It is always difficult, as we read a series of works upon a given subject, to assign their just dues, enough and not too much, to the earlier authors. I think, as Messer himself thinks, that this notion of an unconscious, merely dispositional problem was clear to Watt. It is also clear to Ach, who, however, believes that determination of consciousness is accompanied, practically without exception, by an awareness of determination,[23] and who in so far challenges Marbe's introspections. Nevertheless, there can be no doubt that the work of the later investigators, Ach and Messer, has made the relation between Watt and Marbe much closer than Watt realised when he wrote his paper.

We may conclude our present account of Watt's theory by quoting from his own summary:

"The reproductive tendencies represent the mechanical factor in thinking, while the problem is what makes it possible that ideas shall be significantly related."[24] "There are, then, three fairly well-defined spheres of influence: that of the reproductive tendencies themselves, the ground and basis of everything else; that of the problem; and that of the coconsciousness and coconscious activity of problem, on the one hand, and of contents, that may be relatively independent, on the other." If we seek to relate these three spheres of influence to the theory of apperception, we may say that "to the first belongs the process known as apperceptive choice (*die sog. Wahl einer apperzeptiven Tätigkeit*); to the second, whatever in the modern idea of apperception is derived from the apperception of the Herbartian psychology; and to the third apperception proper, the core or nucleus of the Wundtian doctrine."[25]

Ach we may dismiss still more briefly, since his exposition, so far as concerns our present topic, is in close agreement with that of Watt. The observer's consciousness, during the fore period, is dominated by a purpose (*Absicht*). The idea of end, the *Zielvorstellung,* subexcites its correlated reproductive tendencies, and is therefore accompanied by an awareness of meaning. The tendencies so aroused are, further, brought into relation with the idea of object, the *Bezugvorstellung,* which they accordingly influence in the sense of the idea of end. "The establishment of these relations between idea of end and idea of object I term a purpose."[26] We should thus have, as constituents of the purpose-consciousness, the idea of end, given, perhaps, in terms of internal speech; the awareness of the meaning of this idea ; the awareness of the idea of object; and, I suppose, the awareness of the relations obtaining between the two ideas, of end and of object. We may also have, Ach says, a relation to the future, since the purpose is directed upon the perception of object which the future is to bring.[27]

The idea of end is, evidently, very much the same thing as Watt's *Aufgabe,* and the relation which the idea of end sustains to the present idea and future perception of object covers much the same ground as Watt's coöperation of problem and stimulus. The idea of end is also, like the *Aufgabe,* the point of departure of determining tendencies. Although it seldom appears in consciousness when the object is perceived, the stimulus presented, it nevertheless determines our reaction upon the object. Suppose, for example, that the stimulus consists of the figures 6 and 2, divided by a vertical line — 6|2. According as the task prescribed is addition, subtraction or division, the ideas reproduced by the stimulus will be 8, 4 or 3; the *Aufgabe,* the *Zielvorstellung*—itself unrepresented in consciousness—has raised to supraliminal intensity the single reproductive tendency that accords with the purpose of the observer.[28] "These dispositions, unconscious in their operation, which take their origin from the meaning of the idea of end and look towards the coming perception of object,—these dispositions," says Ach, "that bring in their train a spontaneous appearance of the determined idea, we call determining tendencies."[29]

All this might easily be translated into Watt's terminology: so easily, that we are likely to forget the difference of subject-matter, to forget that Watt is dealing with the judgment, and Ach primarily with the voluntary action. That difference comes back to us with a sort of shock, and, when it comes, sets up the *Bewusstseinslage* of doubt. How can the concepts of purpose and problem be adequate to the psychology of thought, if they serve equally well for the psychology of volition?

So we are obliged—there is no help for it— to start over again, and to scrutinise the definitions of judgment offered by Marbe and Watt. And it seems to me that a very brief scrutiny shows these definitions to be too wide. "All experiences may become judgments," Marbe told us, "if it lies in the purpose of the experiencing subject that they shall accord, either directly or in meaning, with other objects."[30] Now let me read you a significant passage from his book:

"The purpose that is characteristic of judgment, the accordance of the experiences or their meanings [with the objects to which they refer], may be effective only secondarily, alongside of other purposes. When, for instance, an actor is playing a part, he utters words

which he intends to agree with the words chosen by the
dramatist.   But as he speaks, he is pursuing a whole
number of other purposes.   He aims to impress his hearer
in various ways; he tries, perhaps, to sink himself wholly
in his part, . . . and so on.   When experiences are
evoked in this way, when the purpose that is characteristic of judgment is forced into the background by
other, concomitant purposes, it hardly seems correct
to term the experiences judgments.   Or take another
example.   In some of our experiments, the observer was
asked to sing a tone of the pitch of a given tone, and
no one would hesitate to call the tone sung a judgment.
But we should hesitate to say of a singer who took the
part of Lohengrin that he had, by his singing, judged
rightly or wrongly.   Nevertheless, there is no sharp line
of distinction between our experiment with the sung
tone and the case of this opera singer that should lead
us in the one instance to speak of judgment and in the
other not.   The fact is that, as the purposes concerned
in the origination of an experience (over and above the
purpose that is characteristic of judgment) become
more and more numerous, we grow less and less inclined
to consider that experience as a judgment."[31]

Does not that sound a little apologetic?   Surely,
it is not impossible that an actor should read his
part with the single-minded purpose of expressing his author; surely, it is not impossible that
he should take it mechanically, as a matter of
course, because he is an actor and that is the
part to take,—precisely as Marbe's observers
sang the tone because they were psychological

observers and that was the tone to sing. These things are possible. And, on the other hand, a plurality of purposes is not fatal to judgment. You may review a book in order to show that you think it important, in order to make its writer better known, in order to see your own name in print, in order to earn some money: your estimate of it is still right or wrong. Unless, then, we give up altogether the attempt to mark off judgment as a special subject of psychological inquiry, we must say that Marbe's definition is too wide.

Watt defines judgment as "a sequence of experiences whose procession from its first term, the stimulus, has been determined by a psychological factor now past as conscious experience, but persisting as an appreciable influence,"[32] and declares that 'all his experiments were judgments.'[33] But then one rather wonders if there is anything in the mental life, of the sequential type, that is not a judgment. In reproducing a series of nonsense-syllables, for instance, the observer is determined by the *Aufgabe;* and it may be questioned whether the same thing does not hold—I quote Ach's examples—of the freest play of imagination and the most abstract form of æsthetic contemplation. Messer points a like criticism by reference to gymnasium work. The

instructor formulates the exercise in some stereo-
typed phrase, and then counts one, two, three;
the exercise is gone through at the word of command. Here, then, we have a sequential experience that is conditioned upon the stimulus, the
number called, and that takes place under the
persistent influence of a foregone conscious experience, the hearing of the original prescrip-
tion. And so a raising of the arm or a bending
of the body would be a judgment.[34]

Well! what, then, does Messer offer by way of
definition? His observers were instructed, from
the first, to "understand by judgment that process of thought which finds its complete linguistic expression in a predicative proposition
(*Aussagesatz*), which must, of course, be significant."[35] And when he examines the introspective reports, Messer discovers—what the rest
of the world would probably have expected, but
what apparently comes to him as a pleasant surprise—that the observers agree in their view of
the essential character of the judgment consciousness. It is essential to judgment, they
say, "that a relation between stimulus-idea and
idea of response, a relation that is more particularly characterised as a relation of predication
(*Aussage-Beziehung*), shall be willed, 'intended,'
or at any rate accepted (*anerkannt*)."[36] But a

significant relation of predication was what they
had been told to find; and when we remember
that three of the six observers (Watt himself was
one) had taken part in Watt's investigation, that
two of the three had acted as observers for Ach,
and that the work was done, largely with Watt's
apparatus, in the laboratory in which Watt's
study had just been completed,[37] we shall hardly
be overwhelmed by the 'willed' or 'intended.' I
do not say that Messer is wrong; but I gather
that he took out of his experiments, in this regard, pretty much what he put in. However,
it is more important to consider his analysis.

What, first of all, of the relational experience?
Can it be analysed? The observers were not
able to define it positively in its specific character (*die Beziehung in seiner spezifischen Eigen-
art positiv zu bestimmen*). They did, in some
cases, distinguish it from the attributive relation:
attribution narrows consciousness, restricts the
sphere of meaning, predication extends it: but,
even so, "the limits between predicative and attributive relation are fluctuating (*fliessend*)."
On the whole, then, "the exact analysis and characterisation [of this relation] must be left to
later investigators."[38] The willing or intending,
on the other hand, is ordinarily a matter of the
problem set to the observer by the instruction

of the experimenter,—"on the assumption, of course, that the observer understands the instruction and has the 'will' to react in accordance with it."[39]

So far, therefore, we have Watt's *Aufgabe,* and the experience of a predicative relation. Marbe had no psychological criterion of judgment; Watt had one; Messer has two. But Messer seeks, further, to bring the *Aufgabe*-psychology into relation with the objective reference of the Austrian school. I am not sure that I wholly understand him; but I will give you what I take to be his meaning.

Ordinarily, Messer says, in the everyday life of mind, our experience is intentional, directed upon objects.[40] This reference is due to an *Aufgabe*, the normal, self-evident and therefore unconscious purpose 'to cognise.'[41] Now this natural and normal attitude of mind may or may not be carried into the laboratory. We exchange it for an unusual and, in a way, artificial attitude when we are studying sensations and ideas (that is, reproduced sensations or reproduced complexes of sensations) ; we seek, in their case, to describe consciousness as it is, to discriminate the qualities of conscious contents; the contents themselves, and not their meanings, are in the focus of attention.[42] Contrariwise, we retain it, and we must retain it, when we are studying the processes of cognition, perception and thought (judgment); we have, in their case, to take account of the fact of transcendence, of the things and the properties of things to which the cognitive experiences refer. "The psychologist who should suppose that perception and thought may be adequately characterised by the simple ascertainment of the sensations and ideas present in consciousness would be like a man who should seek to apprehend the real nature of money by simply investigating the materials of which money is made."[43]

The nature of the *Aufgabe*, then, is of very great importance. The *Aufgabe* of existence, with its consequent internal predisposition (*Einstellung*), gives us the psychology of sensation and idea and the association of ideas; gives us, among other things, Ebbinghaus' work on memory. The *Aufgabe* of objective reference, with its predisposition, gives us the psychology of perception and judgment. The shift from this, the customary attitude of everyday life, to the other, the unusual attitude of the descriptive psychologist, is justified on two grounds: first, because it ensures an exact psychology of the processes investigated;[44] and secondly, because it brings to light what otherwise, from sheer force of habit, we should have overlooked,—*e.g.,* the "peculiar experience of specific conscious quality"[45] that forms part of the judging consciousness, the volition or intention of the introspective reports. For transcendence or intentional relation inheres in thought as conscious experience: we have only to lay an associative reaction and a judgment reaction side by side, and it appears at once. If Marbe's observers missed it, that was because their problems were not sufficiently varied. Marbe himself implies it, when he says that "all experiences may become judgments if it lies in the purpose of the experiencing subject that they shall accord with other objects"; for this statement, translated into other terms, means precisely what we have already said,—that the obvious and therefore unconscious purpose of cognition is decisive for the judgment-character of experience.[46]

In summary, therefore, we have in the judgment, first, the experience of a predicative relation; secondly, the control or direction of the course of consciousness by an *Aufgabe* that usually does not show in consciousness; and thirdly, the qualitatively specific experience of willing or intending the predicative relation, due to the fact that the *Aufgabe* is that of objective reference, that the 'purpose' of the observer is 'to cognise.' But the relation, you will remember, is not necessarily willed or intended; it may be merely accepted. What does this mean?

It means that we are to go the whole way with Brentano's school, and to distinguish act and content,—or rather, in this case of judgment, act and objective.[47] Primarily, Messer says, the distinction is concerned only with the significance or meaning of the judgment, and is therefore logical, not psychological. Nevertheless, it comes into psychology, if only in secondary fashion. For whenever a judgment, a predication, is questioned, tested, examined by the judging subject, then act and objective, acceptance or rejection and matter accepted or rejected, appear in psychological guise, as discriminable factors of his experience.[48] If, then, the *Aufgabe* has not been fully effective; if the volition or intention has, for some reason or other, failed of realisation, so that the peculiar *quale* of the judging consciousness is absent, and the observer turns round upon his *Aussage* in critical mood; then the judgment may be completed by the specific act of acceptance.

I have stated Messer's position as accurately as I can. But I do not find it clear. I have the impression that he is confusing two different things: the nature of mental experience as de-

termined by various problems, and its nature as
given apart from any problem. I can see that
the setting of a problem might, as Ach says it
does,[49] lead to novel modes of mental connection;
I cannot see how it should actually generate a
specific conscious quality. I fail, also, to see
the ground of Messer's classification of the subject-matter of psychology. Memory is, surely,
as intentional as perception or thought. If, not-
withstanding, Ebbinghaus' existential treatment
of memory promises us an exact psychology,
why should not an existential treatment of perception and thought be both possible and hope-
ful? Or, in other words: if perception and
thought are intrinsically something other than
existent qualities, as money is something intrinsically other than paper and gold and silver,
then, of course, their objective reference must
always be considered, whatever the *Aufgabe* of
the moment may chance to be. If, however, the
objective reference is itself due to *Aufgabe,* then
a shift of *Aufgabe* from that of everyday life
to that of the laboratory should yield results as
valuable as those obtained in the sphere of sensation and the association of ideas. Messer speaks
of a 'divergence of the lines of psychological
inquiry,'[50] as if there were a single original path
which now branches into two, the one taking us

to sensation and idea, and the other to perception and judgment.   But the original path, so
far as I can discover, is simply the path of popular psychology, which is straightly continuous
with the road to perception and judgment; the
second path, that Ebbinghaus followed, is the
little travelled and artificial way of existential
or 'exact' psychology.   It would seem wiser, if
we are to pay regard to objective reference at
all,—and I need not here discuss that question,—
to lay double tracks from the very beginning.

However, I am now criticising Messer's position, whereas I set out to criticise his statement
of the position.   I find the statement confused,
in this matter of objective reference; and I find
it still more confused in the matter of act and
content.   I must read you a longish passage.

"This act of judgment," Messer writes, "this act of
acceptance and rejection, appears not only in connection with objectives of judgment, that is, with thought-
contents that stand in predicative relation and find their
linguistic expression in the predicative proposition, but
is of frequent occurrence in all our experimental series.
Whether the problem is that of formulating a proposition, or merely that of designating an idea or an object
or what not, again and again we have the experience
reported that conscious contents, of one kind or another,
offer themselves as solution of the problem, and that
they are accepted or rejected; oftentimes the verbal

idea Yes or No is discovered in consciousness. And this experience of approval and disapproval, this utterance of Yes or No, is termed, by all observers alike, a 'judgment.' We have ourselves limited the term judgment to the thought-content of the predicative proposition, but we may very well apply the name 'act of judgment' to the experience in question. Acts of judgment, in this sense, may appear wherever 'problems' are set to thought, and wherever the contents supplied by the mechanism of association are brought into relation with the 'problem,' examined as to their adequacy to its solution, and accordingly accepted or rejected. Now in these facts, that certain contents acquire the character of problems, and further that acts of acceptance and rejection occur in the manner described, we have psychical experiences that are evidently inexplicable from the uniformities of simple reproduction and association, and that justify our distinguishing the processes of thought from those of associative reproduction."[51]

I say nothing of the point that, in this passage, the mechanism of association apparently furnishes contents of a certain sort apart from any problem whatsoever: that difficulty we have already mentioned. The particular difficulty here is that an act of judgment may appear in consciousness without the content of judgment, that the *Urteilsakt* appears along with a *Begriffsinhalt*. How is such a state of affairs possible, if act and content are correlative? I can explain Messer's view only if I suppose that, as regards both the act of judgment and the specific experience of volition or intention, he moves back and forth between his two types of *Aufgabe,* the existential and the relational. When he affirms that the relational problem brings into being a specific conscious quality, and when he affirms that the act of judgment, as acceptance or rejection, may accompany a single significant term as well as a predicative proposition, he seems to me to be regarding intention and acceptance, after all, as existential contents, on the same level with sensations and ideas. If I am right, Messer is confused in his thinking. If I am wrong, then I must still believe that he is confused in his writing.

Let us, however, summarise once more. The observer is given a certain problem. The problem finds representation in consciousness, verbal or other; the observer understands it, has the attitude or *Bewusstseinslage* of meaning; and has the good-will to follow instructions. This good-will, which may also be termed a preparedness for the particular mode of reaction, is represented in consciousness by a definitely directed expectation, by a 'feeling' of clearing obstructions out of the way, and so on.[52] The stimulus comes, and the judgment runs its course. It is characterised formally, by its determination;

materially, by the experience of a predicative relation, and also, as a rule, by a volition or intention, the specific conscious quality of the relational problem, the problem of objective reference. If this quality is lacking, then the predicative relation appears along with an act of judgment, the qualitatively specific experience of acceptance or rejection.

That is Messer's analysis; and it contains, evidently, much more than we find in Watt. At the same time, a good deal of the new matter implies the doctrine of conscious transcendence; and a psychologist who, like Bühler, banishes transcendence from psychology will make short work of it. Moreover, the predicative relation was, as I pointed out, not the discovery of the observers but an explicit feature of Messer's instruction to them; and we have seen that they insisted, despite the instruction, on following out some prior suggestion and giving the name of judgment to the experience of acceptance or rejection. All this leaves us in uncertainty as regards the net value of Messer's contribution to our subject. And when we read, later on, that "thinking may be counted among the voluntary actions,"[53] we may even doubt whether we have advanced appreciably beyond our starting point. For what we need is not a genus but a difference: Watt and Ach gave us the genus. And if the predicative relation is the *differentia* required, we want the observers to find it for themselves, and not to take it from the experimenter; we want them to tell us what it is like, and not to leave its description to future investigations; and we want them to stick to it, and not to apply the term judgment to something quite different. For the rest, there are plenty of 'judgments' classed by Messer as 'reproduced,' 'abbreviated,' 'preparatory,' 'borrowed,' that on his own definition should not be classified as judgments at all.[54]

So Messer passes from the scene. I have dealt somewhat severely with his psychology of judgment. Let me, all the more for that, remind you that his two hundred pages will well repay your study; let me say again that he is a mine of introspective information; and let me repeat my opinion that his paper is, in many respects, the most valuable of the studies issued from the Würzburg laboratory. We turn now to Bühler.

You remember Bühler's method? He means to make his observers think; and he makes them think by asking them questions that cannot be answered, yes or no, without thought. A first group of questions, suggested by Ach's observations on non-imaginal awareness,[55] takes the

form: Can you, or Do you know:—Can you calculate the velocity of a freely falling body? The
observer replies, yes or no, as soon as he has made
up his mind. In the second and third groups,
which begin with Do you understand, Is this correct, or the like, the experimenter reads off some
condensed and pithy saying,—an aphorism from
Nietzsche, or a verse from Heyse or Rückert. A
fourth group, which aims to induce thoughts of
a synoptic character, comprises large general
questions: What is an ideal? What has Herbart
in common with Hume? And a fifth and final
group, which is intended to bring out the relation between thought and idea, contains such
questions as: Do you know how many primary
colours the Sistine Madonna is painted with? In
every case, the observer gives a full account of
his experience.[56]

We find in the introspective reports ideas, feelings, attitudes. But, Bühler says, this is not all.

"The most important items of experience consist of
something that is not touched at all by any of the
categories by which these formations are defined (I abstract for the time being from the attitudes, whose
position is peculiar): something that shows no trace
of sensible quality or sensible intensity: something of
which we may rightly predicate degree of clearness,
degree of assurance, a certain vividness whereby it appeals to our mental interest, but which in content is

determined quite differently from anything that in the last resort may be reduced to sensations; something about which it would be nonsense to enquire whether it possessed a higher or lower degree of intensity, and still greater nonsense to ask what sensible qualities it could be resolved into. These items are what the observers have termed, with reference to Ach, aware-nesses, or sometimes knowledge, or simply 'the conscious-ness that,' but most frequently and most correctly thoughts."[57] "The essential constituents of our thought-experiences are thoughts and thoughts alone."[58]

We may say at once that Bühler interprets the attitude (*Bewusstseinslage*) in terms of this theory as "a consciousness of the process of thought, and more especially of the turning-points of this process in experience itself,"[59]— just as Watt, we may add, interprets it, in terms of his problem-psychology, as a problem without a name.*[60]

This, then, is the thesis of all Bühler's publi-cations,—that "there are thoughts without any

---

* Both in Watt and in Bühler, the theory of attitude is merely an incident in the theory of thought. "A problem," Watt says, "is a state of consciousness that exists only in order to determine a certain significant series of reproductions; that can be specified only by reference to, and indeed comes to consciousness only as, this series: an attitude is the same thing without a special name. In the case of the problem, we can specify both the name and the meaning of the contents reproduced by it." This account, of course, leads to the difficulty which we discussed above, p. 130. Bühler speaks of attitudes as "eigentümliche mehr zuständliche Erlebnis-strecken," and then defines them in the words of the quotation.

the least demonstrable trace of any sort of imaginal groundwork;"[61] "knowledge (*Wissen*) is a new manifold of modifications of our consciousness,"[62] covering the variety of thoughts as the general term sensation covers the variety of sensations. He accordingly defines thought as a mental element, "the ultimate unit of experience in our thought-experiences," as "the least item of a thought experience; that in which a progressive definitional analysis can discriminate no independent items but only dependent parts."[63] And he proceeds at once to classification.

Into this classification I shall not follow him, because I believe that his method leads to erroneous results. I can best indicate my line of criticism by taking a very simple instance. When a student begins work in the psychological laboratory, and more particularly when he begins work by any one of the metric methods of psychophysics, he is very likely to fall into what we term, technically, the stimulus-error.[64] He is instructed to attend to sensation, but in reality he attends to stimulus. Instead of comparing two noise-intensities, he will compare the imagined heights from which the balls fall that give the noise-sensations; and, in general, he will concern himself not with greys but with grey

10

papers, not with kinæsthetic sensations but with weights, not with visual magnitude but with the size of objects. The error is both insidious and persistent; I could quote you a long list of warnings to avoid it; and I could show you that those who give the warnings do not always themselves escape the error. It is, as Messer said, natural and customary to think, not of mental processes, but of the things and events about us,—while it is, as I believe, absolutely necessary to get rid of things, and to think only of the mental processes, if we are to have a science of psychology. Well! my criticism is that Bühler's observers fell into an error of the same sort as the stimulus-error. They were men of wide psychological experience, of long technical training, of undisputed ability: but they were given an immensely difficult task, in terms of a very poor method. How difficult was the task, you may realise by calling to mind the history of analytical research in the more accessible field of sensation; how poor was the method, you may realise by calling to mind the wealth of experimental appliances which that research has found necessary. Indeed, the method was not only intrinsically crude but it was also suggestive. Let me give an illustration, taken at random.

"Is this true? 'To give every man his own were to

will justice and to achieve chaos.'—Yes.—First of all, a peculiar stage of reflection (*eigentümliches Stadium der Ueberlegung*) with fixation of a surface in front of me. Echo of the words, with special emphasis on the beginning and end of the sentence. Tendency to accept the statement. Then all of a sudden Spencer's criticism of altruism occurred to me, with the thought that Spencer mainly emphasises,—the thought that the end of altruism is not attained. Then I said Yes. No ideas except the word 'Spencer,' which I said over to myself."[65]

Here we have a report of two verbal experiences,—an echo of the stimulus, which we may probably put down to perseverative tendency, and a significant fragment of internal speech. But we have also the report of a peculiar stage of reflection, and of a tendency to agreement. I submit that a method which simply notes experiences of this kind, and leaves them without further attempt at analysis, is a suggestive method. And I submit that the observer is not describing his thought, but reporting what his thought is about; not photographing consciousness, but formulating the reference of consciousness to things: in a word, that he has fallen, in the case of thought, into the error which we should term the stimulus-error in the case of sensation.

Yes! you say,—but the first of these criticisms may be due to sensationalistic bias, and the latter is, after all, a mere record of personal

impression.   To which I reply: Do not try to
separate the criticisms; take them together.   If
I am right in saying that the observers tell us
what their consciousness is about, when they
should be telling us what it is, then evidently the
method is somehow at fault; and its obviously
crude and obviously suggestive nature points at
once, whether we are sensationalists or whether
we are not, to a comparison with the refined and
objective methods employed in the study of sensation and association.   What I have to show,
then, is that my charge of an error akin to the
stimulus-error is well-founded, based on more
than individual impression.   If I can do this, my
criticism of the method, however it was originally prompted, will follow of itself.

I read, first of all, a passage from a critical
essay by von Aster, published last year in
Ebbinghaus' *Zeitschrift*.

"It was my intention to show that Bühler's experiments do not, in themselves, prove the existence of
specific thought-experiences; experiences, that is, which
are unequivocally and adequately definable as a 'knowledge about' or a 'consciousness of'; experiences in whose
nature it lies that, in or by them, we experience, apprehend, have before us a content that must be brought to
expression by words or complete sentences.   No more
is proved, it seems to me, than the fact that the observers
intimated certain definite experiences by these sentences.

But since intimation, with whatever assurance it may be given, is not of itself a *description* or a direct identification (*Konstatierung*), the question now arises, *what experiences lay at the basis of this intimation.*"[66]

Here, it is true, nothing is said of a stimulus-error. But the distinction between intimation and description, between *Kundgabe* and *Beschreibung*, is precisely my distinction between reporting about consciousness and reporting consciousness. Bühler's results, says von Aster, must be psychologically interpreted, in the light of an existentially directed introspection; and they need not be interpreted in Bühler's way. He points out, further, that the change from Marbe's unanalysable 'attitudes' to Bühler's precise and well-defined 'thoughts' itself indicates a change of procedure on the part of the observers: for description, and especially psychological description, is always approximate and rough, while intimation is assured, self-confident, a matter of course.[67]

There, then, is one critic who, in principle, agrees with me. But I can call another witness on the same side,—and, this time, one of Bühler's two preferred observers. Dürr, in a later number of Ebbinghaus' *Zeitschrift,* writes as follows:

"I have followed the course of Bühler's investigation, in which I was privileged to take part as observer, with keen interest. And I have been led to a rather curious result, which has altogether changed my ideas of the best method for the conduct of thought-experiments. Over and over again, as I was observing for Bühler, I had the impression, though I was not able at the time to formulate it very clearly, that my report was simply a somewhat modified verbal statement of the thoughts aroused in me by the experimenter, and that this verbal statement could not properly be regarded as a psychological description of the thoughts. What I mean by this antithesis of verbal expression and psychological description will perhaps become clearer if I suggest that the layman in psychology would be giving introspective reports every time that he exchanged thoughts with a friend, unless there were some distinction between verbal expression and psychological description."[68]

The psychologically trained observer is, of course, not so naïve as this layman; his report, as Dürr says, is a somewhat modified verbal statement (*eine irgendwie modifizierte sprachliche Darstellung*) of his thoughts; but, in the last resort, he too is stating, not describing. And so, Dürr continues,

"I maintain that Bühler, despite the ingenuity and care which he has shown in his experiments, has not attained to a correct apprehension of the nature of the thought-processes. The path that he has travelled will, in all probability, never lead us to the desired results."[69]—

I have offered you these quotations from von

Aster and Dürr, instead of giving a summary
of their criticism in my own words, because I
wish to convince you that the objection which
they raise to Bühler's work, though it is somewhat differently phrased, is in fact identical with
my charge of an error which is of the same genus
as the stimulus-error. I say that the observers
tell us, not what consciousness is, but what it is
about; von Aster says that they intimate, and
do not describe; Dürr says that they state, ver-
bally express themselves, but do not describe.
In view of this agreement, I shall not follow
Bühler further into his experiments upon
thought-memory.

But there are still two investigations, those of
Binet and Woodworth, which I may seem to
have unduly neglected. I think, however, that
what applies to Bühler applies also to them.
Binet's observers often reported *réflexions,
idées, pensées,* imageless thoughts which they
distinguished from *images.*[70] I pointed out, in
the last Lecture, that many of these thoughts
may be regarded as attitudes, *Bewusstseinslagen.*
In so far as they seem, further, to imply a specific thought-process, Bühler's *Gedanke,* they are
open to the objection that we have just raised
against Bühler's thought-elements,—and in increased measure. For you will perceive that, if

trained psychologists are liable to confuse description with intimation, children of thirteen and fourteen, however patient, however responsive, however psychologically gifted, will be still more liable to slip from fact to meaning, from observation to objective reference. It would be strange indeed if Marguerite and Armande resisted a temptation to which Külpe and Dürr succumbed! And Woodworth's results by the method of questions must be judged by the same standard. It may very well be true that "the thought of diamonds was there before the sound of the word," and that "you know what you want to say" in conversation before the words themselves appear.[71] But what is a thought-of? and what is a knowing? The method is at fault here, as it was with Bühler; experience is indicated, intimated, not described.

There remain Woodworth's and Störring's experiments by the methods of rule-of-three and of syllogism. Woodworth finds that the transfer of the relation from the first pair of terms to the case suggested by the third term may take place without consciousness, simply as a result of the *Aufgabe;* or that the transferred relation may have a name or an image as its vehicle; or again that it may be in consciousness, as 'imageless thought,' without any vehicle. To meet this

last case, he postulates 'feelings of relation,' of
the same psychological order as "feelings of
sensory qualities. Each feeling of relation is a
simple quality."[72] The assumption seems unnecessary,—at any rate until we have finally
decided that the 'feelings of relation' do not constitute transitional forms of a *Bewusstseinslage,*
of the kind to which Messer has called attention;[73] the series 'image or word, imageless
thought, no consciousness' is characteristic of
these 'attitudes.' Störring's work, again, touches
that of the Würzburg school at various points,—
as regards the influence of the *Aufgabe,* or as
Störring calls it, the *Anweisung,* the instruction;
as regards the mechanics of introspection, and
so on,—but, dealing as it does with inference,
and not with concept or judgment, it moves
in general upon a higher plane, and takes the
results of the earlier studies for granted.
Consciousness of identity, consciousness of assurance, consciousness of understanding, consciousness that something is coming,—phrases of this
sort meet us at the threshold.[74] But these are
the very things whose psychology we have been
discussing.—

I said, in the last Lecture, that in 1905 the
outlook for an experimental psychology of
thought was distinctly promising; but that

Messer then essayed a task which was too great
for him, and that Bühler gave a turn to the
inquiry which has served rather to retard than
to advance the progress of our knowledge. We
have now reviewed the various experimental
studies, under the heads of the conscious attitude
and the thought-element, and you agree, I hope,
that my criticism was sound. I cannot subscribe,
as Dürr and Bühler himself cannot subscribe, to
all that Wundt urges against the *Ausfragemethode;* but I believe, with Dürr and von Aster,
that in Bühler's hands the method, so far as its
immediate purpose is concerned, has proved a
failure. I have now to undertake, in a conclud-
ing Lecture, two tasks of very different degrees
of difficulty: a general appraisement of the work
so far done, and a defense of a sensationalistic
psychology of thought.

LECTURE V
THE EXPERIMENTAL PSYCHOLOGY
OF THOUGHT

LECTURE V

THE EXPERIMENTAL PSYCHOLOGY OF THOUGHT

I

THERE is a type of review, known to everyone who has written a book, which begins with a compliment, disapproves steadily of the contents of the successive chapters, and ends by saying that the author has made a valuable contribution to his subject. Now I believe very thoroughly in criticism; and I think that the rather haphazard and planless sort of criticism that we are apt to get in experimental psychology, criticism that is either perfunctory and therefore unhelpful, or else due to a personal interest in the writer and therefore biased,—I think that the relatively large proportion of this sort of criticism is a plain indication of the immaturity of our science. But I believe also in appreciation, and I think that appreciation should be as explicit and as technical as criticism. I shall therefore try to state, in definite terms, the advantage that, as I see things, has accrued to psychology from the series of investigations which we have been discussing.

I see, then, in the first place, two advantages that are closely bound together, as closely as problem and solution, or question and answer. It is a great thing that consciousnesses like doubt, hesitation, trying to remember, feeling sure, have been dragged into the daylight, and lie now in plain sight, a challenge to the experimental method. And it is a great thing that the fact of determination, the influence of *Aufgabe,* has been expressly recognised, in strict laboratory procedure, as a principle of explanation. Let me enlarge, for a moment, upon these two aspects of our thought-psychology.

Whether we look back over the course of experimental psychology as exhibited in text-books and journals, or whether we search our own hearts, there is no escape from the conviction that sensationalism has been taken too easily. I tried to show, in my first Lecture, how the sensationalism of experimental psychology differs from the traditional sensationalism of the English school. All that I then said I hold to. But I add now that we have not been serious enough with our canons and rules of procedure; having gone so far, we have retraced our steps and gone so far over again, but more carefully; we have not pushed out into the unknown. I can illustrate what I mean by reference to a piece of

work published some years ago from the Cornell
Laboratory,—work which I am not likely to
underestimate, and whose solid merits have been
recognised both at home and abroad. Bagley,
in his *Apperception of the Spoken Sentence,*
takes issue with Stout on the matter of imageless
thought. "From the series of observations which
were made in the course of our experiment," he
says, "no conscious 'stuff' was found which
could not be classed as sensation or affection,
when reduced to its ultimates by a rigid analysis"; and he gives a wealth of introspective detail. But it is a question, you see, whether his
observers were not unconsciously set, disposed,
prejudiced towards sensationalism; it is a question whether, had they been born and bred in
Stout's briar-patch, they would not have discovered an 'imageless apprehension.'[1] At any rate,
what we have now to do is to grapple with the
alleged imageless experiences, one by one; to
look them squarely in the face, from our sensationalistic standpoint; and either to carry our
analysis triumphantly through, or to make open
confession of failure.

I have sometimes fancied—though the effort
to be impartial may easily carry one too far—
that the lack of sensationalistic enterprise, of
which Marbe and the rest have convicted us,

may have been due, in part, to a feeling that we could all shelter ourselves, in time of need, behind Wundt's apperception. The Wundtian doctrine is a psychological achievement of the first rank, although we stand, perhaps, too near for a just appraisement of its real magnitude. Not everybody has taken the trouble to understand it,—and, like all large thought constructions, it requires understanding. But everybody has known that it was there, a living witness to the inadequacy of associationism; and as Wundt operates only with sensations and affections, we have had the comfortable assurance that we might safely do the same thing. However that may be, and I offer it as the merest suggestion, there can be no doubt that the imageless psychologists have done us the same kind of service in the sphere of thought that the James-Lange theory did us in the sphere of emotion. We had become too civilised, too professional, too academic, in our accounts of emotion; and James, with his reverberation of organic sensations, brought us back to the crude and the raw and the rank of actual experience. James' lion has now been pretty thoroughly assimilated by the academic lamb, who is the better and stronger for the meal. Whether the sensationalists can, in like manner, assimilate attitudes and awarenesses and thought-elements remains to be seen. They have at least been stirred up to a healthful activity; and if the outcome of the struggle is a dual control, their position will certainly not be weaker than it now is, but rather made more secure within a fixed boundary.

There, then, is the problem which the recent psychology of thought sets to psychology at large,—and of which it at once offers a partial solution in the doctrine of the problem, the *Aufgabe,* itself. The notion of an external and precedent determination of consciousness is, of course, familiar enough; we speak of command, of suggestion, of instruction, of the influence of surroundings, of class-room atmosphere and laboratory atmosphere, of professional attitude, of class bias, of habit and disposition, of temperamental interests and predilections, of inherited ability and inherited defect; and in all these cases we imply that the trend of a present consciousness, the direction that it takes, is determined beforehand and from without, whether in psychophysical or in purely physiological terms. But a thing may be a commonplace of the text-books, and yet have escaped experimental study. Thus laboratory psychology has, until very lately, looked askance at hypnosis as a method of psychological investigation; the treatment of sug-

11

gestion has therefore, to a large degree, been left to the psychopathologists and the psychologists of society, and we have borrowed from them as occasion arose. Things are changing; Ach and Martin have employed hypnosis in the laboratory. Things will change still more, now that experimental results in general are seen to be functions of the instructions given.

I do not know where the first hint of this determination of consciousness is to be found. Müller and Schumann are on the track of it in 1889, when in reporting their experiments with lifted weights they describe the phenomenon of motor *Einstellung,* motor predisposition.[2] Külpe in 1893 works it out explicitly for the case of voluntary action; "the preceding state of consciousness," he declares, "is of first importance in all reaction-time experimentation," and he distinguishes the sensorial from the muscular type of simple reaction, and the simple sensorial from the cognitive reaction, on the ground of difference in the preparation of the reactor; indeed, his whole polemic against the subtractive procedure, the measuring of time of cognition, time of discrimination, time of choice by the successive subtraction of the times of simpler reactions, is based upon the argument that reaction-psychology must be essentially a psychology, not of

contents, but of preparation.[3] To some extent,
this same idea was present to Martius in 1891,[4]
to Münsterberg in 1889,[5] to Lange in 1887.[6] On
the non-experimental side we may go back to
Hobbes, who in the *Leviathan* distinguishes
mental discourse that is unguided, without design and inconstant, from mental discourse that
is regulated by some desire or design;[7] or we
may start with Volkelt, who in 1887 emphasised
the importance of the *Vorsatz,* the plan or design, for the results of observation.[8] On the
whole, it is probably true to say that this notion
of the external and precedent determination of
consciousness comes into experimental psychology, by hints and partial recognitions, in the
late eighties of the last century.

However, I am not disputing the originality
or the service of Watt and Ach. It is they who,
by systematic experimentation, have given us the
Aufgabe and the *determinierende Tendenzen*,
and the gift has made it impossible for any future psychologist to write a psychology of
thought in the language of content alone. I
believe, indeed, that the principle of determination, taken together with what I may call a
genetic sensationalism, furnishes a trustworthy
guide for further experimental study of the
thought-processes; and I think that the work

immediately before us is, under this guidance, to bring the processes, little bit by bit, under rigorous experimental control.

We are further indebted to the subjects of our inquiry for a great volume of introspective *data,* a mass of introspective material that for bulk and value is, I suppose, without a parallel. Grant that the reports need, in many cases and in various ways, a psychological reinterpretation: they stimulate to that interpretation. Grant that they set more problems than they solve: they set those problems in clear and positive form. Raise whatever objection you will: the fact remains that a large proportion of this analysis is solid and stable, and that none of it need be misleading. If it had merely retaught the old lesson that the stronghold of mind is not to be taken by storm, but must be reduced by patient siege, we might still have been grateful; we cannot too often be reminded that the method of psychology is an experimental introspection,—that observations must be repeated, that the process observed must be set apart, in isolation from other processes, that variation of experience must follow and tally with variation of conditions, if we are to build the science on a firm foundation.[9] The printed records show us this; they justify to the utmost that painstaking regard for method that

has now and again been made our reproach: but
the proof and the justification are positive as
well as negative, given with success as well as
with failure.   One feels—I have felt—a certain
aversion to the scores of closely packed and
spottily printed pages of the *Archiv*; and the
writers, surely, have a good deal to learn on the
score of literary presentation; there is no reason
why they should be quite as full, quite as chatty,
confidential, platitudinous, formless, as they
actually are.   But after a first reading, when
one has the clue to the labyrinth, the real and
permanent value of the 'protocols' is plain
enough.

A specific problem set: a principle of explanation discovered: a volume of untrimmed introspections offered in evidence:—those, I should
say, are the three things that we may be grateful
for.   Those are, at any rate, the three most
tangible things.   There is much more to be
learned: useful hints are given for the conduct
of experiment, individual differences are in-
structively displayed, sources of suggestion may
be traced and their influence noted, mistakes are
made and their consequences may be followed
up, and so on and so forth.   But help of this sort
is, after all, the help that we derive from any
serious and extended piece of work, while the

three points that I have just mentioned are characteristic and new.

II

And now I am to attempt construction, and to set forth my own ideas on the psychology of thought! I am not happy in the prospect. But I am committed to certain principles, and I must do what I can—though there is time only for fragments and outline sketches—in their defense. And first I offer a word upon the regulative maxims that should, as I believe, direct our inquiry.

I assume that we are to attempt a psychology, and that psychology has here to pick its way between logic or theory of knowledge, on the one hand, and common sense on the other. When we are instructing our students in the psychology of sensation and of the simpler sense-complexes, we have to steer this same sort of middle course, only that there the course lies between physics (under which I include physiology) and common sense. The psychological process is so unlike both the nerve-process and the thing of common-sense thinking that our task, in the case of sensation, should be relatively easy. You know that it is not; you know that while students will profess that they clearly see the differences

as described, it is exceedingly difficult to get
them to take up the psychological attitude for
themselves, to psychologise; the solid, palpable
facts of natural science and the prejudices of
common sense are for ever in the way. Well!
this difficulty is increased tenfold in the case of
thought. For the psychology of thought leads
straight up to, passes directly over into, a functional logic, a theory of knowledge; you may love
the one and hate the other, but you cannot be
sure that you are always on your own side of
the line; you are interested to work out an application, or you give the rein to your reproductive
tendencies, and behold! you have overstepped
your limit. Common sense tempts you: for
common sense, however illogical itself, is very
fond of logic, and oftentimes joins forces with
logic to wean you from your psychological
allegiance. I speak abstractly; but it is only
a step to the concrete. Nothing is more striking, nothing in its way is more amusing, than
the constant recurrence of the charge of logical
bias in others, and the honest ignorance of logical
bias in oneself, that characterises the authors we
have been reviewing. Woodworth 'smarts under the epistemological whip' of sensationalism,
and will go to the observed facts; he therefore
proceeds to write several pages of epistemology.

Bühler regrets that Messer should have been dominated by Erdmann's logic, and will himself go to the observed facts; he prepares for the expedition by putting on a fairly complete suit of logical armour. It seems to me that the charge, as made in the particular instances, is for the most part justified, and that the mutual— shall I say, recrimination? has its allotted place in thought-psychology; the more we are criticised, the more careful shall we be. Only, it would be foolish to suppose that we are ourselves, *ex officio,* free from an error that we discern in everyone else. Let us remember that the chances of error are legion, and not be surprised if we succumb. But let us cling to the ideal of writing a psychology; let that *Aufgabe* be perpetually present in consciousness; let us adopt it as a regulative principle of our procedure.

I assume, secondly, that wherever we have to deal with a closed consciousness, simultaneous or sequential,—I can think of no better adjective than 'closed'; I mean such things as a perception, an action, a thought,—the analytical consideration of mind must be supplemented by the genetic, and that this genetic consideration must be twofold, individual and racial. I have been so generally misunderstood and so seriously (though I have no doubt unintentionally) misrepresented in this connection that you will, perhaps, pardon a somewhat elementary discussion of the postulate: I desire to be quite explicit.

The immediate task of analysis, in face of any complex mental process, I take to be itself twofold. We have to regard the process both in transverse and in longitudinal section; to determine the nature and number of the elementary processes into which the complex may be resolved, and to determine, again with reference to these elementary processes, the type and duration of its temporal course. When, however, we are dealing with what I have called the closed consciousnesses, a single application of this analytical procedure is not enough; on the contrary, we must analyse again and again, at the various formative levels of consciousness; we must follow out the operation of that general law of growth and decay to which I referred in the first Lecture.* An obvious illustration of this necessity is furnished by the psychology of action. To understand the action consciousness we must trace the rise and fall of the impulse within the individual mind: its rise to volition and selective action, its fall to the ideomotor and secondary reflex forms. But we must go even still further afield; we must transcend the limit

* P. 33.

of the individual mind; we must raise the ultimate question whether the earliest organic movements were conscious or unconscious. There is no other way, as things are, to approximate explanation in this department of psychology,—and we have said that psychology is to be both descriptive and explanatory. We find, in fact, that analytical psychology always takes this way: I instance only such well-known things as Wundt's theory of space-perception and Stumpf's theory of tonal fusion.[11]

There are, then, in these cases, two analytical and two genetic problems: the examination of present process in transverse and in longitudinal section, and the examination of formative levels in the history of the individual and of the race. Now arises the question with which we are here directly concerned: What shall be adopted, in these various examinations, as the criterion of a mental element?

I regard as a mental element any process that proves to be irreducible, unanalysable, throughout the whole course of individual experience. Consider, for instance, the processes of sensation and affection. They have certain salient characteristics in common; they suggest the biological analogy of two species of the same genus; I have felt justified in deriving them from a single hypothetical mental ancestor.[12] Nevertheless, I can trace no passage from the one to the other in the individual mind; they seem to be separate and distinct, so soon as nervous organisation is complete; and they must, therefore, I believe, be regarded by analytical psychology as separate elements. Consider, on the other hand, the attitudes and awarenesses of which we have said so much. If we can trace an attitude back, within the same mind, to an imaginal source; if it thus appears not as original endowment but as residuum, not as primule but as vestige, then I should protest against its ranking as a mental element. Even if there are certain minds in which the derivation is impossible, in which the attitude can neither be identified with sensation and image nor referred with certainty to precedent sensory and imaginal experience, I should still hesitate—so long as there are other minds in which the derivation is possible—to adopt the purely phenomenological standpoint, and to class it outright as elementary; I should prefer to term it a secondary element, or a derived element, and so to distinguish it from the elements proper, as defined a moment ago. Classification is, of course, always a matter of expediency, and I have no quarrel with those who differ from me on this particular point. But it seems to me inexpedient to give the rank of element to anything that is not a matter of original and general human endowment.

You see, then, the place that I allow to genetic consideration. The misunderstanding to which I have referred arises, I imagine, from a confusion of two points of view, which may be distinguished as the analytical and the integrative. The analytical psychologist, even when he is occupied with mind in its development, is always trying to analyse. He may, and he does, protest that it never occurs to him to consider sensation, for instance,—the sensation of the adult human consciousness,—as a genetic unit. Nevertheless, what he finds by his genetic consideration must, of necessity, be sensation over again, in some less differentiated form; his problem is analysis, and his results are conditioned by the problem. The integrative psychologist, eager to preserve that continuity of mind which the analyst purposely destroys, and working from below upwards instead of from above downwards, reaches results that, in strictness, are incomparable with the results of analysis: as incomparable, let us say as 'seasonal dimorphism' and 'unstriped muscle.' Incomparables, of course, are not incompatibles; but the attempt to compare them, to bring them under a common rubric as 'facts of psychological observation' or what not, must inevitably lead to misunderstanding.[13]

I have only to add the caution that we must not expect a genetic inquiry to reveal, in every case, a complete series of nicely graded transitional forms. If I may trust some observations of my own, the path that leads, for example, from full imagery to *Bewusstseinslage* is more likely to be broken than continuous; consciousness seems to drop, at a single step, from a higher to a lower level; the progress is effected by substitutions and short cuts, rather than by a gradual course of transformation. This, however, is a matter of descriptive detail, and does not affect the principle which is laid down in the maxim.

I assume, thirdly, that consciousness may be guided and controlled by extra-conscious, physiological factors,—by cortical sets and dispositions; and I agree with Ach that this extra-conscious determination may lead to novel conscious connections, which would not have been effected by the mere play of reproductive tendencies,[14] though I do not agree with Messer that the disposition as such is represented in consciousness by a specific experience.[15] In a paper which is intended to form the basis for a theory of thought, a paper entitled "On the Nature of

Certain Brain States connected with the Psychical Processes," von Kries, in 1895, worked out a theory of *cerebrale Einstellung,* cerebral set or adjustment, with the main features of which I am in entire accord. He distinguishes two types of adjustment, the connective and the dispositional: the former illustrated, in simple terms, by the reading of a musical score in a particular key, the latter by our understanding of abstract words like 'red,' 'triangle.'[16] It is needless to point out that a theory of this sort serves admirably to explain the experimental results of Watt and Ach; indeed, Ach's determining tendencies and subexcited reproductive tendencies are merely specialised types of von Kries' connective and dispositional adjustments.[17] And the idea of determination is now so familiar to us that I need not further discuss it here, or devote further time to my third and last regulative maxim. I pass on to the problems themselves; and I take up first of all the problem of meaning.

III

Some time ago we met with the objection that it is nonsense to call a psychical fact or occurrence the meaning of another psychical fact or occurrence; two ideas are and must remain two ideas, and cannot be an idea and its meaning.   I said, in reply, that in my belief two ideas do, under certain circumstances, make a meaning. What are the circumstances?

I hold that, from the psychological or existential point of view, meaning—so far as it finds representation in consciousness at all—is always context.   An idea means another idea, is psychologically the meaning of that other idea, if it is that idea's context.   And I understand by context simply the mental process or complex of mental processes which accrues to the original idea through the situation* in which the organism finds itself,—primitively, the natural situation; later, either the natural or the mental.   In another connection, I have argued that the earliest form of attention is a definitely determined reaction, sensory and motor both, upon some dominant stimulus; and that as mind developed, and image presently supervened upon sensation, this gross total response was differentiated into three typical attitudes,—the re-

*The term 'situation' seems to me to bring out more clearly than any nearer equivalent of *Aufgabe* the part played in determination by the organism itself.   Externally regarded, a situation is a collocation of stimuli; but it becomes a situation only if the organism is prepared for selective reaction upon that collocation.   An *Aufgabe*, on the other hand, a task or problem, may be set to any organism, prepared or unprepared.   I have no wish to press the word: but I here mean by 'situation' any form of *Aufgabe* that is normal to the particular organism.

ceptive, the elaborative and the executive, which
we may illustrate by sensible discrimination, reflective thought, and voluntary action. Now it
seems to me that meaning, context, has extended
and developed in the same way. Meaning is,
originally, kinæsthesis; the organism faces the
situation by some bodily attitude, and the characteristic sensations which the attitude involves
give meaning to the process that stands at the
conscious focus, are psychologically the meaning
of that process.[18] Afterwards, when differentiation has taken place, context may be mainly
a matter of sensations of the special senses, or
of images, or of kinæsthetic and other organic
sensations, as the situation demands.[19] The particular form that meaning assumes is then a
question to be answered by descriptive psychology.

Of all the possible forms, however,—and I
think they are legion,—two appear to be of
especial importance: kinæsthesis and verbal
images. We are animals, locomotor organisms;
the motor attitude, the executive type of attention, is therefore of constant occurrence in our
experience; and, as it is much older than the
elaborative, so it is the more ingrained. There
would be nothing surprising in the discovery
that, for minds of a certain constitution, all non-

verbal conscious meaning is carried by kinæsthetic sensation or kinæsthetic image.   And
words themselves, let us remember, were at first
motor attitudes, gestures, kinæsthetic contexts:
complicated, of course, by sound, and therefore,
fitted to assist the other types of attention, the
receptive and the elaborative; but still essentially
akin to the gross attitudes of primitive attention.
The fact that words are thus originally contex-
tual, and the fact that they nevertheless as
sound, and later as sight, possess and acquire a
content-character, these facts render language
preëminently available for thought; it is at once
idea and context of idea, idea and meaning; and
as the store of free images increases, and the elaborative attitude grows more and more natural, the
context-use of words or word-aspects becomes
habitual.   The meaning of the printed page may
now consist in the auditory-kinæsthetic accompaniment of internal speech; the word is the
word's own meaning;[20] or some verbal representation, visual or auditory-kinæsthetic or visual-
kinæsthetic or what not, may give meaning to a
non-verbal complex of sensations or images.
There would, again, be nothing surprising—we
should simply be in presence of a limiting case—
in the discovery that, for minds of a certain con-

12

stitution, all conscious meaning is carried either
by total kinæsthetic attitude or by words.

As a matter of fact, meaning is carried by all
sorts of sensational and imaginal processes. Mental constitution is widely varied, and the mean-
ing-response of a mind of a certain constitution
varies widely under varying circumstances. A
descriptive psychology is primarily concerned
with types and uniformities; but if we were to
make serious work of a differential psychology
of meaning, we should probably find that, in the
multitudinous variety of situations and contexts,
any mental process may possibly be the meaning
of any other.

But I go farther. I doubt if meaning need
necessarily be conscious at all,—if it may not be
'carried' in purely physiological terms. In rapid
reading, the skimming of pages in quick succession; in the rendering of a musical composition
in a particular key; in shifting from one language to another as you turn to your right or
left hand neighbour at a dinner table: in these
and similar cases I doubt if meaning necessarily
has any kind of conscious representation. It
very well may; but I doubt if it necessarily does.
There must be an *Aufgabe,* truly, but then the
Aufgabe, as we have seen, need not either come
to consciousness. I was greatly astonished to

observe, some years ago, that the recognition of shades of grey might be effected, so far as my introspection went, in this purely physiological way. I am keenly alive to the importance of organic sensations and, as I shall show in a moment, to that of reduced or schematic kinæsthetic attitudes. I was not at all astonished to observe that the recognition of a grey might consist in a quiver of the stomach. But there were instances in which the grey was 'recognised' without words; without organic sensations, kinæsthetic or other; without the arousal of a mood; without anything of an appreciably conscious sort. I found not the faintest trace of an imageless apprehension, if that apprehension is supposed to be something conscious over and above the grey itself. I cannot further describe the experience: it was simply a 'recognition' without consciousness.

Nevertheless, you may say, there must have been something there; you would have had a different experience had the grey not been recognised. So a word that you understand is experienced otherwise than a nonsense word or a word of some unknown foreign language. Certainly! But my contention is that the *plus* of consciousness, in these comparisons, lies on the side of the unrecognised, the unknown, and not on the side

of the recognised and known. There was plenty
of consciousness, in the experiments to which I
am referring, when a grey was not recognised:
the point is that there was sometimes none at all
when there was recognition. But let me repeat
that this statement is made tentatively, and subject to correction; I believe it to be true of myself, but it requires confirmation from others.[21]

What, then, of the imageless thoughts, the
awarenesses, the *Bewusstseinslagen* of meaning
and the rest? I have, as you may suppose, been
keeping my eyes open for their appearance; and
we have several investigations now in progress
that aim, more or less directly, at their examination. What I have personally found does not,
so far, shake my faith in sensationalism. I have
become keenly alive, for instance, to the variety
of organic attitude and its kinæsthetic representation. I am sure that when I sit down to the
typewriter to think out a lecture, and again to
work off the daily batch of professional correspondence, and again to write an intimate and
characteristic letter to a near friend,—I am sure
that in these three cases I sit down differently.
The different *Aufgaben* come to consciousness, in part, as different feels of the whole
body; I am somehow a different organism, and
a consciously different organism. Description

in the rough is not difficult: there are different visceral pressures, different distributions of tonicity in the muscles of back and legs, differences in the sensed play of facial expression, differences in the movements of arms and hands in the intervals between striking the keys, rather obvious differences in respiration, and marked differences of local or general involuntary movement. It is clear that these differences, or many of them, could be recorded by the instruments which we employ for the method of expression, and could thus be made a matter of objective record. But I have, at any rate, no doubt of their subjective reality; and I believe that, under experimental conditions, description would be possible in detail. I find, moreover, that these attitudinal feels are touched off in all sorts of ways: by an author's choice and arrangement of words, by the intonation of a speaking voice, by the nature of my physical and social environment at large.[22] They shade off gradually into those empathic experiences which I mentioned in the first Lecture, the experiences in which I not only see gravity and modesty and pride and courtesy and stateliness in the mind's eye, but also feel or act them in the mind's muscles. And I should add that they may be of all degrees of definiteness, from the relatively coarse and heavy outlines of the typewriting illustration, down to the merest flicker of imagery which lies, I suppose, on the border of an unconscious disposition.

I do not for a moment profess to have made an exhaustive exploration of my own mind, in the search for *Bewusstseinslagen*. But if there were any frequent form of experience, different in kind from the kinæsthetic backgrounds that I have just described, I think that I am sufficiently versed in introspection, and sufficiently objective in purpose, to have come upon its track. I have turned round, time and time again, upon consciousnesses like doubt, hesitation, belief, assent, trying to remember, having a thing on my tongue's tip, and I have not been able to discover the imageless processes. No doubt, the analysis has been rough and uncontrolled; but it has been attempted at the suggestion of the imageless psychologists, and with the reports of their introspections echoing in my mind. Bühler's thought-elements I frankly disbelieve in.[23] The unanalysable and irreducible *Bewusstseinslagen* of other investigators may, I conceive, prove to be analysable when they are scrutinised directly and under favourable experimental conditions. If they still resist analysis, they may perhaps be considered as consciousnesses of the same general sort as my attitudinal feels, but as consciousnesses that are travelling toward the unconscious by another road. It is conceivable, in other words, that while, in my mind, the attitudes thin out, tail off, lose in bulk, so to say, as they become mechanised, in minds of a different type they retain their original area, their extension, and simply become uniform and featureless, as a variegated visual surface becomes uniform under adaptation. If that hypothesis is worth consideration, then the first problem for experiment is, as I have earlier suggested, to trace this course of degeneration within the same mind. Whether the featureless fringes or backgrounds shall be classified as a secondary kind of mental element—in any event, as we have seen, a question of expediency—would then depend upon the success or failure of the search for intermediaries that should link them to imagery.[24]

As for Ach's theory of the subexcitation of a field of reproductive tendencies, I confess that I have been in many minds about it. The objection that a mere glow or halo in consciousness could not be the vehicle of anything so clear and definite as a specific knowledge, I discount altogether; there is no necessary relation, in my experience, between indefiniteness of conscious

contents and haziness of meaning. The doubt
that I have is, first of all, whether the theory is
necessary, whether the awarenesses (which, remember, I do not myself experience as awarenesses) may not be traced down from imaginal
complexes; and secondly, whether it is psycho-
physically possible that excitations which are
individually subliminal shall by their combination
produce an effect in consciousness. The case is
not at all parallel to that of Fechner's caterpil-
lars, heard feeding in the wood:[25] for there you
have a simple summation of homogeneous excitations, whereas here you have the faint stirring
up of all sorts of reproductions, the getting
ready of all manner of associated ideas. I cannot quite reconcile myself to the theory,—though
if I were convinced of the ultimate character of
the awareness, I might find it more plausible
than I do.[26]

And what of the feelings of relation? Do I
not grant that they exist? Most assuredly; I
intimated as much in a previous Lecture. It
would be curious indeed if we could talk so
fluently about relations, and yet had no feeling
of them, no conscious representation of relation.
But the phrase 'feeling of relation' is no more
unequivocal, as a psychological term, than the
phrase 'idea of object' or 'consciousness of mean-

ing.   It carries an intimation, an indication, a
statement-about; it does not describe.   And the
question for psychology is precisely that: What
do we experience when we have a 'feeling of
relation'?

What I myself experience depends upon circumstances.   It was my pleasure and duty, a
little while ago, to sit on the platform behind a
somewhat emphatic lecturer, who made great use
of the monosyllable 'but.'   My 'feeling of but'
has contained, ever since, a flashing picture of
a bald crown, with a fringe of hair below, and a
massive black shoulder, the whole passing swiftly
down the visual field from northwest to south-
east.   I pick up such pictures very easily, in all
departments of mind; and, as I have told you,
they may come to stand alone in consciousness
as vehicles of meaning.   In this particular instance, the picture is combined with an empathic
attitude; and all such 'feelings'—feelings of if,
and why, and nevertheless, and therefore—normally take the form, in my experience, of motor
empathy.   I act the feeling out, though as a
rule in imaginal and not in sensational terms.   It
may be fleeting, or it may be relatively stable;
whatever it is, I have not the slightest doubt of
its kinæsthetic character.   Sometimes it has a
strong affective colouring—this statement holds

of all my attitudinal feels—and sometimes it is wholly indifferent.

The kinæsthetic origin of these 'feelings' has recently been urged by Washburn, who however considers them to be, in the human consciousness, "ultimately and absolutely unanalysable and unlocalisable."

"The significance of these ['relational elements']," we read, " . . . is the following. They are remnants of remotely ancestral motor attitudes, and they resist analysis now because of their vestigial nature. Take the 'feeling of but,' for example: the sense of the contradiction between two ideas, present when we say 'I should like to do so and so, *but*—here is an objection.' If we trace this back, what can it have been originally but the experience of primitive organisms called upon by simultaneous stimuli to make two incompatible reactions at once, and what can that experience have been but a certain suspended, baffled motor attitude? Similarly with the 'feeling of if' . . . ."[27]

We all appeal, at times, to the primitive organism—who is a useful creature—and I have no doubt that, in this particular case, the appeal is justified. But, in my own experience, an organism need not be more primitive than a professor of psychology in an American university to feel the suspended motor attitude. And while the analysis and localisation of my particular feeling of 'but' has value only for individual psychology, I do roughly localise it and I can roughly analyse it into constituents.

It follows from what has been said that I fully agree with Woodworth as regards the unit-character, the psychological completeness and independence, of the 'feeling of relation'; Calkins' characteristic of 'belonging to' something else appears to me to derive from reflection, not from introspection.[28] Where I differ is in my sensationalistic reading of the relational consciousness. It is, however, always possible, as I explained a little while ago in the case of meaning, that we are in presence of individual differences, and that the champions of the element of relation have moved farther than I along the path to automatism or mechanisation. It would then again be a question of expediency whether we set this unanalysable degenerate in a class by itself, or whether we give it a place among the ideational contents of consciousness. In either event we shall have to qualify our choice, to state that another mode of classification is possible.

That the path of habit does, in fact, lead here to mechanisation, I am as sure as, without strict experimental proof, I can be. Over and over again I have noticed how consciousness may be switched into a new direction by a relational word, without any traceable representation of

the relation within consciousness. The function
of the word is like that of the mysterious button
at the side of the barrel-organ, which when
pressed by the grinder changes the resulting
tune. I must declare, at the risk of wearying
you with declarations, that I can bear witness
both to kinæsthesis and to cortical set, but that
between these extremes I find nothing at all.

So much, then, for meaning and attitude and
relation. Even the little that I have been able
to say about them shows, I hope, that the sensationalistic position is still tenable. I wish that
I could offer some positive contribution to the
psychology of judgment; but the insuperable
difficulty there is that we do not yet know what
judgment is. It is an anomalous position! We
are committed to a 'psychology of judgment'; we
can no longer say, with Rehmke, that the phrase
is a contradiction in itself,[29] or with Marbe that
there is no psychological criterion of judgment;
and yet no one, psychologist or logician, can
furnish a definition that finds general acceptance.[30] And this lack of a settled psychological definition is not a matter simply of different
points of view, as it is, for instance, in the case
of sensation and idea. There the differences
of opinion are natural, traditional, intelligible
from the history of human thought; here there

is actual uncertainty regarding the nature and limits of the process to be defined.

When, years ago, I was writing a text-book of psychology, and felt the need of a paragraph upon judgment, I adopted Wundt's description of the play of active attention upon an aggregate idea; and in order to give judgment a definite place in the system, I named it an association after disjunction, and classified it with the successive associations. I took Wundt's description because it was couched in terms of content, and because I could verify it in my own experience. Bühler and his observers have recently borne witness to its truth;[31] and, indeed, I suppose that no one denies the occurrence of the particular type of consciousness to which Wundt refers. For the same reason, when a reviewer observed that I had given an account only of the analytic, and not of the synthetic judgment, I replied in good introspective faith that my account was intended to cover both forms.[32] It is clear, however, that the discovery of the *Aufgabe* makes all content-psychology of the Wundtian sort, however accurate within its limits, appear partial and incomplete.

When, again, I was looking about for instances of the judgment, I took it for granted that such statements as 'Socrates is a man,' 'Hon-

esty is the best policy' are not judgments at all,
in any distinctive sense,—that they are, on the
contrary, just as mechanical as is the pianist's
rendering of a certain composition in a certain
key. Marbe's investigation of judgment seems
to me to be open to the criticism that, in a great
many of his experiments, no judgment is involved. When, for instance, he asks Külpe,
pointing at the same time to an object on the
table, "What is that?" and Külpe answers "An
ink bottle," there is a touch of comedy in the
zugehörige Aussage that the answer came 'quite
reflexly.' How else should it have come? Well!
now hear Watt on the other side:

"There is no reason to suppose," he tells us, "that a
certain typical course of consciousness is the indispensable condition of logical thinking. We have to fix
our attention upon the result (*Leistung*) and upon
that alone; we need not assume that a certain rapidity
of reproduction and mode of apperception are essential
conditions of a logical act. I find no logical difference
between the first, slow, hesitating reproduction of an
idea and the quickest, such as we have in the pair rat-
bat. It has, however, become the rule with many psychologists to speak of a thinking that has grown
mechanical by practice, in opposition to a thinking that
is active, novel and valuable. This is a vulgar difference, which has little import for psychological analysis
and for experiment."[33]

I can only say that, so far as I see, the difference—be it as vulgar as possible—has a great deal of import for analysis and experimentation. Watt, I may remind you, is convinced that all his experiments were judgments, because all alike stood under the influence of the *Aufgabe*. But, if we find that consciousness under that influence shows all manner of variation, it is our business, as psychologists, to make the variation explicit; to bring the different forms, by experimental control, to a psychological analysis. At the same time the fact that Watt adopts so general a criterion of judgment shows the uncertainty of its psychological definition; just as the adoption of a similarly general criterion of voluntary action, by Thorndike and Woodworth, shows how far we are, in that field also, from clear-cut distinctions.[34] Any proposed definition must have something personal and arbitrary about it.

Yet Bühler started out with the simple intention of making his observers think, and I have been saying that his method was a failure! Yes,—not because the intention was wrong, but because the method at once escaped experimental control and put a premium on the stimulus-error. I venture to propose a middle way. I have pointed out that we are all exposed to infection from logic, though we recognise the symptoms of the disease in others more readily than we observe them in ourselves. Now let us face the facts; and, if we can, let us agree with Royce that "every advance upon one of these two sides of the study of the intellectual life makes possible, under the conditions to which all our human progress is naturally subject, a new advance upon the other side."[35] Then a programme for the experimental study of judgment lies before us. We have to work steadily and one by one at the part-problems set by the investigations already made, and we have to compare our results with the teachings of the standard books on logic. The logicians disagree, as the psychologists disagree. But we shall find out, by our comparison and by the suggestion of further work that issues from it, what types of consciousness there are that correspond with current logical definitions of judgment. As the exploration goes on, uniformities will appear of themselves; and ultimately we shall be able to decide whether judgment is a general term for a great variety of consciousnesses, a name like 'perception,' or whether it is, like 'fusion,' the name of a specific mode of conscious arrangement. To make the idea more concrete, I propose, for instance, that we combine Wundt's notion of the apperceptively analysed aggregate idea with the doctrine of

Aufgabe, and discover experimentally how far
the combination takes us. Or, to illustrate it
from another point of view, I suggest that Messer's mistake lay in his outright acceptance of
Erdmann's definition of judgment; that he
should not have instructed his observers to find
the predicative relation, but should have put
them under conditions where they might find it
if it was there. The advantages of this procedure
are that we secure a definite starting point for
experimental work, and carry on that work under
the guidance of some definite hypothesis. The
obvious disadvantage is the dependence of a psychological enquiry upon logical presuppositions.
But we ought to have our eyes open: and, if we
nod, our friends will not scruple to arouse us.[36]

It is, as everyone knows, far easier to propose
than to carry the proposal out in experimental
performance. Once upon a time, I innocently
gave a trio of students the topics of expectation,
practice and habituation, with the idea that a year's
experimental work would reveal everything about
them that we need to know. The three reports
are still extant, and I find their perusal whole-
some. It is easy to suggest: but here there has
been no alternative,—or at best the alternative
of a sheer dogmatism. My task has been to per-
suade you that there is no need, as things are, to

13

swell the number of the mental elements; that the psychology of thought, so far as we have it, may be interpreted from the sensationalistic standpoint, and so far as we still await it, may be approached by sensationalistic methods. What the future will bring forth, no one can foresee: it may be that the essential problems are already before us, or it may be that we are still at the threshold of a thought-psychology, that, psychologically as well as logically, judgment is but the first step on a long road of scientific inquiry. In any event, I see less prospect of gain from a revolution than from persistent work under the existing régime.

We have acknowledged our indebtedness to the psychologists of imageless thinking. We have admitted and considered the fact of constitutional bias. On the other hand, we have proved that much can be analysed which had been pronounced simple and unanalysable, and we have found a direction for research that is proving itself practicable in the laboratory. The final decision between the opposing views may now be left, with confidence, to the outcome of future experiment.

NOTES

NOTES TO LECTURE I

[1] K. Marbe's work on judgment (1901) has proved to be the starting-point of a long and important series of investigations, and it is becoming customary to date the experimental psychology of thought from the appearance of the *Experimentell-psychologische Untersuchungen über das Urteil, eine Einleitung in die Logik,** as we date the experimental psychology of memory from Ebbinghaus' *Ueber das Gedächtnis.* I have, naturally, no wish to detract from Marbe's service and originality. But in fact there were experiments on thought before 1901; Binet seems to have known nothing of Marbe when he wrote his own book; and Marbe's work—with its negative result on the side of psychological analysis, and its strongly logical leanings—would hardly have had the influence that it has actually exerted unless the ground had been prepared to receive it. Hence it would, perhaps, be more nearly true to say that Marbe stands to the experimental psychology of thought as Lehmann (with his *Die Hauptgesetze des menschlichen Gefühlslebens,* 1892) stands to the experimental psychology of the affective processes.

[2] So A. Binet, *L'étude expérimentale de l'intelligence,*† 1903, 1 f. "Il est incontestable, pour ceux qui suivent les progrès de la psychologie expérimentale, que cette science subit en ce moment même une évolution décisive. . . . Le mouvement nouveaù . . . consiste à faire une

* Cited, in the following Notes, as 'Marbe.'
† Cited, in the following Notes, as 'Binet.'

plus large place a l'introspection, et à porter l'investigation vers les phénomènes supérieurs de l'esprit, tels
que la mémoire, l'attention, l'imagination, l'orientation
des idées."

[3] *Völkerpsychologie. Eine Untersuchung der Ent-
wicklungsgesetze von Sprache, Mythus und Sitte.* I.
Die Sprache, 1900; second edition, 1904.

[4] *Principles of Physiological Psychology,* i., 1904, 5;
Grundzüge der physiologischen Psychologie, i., 1908,
5. The idea is implied *ibid.,* 1874, 5, but is not
clearly expressed before i., 1887, 5 f. See also *Beiträge
zur Theorie der Sinneswahrnehmung,* 1862, Einleitung;
Essays, 1885, 144 ff. (1906, 207 ff.); Ueber Ziele
und Wege der Völkerpsychologie, *Philosophische Studien,*
iv., 1888, 1 ff.; Ueber Ausfrageexperimente und über die
Methoden zur Psychologie des Denkens, *Psychologische
Studien,* iii., 1907, 340 ff. Ct. N. Ach, *Ueber d.
Willenstätigkeit u. d. Denken,* 1905, 21.

I have spoken in the text of Wundt's overt challenge
to the experimentalists. It should be remembered, further, that the *Psychology of Language* is itself couched
throughout in terms of a definite systematic psychology,
and therefore challenges by implication all those who
are unable to accept the system.

[5] All these and other, similar influences are traceable
in the German work. The most important references
are:

B. Erdmann, *Logik,* i., 1892, 1907.
> Die psychologischen Grundlagen der Beziehungen zwischen
> Sprechen und Denken, *Arch. f. syst. Philos.,* ii., 1896, 355-416;
> iii., 1897, 31-48, 150-173.
> Umrisse zur Psychologie des Denkens, in *Philosophische
> Abhandlungen, Chr. Sigwart zu seinem 70. Geburtstage
> gewidmet,* 1900, 3-40.

E. G. Husserl, *Logische Untersuchungen*, *i. Prolegomena zur reinen Logik*, 1900. *ii. Untersuchungen zur Phänomenologie und Theorie der Erkenntnis*, 1901.

T. Lipps, *Einheiten und Relationen, eine Skizze zur Psychologie der Apperzeption*, 1902.

Vom Fühlen, Wollen und Denken, 1902.

Einige psychologische Streitpunkte: iii. Die Relation der Aehnlichkeit, *Zeits. f. Psychol.*, xxviii., 1902, 166-178.

Fortsetzung der "Psychologischen Streitpunkte": v. Zur Psychologie der "Annahmen," *ibid.*, xxxi., 1903, 67-78.

Leitfaden der Psychologie, 1903, 1906.

Bewusstsein und Gegenstände, *Psychologische Untersuchungen*, i., 1905, 1-203.

Inhalt und Gegenstand; Psychologie und Logik, *Sitzungsber. d. philos.-philol. Kl. d. k. b. Akad. d. Wiss. zu München*, Jahrgang 1905, 1906, 511-669.

A. Meinong, Zur Psychologie der Komplexionen und Relationen, *Zeits. f. Psychol. u. Physiol. d. Sinnesorgane*, ii., 1891, 245-265.

Beiträge zur Theorie der psychischen Analyse, *ibid.*, vi., 1893-4, 340-385, 417-455.

Ueber Gegenstände höherer Ordnung und deren Verhältniss zur inneren Wahrnehmung, *ibid.*, xxi., 1899, 182-272.

Abstrahiren und Vergleichen, *ibid.*, xxiv., 1900, 34-82.

Ueber Annahmen, 1902.

Untersuchungen zur Gegenstandstheorie und Psychologie, 1904: Ueber Gegenstandstheorie, 1-50.

Ueber die Stellung der Gegenstandstheorie im System der Wissenschaften, *Zeits. f. Philos. u. philos. Kritik*, cxxix., 1906, 48-93; 1907, 155-207; cxxx., 1907, 1-46.

In Sachen der Annahmen, *Zeits. f. Psychol.*, xli., 1906, 1-14.

C. Stumpf, *Erscheinungen und psychische Funktionen*, 1907. (Aus den Abhandlungen der königl. preuss. Akademie der Wissenschaften vom Jahre 1906.)

Zur Einteilung der Wissenschaften, 1907. (Aus den Abhandlungen der königl. preuss. Akademie der Wissenschaften vom Jahre 1906.)

The range of discussion, to which these references may serve as introduction, is already wide, and the questions at issue are of great moment for a systematic psychology; they lie, however, beyond the scope of the present Lectures.

[6] R. S. Woodworth, Non-Sensory Components of Sense Perception, *Journal of Philosophy, Psychology and Scientific Methods*, iv., 1907, 170; The Consciousness of Relation, *Essays Philosophical and Psychological in Honour of William James*, 1908, 502; M. W. Calkins, The Abandonment of Sensationalism in Psychology, *American Journal of Psychology*, xx., 1909, 269 ff.

[7] See my *Lectures on the Elementary Psychology of Feeling and Attention*, 1908, 172. Useful references are:

C. Sigwart, Die Unterschiede der Individualitäten, *Kleine Schriften*, ii., 1889, 212 ff.

W. Dilthey, Beiträge zum Studium der Individualität, *Sitzungsber. d. kgl. preuss. Akad. d. Wiss.*, 1896, 295 ff.

M. Dessoir, Beiträge zur Aesthetik, i. Seelenkunst und Psychognosis, *Arch. f. syst. Philos.*, iii., 1897, 374 ff.

L. W. Stern, *Ueber Psychologie der individuellen Differenzen*, 1900. (Bibliography, 133 ff.)

E. Meumann, *Vorlesungen zur Einführung in die experimentelle Pädagogik und ihre psychologischen Grundlagen*, i., 1907, 322 ff. (Bibliography, 552 ff.)

R. Müller-Freienfels, Individuelle Verschiedenheiten in der Kunst, *Zeits. f. Psych.*, 1., 1908, 1 ff.

It was the search for individual differences that prompted Ribot to undertake his study of 'general ideas': Enquête sur les idées générales, *Revue philos.*, xxxii., 1891, 376 ff.; Résultat d'une enquête sur les concepts, *Internat. Congress of Exper. Psych.*, 1892, 20 ff. (remarks by H. Sidgwick, 23 f.; note by E. E. C. Jones, 181); *The Evolution of General Ideas*, 1899, 111 ff. Ribot wished to ascertain if there are types of conception as there are types of imagination or ideation, and found in fact three such types, the concrete, the visual typographic and the auditory. His method (the presentation of single words or of sentences) anticipates in crude form those of Binet, of the Würzburg investigators, and of Woodworth. His most important result is, without question, the discovery that meaning oftentimes has no representation in consciousness. "We learn to understand a concept as we learn to walk, dance, fence, or play a musical instrument; it is a habit, *i.e.* an organised memory" (*General Ideas*, 131).

[8] F. Galton, *Inquiries into Human Faculty and its Development*, 1883. "Scientific men, as a class, have feeble powers of visual representation" (87). "After maturity is reached, the further advance of age does not seem to dim the faculty, but rather the reverse, . . . but advancing years are sometimes accompanied by a growing habit of hard abstract thinking, and in these cases . . . the faculty undoubtedly becomes impaired. . . . Language and book-learning certainly tend to dull it" (99 f.). "I could mention instances within my own experience in which the visualising faculty has become strengthened by practice" (106). "I cannot discover any closer relation between high visualising power and the intellectual faculties than between verbal memory and those same faculties" (111).

Binet is evidently writing from an imperfect memory when he says (Binet, 111): "il y a . . . une opinion très répandue d'après laquelle les images intenses se rencontrent chez les femmes et les enfants, tandis que ceux qui ont l'habitude de l'abstraction, les adultes réfléchis, n'ont pas de belles images de la réalité, mais de pauvres fantômes sans couleur et sans relief. Je suppose que toutes ces questions sont un peu embarrassées d'idées préconçues; ce ne sont point là des observations régulières, et il ne faut pas s'y arrêter trop longtemps." But Galton's statements are both careful and explicit. Cf. W. James, *Principles of Psych.*, i., 1890, 266.

⁹ The following is a characteristic illustration of my use of imagery. I had to carry across the room, from book-shelf to typewriter, four references,—three volume-numbers of a magazine, three dates, and four page-numbers. The volumes and years I said aloud, and then consigned to the care of the perseverative tendencies. Of the four page-numbers, I held two by visual images, one by auditory, and one by kinæsthesis. After I had written the references out, it occurred to me that the procedure—which at the time was adopted naturally and without reflection—had been somewhat dangerous; the record proved, however, to be accurate. Experiences of the sort are, indeed, very common with me, and I should hardly have noted the occurrence had I not been recently engaged in the writing of this Lecture. Similar tricks of retention are, very possibly, employed by imaginal minds at large. But, until we have detailed descriptions, the range of the mixed memory-type must remain uncertain. I put the above observation on record in the hope that it may elicit others of like tenor.—It is, perhaps, scarcely necessary to add that the 'having' of images and the 'using' of images are very different things, and that the determination of type must always take account of conditions. See, *e.g.*, H. J. Watt, Experimentelle Beiträge zu einer Theorie des Denkens,* *Arch. f. d. ges. Psych.*, iv., 1905, 312, 368; *ibid.*, vii., 1906, Literaturbericht, 44, 47; M.

* Cited, in the following Notes, as 'Watt.'

F. Washburn, A. Bell and L. Muckenhoupt, A Comparison of Methods for the Determination of Ideational Type, *Amer. Journ. Psychol.*, xvii., 1906, 126; E. L. Thorndike, On the Function of Visual Images, *Journ. Philos. Psych. Sci. Meth.*, iv., 1907, 324 ff.; J. Segal, Ueber den Reproduktionstypus und das Reproduzieren von Vorstellungen, *Arch. f. d. ges. Psych.*, xii., 1908, 124 ff.

For a discussion of internal speech, see J. M. Baldwin, *Mental Development in the Child and the Race: Methods and Processes*, 1906, 409 ff.

[10] The topic of visual reading is discussed by E. B. Huey, *The Psychology and Pedagogy of Reading*, 1908, 10, 117 ff., 180 f. Huey gives, as a "very rare" instance of rapid reading, the case of a mathematician who "has read the whole of a standard novel of 320 pages in two and one-fourth hours." "I am inclined to think," he says, "that at any such speed the meanings suggested immediately by the visual forms suffice for all but the more important parts, and that these meanings are felt sufficiently, without inner utterance, to permit selection of what is more important, the more important places themselves having a fleeting inner utterance to vivify their meaning. We must indeed experiment further before we can conclude against the possibility of mainly visual reading, at the very high speeds."

I should not have supposed that the rate of reading mentioned by Huey was exceptional; I certainly often read at the same or at a higher speed. But my rate varies enormously, both with the subject-matter of the work read and with my purpose in reading. I usually

take a new book, or a new article, at a rush, and then—
if I want to savour the style or to assimilate the details—
go over it again slowly and minutely. It is surprising
how accurate an impression may be gained by hurried,
selective reading, 'skimming,' if only one has had sufficient practice; I come back to this point in Note 13
below.

There is no question, I think, that purely visual reading is possible, and that its habit may be cultivated.
Here is an instance. I used to read the abbreviation
Vp., in terms of internal speech, as *Versuchsperson.*
Then, for a time, I read it as *Vöp* or *Vup;* later, again,
as a mere breath on the *V;* now I take it altogether by
eye. The same thing holds of such forms as *bzw., u.
dgl. m., m. E., u. s. w., etc.* When I am reading carefully, and when the abbreviations have an argumenta-
tive significance, I take them by a shadowy form of the
kinæsthetic feels discussed in Lecture V.; in ordinary
reading, however, they are simply seen.*

Professor Whipple (whose general type is auditory-
motor) tells me that he has had similar experiences, but
far more frequently with foreign languages than with
English. I have not noticed this difference in my own
case.

* In my study of the authors now under discussion, I at first
read the abbreviation *Bsl.* as *Bewusstseinslage.* This soon simplified to something like 'bizzle.' This, again, simplified to a mixture
of internal speech and vision; the *b* came in terms of speech, and
the *sl* tailed off in terms of sight alone. Oftentimes there was
an unpleasant hitch or catch in consciousness ("I can't pronounce
that!"), which was due, apparently, to a momentary inhibition of
breathing, accompanied by an incipient shrug. At present, I get
either the speech-sight mixture without the hitch, or I read over
the abbreviation visually.

[11]I have practically no gift of musical composition, and my skill as a performer is below zero. On the other hand, I come of a musical family, and was fortunate enough to hear a great deal of the best piano music in my childhood. My musical endowment—apart from this haunting by orchestral performances—consists in a quick and comprehensive understanding of a composition, a sort of logical and æsthetic *Einfühlung*, an immediate (or very rapid) grasp of the sense and fitness of the musical structure. There is thus a fairly close analogy between my apprehension of music and the visual schematising of arguments which is described in the Lecture. It would be interesting to know whether the correlation is at all general.—Cf. Lecture V., Note 22.

My use of the visual schema itself suggests the recourse to simple mechanical analogies (models of the atom, representation of gravitational attractions by means of pulsating bodies in a liquid medium, etc., etc.) for the illustration of physical phenomena of a more complicated kind, which is often said to be characteristic of British physicists. Galton mentions physicists only casually (113).

[12] In this regard, my type is that of Marguerite and not of Armande: see Binet, 155 ff. Galton (*Inquiries*, 109) speaks of persons who "have a complete mastery over their mental images," and remarks that "this free action of a vivid visualising faculty is of much importance in connection with the higher processes of generalised thought, though it is commonly put to no such purpose." It is, accordingly, only natural that I have no such imaginal experiences as those of Goethe (series

of unfolding roses; *Werke,* Weimarer Ausgabe, Abth.
2, xi., 282) or of G. Henslow (spontaneous transformation of images: Galton, *Inquiries,* 159 ff.).

[13] Huey, in discussing aids to quick and selective
reading (*op. cit.,* 411, 423), mentions with approval
the German use of capital initials for substantives, the
use of italics, etc. "The special temporary characterisation of the important words or phrases in any given
article, by changes in type, etc., may also aid much in
speed and ease of reading whenever the reader's aim is
selective, purposing to get quickly the kernels or gist of
the matter read." The German capitals become so accustomed that I doubt if they do any service. Wundt,
it is true, argues that "jede Einbusse an differenzirend-
en Merkmalen eine Erschwerung der Unterscheidung
bedeutet, die dadurch, dass man sie nicht mehr bemerkt,
noch nicht verschwindet" (*Physiol. Psych.,* iii., 1903,
608); but an argument of this sort may easily be pushed
too far. On the other points I was formerly of Huey's
opinion; now, however, I rather suspect the value of the
change of type. For one thing, spaced or italicised
matter is difficult to read; the eye balks at it. For another, I very often find that the spaced or italicised
items are not those that I myself should wish to have
emphasised. Just as a summary, while useful in its
way, is a very dangerous substitute for the article
which it professes to reproduce, so are the author's italics very unreliable guides to the contents of his pages;
for the motives that prompt the writer to accentuate are
not necessarily those that dominate the reader. It is
both amusing and instructive to have one of your own
essays read aloud by an intelligent student, and to note

the slurring of what you thought important and the stressing of what appeals to the reader.

So I should suppose that the ideal arrangement for a text-book, *e.g.*, is that which allows of short and sharply separated paragraphs, as an aid to the untrained attention, but which within the paragraph keeps as a rule to a strict uniformity of type. "Any arrangement," Huey tells us, "which makes comprehensive skimming an easy matter will be of great benefit for large parts of our reading": but the skimming which relies upon italics or black-faced type is scrappy rather than comprehensive. The ability to skim, like the ability to cram, is a valuable intellectual asset; only one must learn to skim for oneself, as one must learn to prepare one's own abstract or digest for memorising.

In my experience, the headlong first reading of a new work, to which reference was made in Note 10 above, is for the most part visual and diffusedly organic in character. I have never attempted its analysis, under experimental conditions; and the procedure is so habitual that a complete analysis would at the best be exceedingly difficult. On the side of vision, I seem to pay little regard to headings or italics; I read straight ahead, taking in the first few words of a sentence and then jumping to catch-words; sometimes I skip entire sentences, even entire paragraphs. If there is a hitch of any sort, breathing is inhibited, and internal speech appears. The organic reaction is wide-spread, and strongly affective. I warm eagerly to any novelty of method, to the original application of a familiar idea, to any extension of experiment, to anything that supports or amplifies my own thinking; I am troubled and restless when I find a discrepancy between evidence and inference, a reference omitted, a set of observations that threatens to overturn a belief. There is also, I think, a fairly marked play of facial expression; I have caught myself smiling or frowning, pursing the lips or raising the eyebrows (see Lecture V., Note 22). This is a clumsy and banal account of a very vivid and varied experience; it may, however, have been worth while to emphasise the fact that sight and attitudinal feel (Lecture V.) do my skimming for me, with only occasional assistance from internal speech.

[14] Galton (*Inquiries*, 157 f.) remarks that a "curious and abiding fantasy of certain persons is invariably to connect visualised pictures with words, the same picture to the same word." The figures "are not the capricious creations of the fancy of the moment, but are the regular concomitants of the words, and have been so as far back as the memory is able to recall." Galton does not explain whether these visual pictures are merely accessory, or whether they form part of the psychological meaning of the words.

One of Messer's observers replies to the stimulus-word *Christin* as follows: "Als ich 'Christ—' gelesen hatte, optisches Bild einer weissen Wachskerze (diese Vorstellung habe ich immer bei 'Christ'; sie erscheint mir blödsinnig) . . ." Here, too, we are left in doubt whether the visual associate is accessory or has its share in meaning; the 'foolishness' of the image, to a later reflection, is not decisive. See A. Messer, Experimentell-psychologische Untersuchungen über das Denken,* *Arch. f. d. ges. Psych.*, viii., 1906, 68. Another instance is fur-

* Cited, in the following Notes, as 'Messer.'

nished by H. Sidgwick (*Internat. Congress of Exper. Psych.*, 1892, 24). "In his reasonings on political economy he found that the general terms were almost always accompanied by some visual image besides and along with the image of the word itself; but the images were often curiously arbitrary and sometimes almost undecipherably symbolic. For example, it took him a long time to discover that an odd symbolic image which accompanied the word 'value' was a faint, partial image of a man putting something in a scale. On the other hand in logical or mathematical reasoning he could usually detect no image except that of the printed word." Cf. W. C. Bagley, *Amer. Journ. Psych.*, xii., 1900, 118 f.; Binet, 100.

Many of my own students, and a number of persons in my audience at the University of Illinois, have informed me that the visual, pictorial representation of meaning is natural and familiar to them. But like attracts like; and we shall not know the relative frequency of the type until we have made one of those statistical investigations which Binet (299) hands over to "les auteurs américains, qui aiment faire grand."—

In general, there seems to be no more reason to doubt the occurrence of pictorial, non-verbal thinking than there is to doubt that of a purely visual reading. Watt became familiar with it: "da werden die Gesichtsvorstellungen oft Arbeitsplätze für das Denken" (312; cf. the discussion of visual ideas, 361 ff., 432 f., and the recommendation of further enquiry, 436); and Messer accords it a certain place in the process of thought (87); cf. also Bovet, *Arch. de Psych.*, viii., 1908, 26, 37. For certain minds, at certain times, Taine's statement

14

that "l'esprit agissant est un polypier d'images mutuellement dépendantes" would then be strictly and literally true (*De l'intelligence*, i., 1883, 124).

[15] J. Locke, *An Essay Concerning Human Understanding*, [1690] Bk. iv., ch. 7, §9.

[16] G. Berkeley, *A Treatise Concerning the Principles of Human Knowledge*, [1710] Introduction, §§10, 13. The passages have been rearranged. D. Hume, *A Treatise of Human Nature*, [1739] Bk. i., pt. i., §7.

[17] W. Hamilton, *Lectures on Metaphysics*, ii., 1859, 300 (Lect. xxxv.).

[18] T. H. Huxley, *Hume*, 1881, ch. iv., 96 f.

[19] See the discussions of Binet, 113, 141 ff., 150, 153; Watt, 364 f., 431 ff.; Watt, Literaturbericht, *Arch. f. d. ges. Psych.*, vii., 1906, 42 ff.; Messer, 55 f., 85 ff.; K. Bühler, Tatsachen und Probleme zu einer Psychologie der Denkvorgänge, i. Ueber Gedanken,* *Arch. f. d. ges. Psych.*, ix., 1907, 363 f. (cf. 352); A. Wreschner, *Die Reproduktion und Assoziation von Vorstellungen*,† 1907-1909, 158 ff., etc.

Messer writes (85 f.): "je lebhafter und anschaulicher, je reicher an individuellen Zügen [die reproduzierten Gesichtsvorstellungen] sind, um so weniger decken sie sich mit der mehr oder minder *allgemeinen* Bedeutung der Worte. . . . Je schematischer, blasser, unbestimmter und insofern 'allgemeiner' die optischen Vorstellungen sind, un so weniger unterscheiden sie sich also im Grunde von jener anderen Klasse der (unanschaulichen) Bedeutungserlebnisse." He seems, however, to have anticipated this result; at any rate he takes it as

* Cited, in the following Notes as 'Bühler.'
† Cited, in the following Notes, as 'Wreschner.'

a matter of course. I give my own experience in the text.

[20] A. Fraser (Visualisation as a Chief Source of the Psychology of Hobbes, Locke, Berkeley and Hume, *Amer. Journ. Psych.*, iv., 1891, 230 ff.) remarks that "in Berkeley and Hume we have the philosophy of youth. At the age of twenty-five both these men had completed their chief philosophical works. And here again we have an illustration of Galton's results. Their powers of visualisation were much higher than in the case of [Hobbes and Locke]—so high, in fact, that they could visualise enough to make them believe that anything they couldn't visualise did not exist" (241). Locke "was somewhat advanced in years when he presented his philosophical works . . . ; and . . . his philosophy . . . was under the necessity of leaving a great part of the verbal web untranslated" (*ibid.*). Fraser does not discuss the passage from the fourth Book.

This argument can hardly be accepted in its application to the general idea; conceptualism as well as nominalism may have a basis in visualisation (cf. Fraser's own admission, quoted in the following Note); Locke and Berkeley differed in the mode or character of their visualisation, but not necessarily in visualising power. The argument would apply only if we could believe that Locke did not actually see his "general idea of a triangle," but—to put it bluntly—made up the idea out of words. I grant that there is something, both in context and style, to suggest that view. Nevertheless, I get the definite impression that Locke is writing from an introspective cue; we have, in the passage, simply one of those bits of translation out of psychology into the logic of common sense with which the *Essay* abounds. The logical aspect is again to the fore in Bk. ii., ch. xi., §9. But in Bk. ii., ch. xxxii., §8 we are told that the abstract idea is "something in the mind between the thing that exists, and the name that is given to it"; and in Bk. iii., ch. iii., §9 the introspective appeal is directly made.

It is very instructive to compare the parallel passages in the writings of J. S. Mill. If we had no more than the bare references to the selective power of attention in the *Logic* (1846,* Bk. ii., ch. v., §1; Bk. iv., ch. ii., §1), we might well suppose that Mill was arguing only, and not introspecting. But the passage in *An Examination of Sir William Hamilton's Philosophy*, 1865, 320 f., bears all the marks of a first-hand observation,—marks that are made the plainer by the writer's theoretical confusion (James, *Princ. of Psych.*, i., 470). And observation reappears in the note to J. Mill's *Analysis of the Phenomena of the Human Mind*, i., 1869, 289, where the artificiality of Locke's account of the idea of triangle is expressly recognised. Mill's psychology is annoyingly schematic; but I do not think that any reader of psychological insight will doubt that he is psychologising.—

Relevant observations are noted by Binet, 153; Messer, 54. Cf. also the ideation of *Eigenschaften*, Messer, 56 f.

[21] So Fraser (*op. cit.*, 244): "In this case the generic character does not consist in the name, it is in the idea. Neither is the idea a 'blur,' it is clear and distinct. To what extent this degree of visualisation exists in the

* I have not been able to consult the first edition, of 1843.

world I cannot say, but there can be no doubt as to its possibility." Binet (146 f.) is somewhat sceptical. "L'idée de cette combinaison [d'images particulières, individuelles], qui est toute gratuite, car personne n'a pu l'observer, appartient à Huxley, qui a donné une forme très originale à son hypothèse en comparant la formation des idées générales à ces photographies composites que Galton a obtenues en superposant sur une même plaque les images de plusieurs objets un peu analogues. . . . L'explication de Huxley fut d'abord acceptée avec faveur, généralisée sans retenue, et finalement elle a été réduite par Ribot à un rôle plus modeste. . . . Je n'ai point rencontré chez [mes deux sujets] d'images dans lesquelles se marquerait avec évidence la combinaison de plusieurs perceptions différentes." Of course, the whole question is a matter of individual psychology : but I have no doubt that Huxley did, in his own case and under the conditions of his special occupation, observe the formation of the type-idea, in stages, from the combination of individual perceptions.

[22] Hamilton, *op. cit.*, 312.

[23] Bühler, 363.

[24] Further instances were supplied by members of my audience at the University of Illinois. I mention one case only, that of a trained psychologist. Meaning, for this observer, consisted psychologically in the kinæsthetic image (sometimes connected with actual innervation) of lifting the right hand and arm, as if to open a closed box. Here, as in the examples given in the text, the explanation comes *ex post facto;* the experience of meaning, as such, has nothing in it to suggest or recall the opening of the box; but reflection

shows that the imaged gesture is of the box-opening kind. Meaning, therefore, is something that you reveal or disclose.

[25] Organic Images, *Journ. Philos. Psych. Sci. Meth.*, i., 1904, 38.

[26] I find a similar observation in Messer (59). One of the observers reports "eine gewisse innere Zuneigung. Wenn ich nachträglich versuche, eine gleichartige Bewegung auszuführen, wie sie mir gegeben zu sein schien, so sehe ich, dass die Bewegungen alle viel zu lebhaft *und grob* ausfallen als die früher erlebten" (italics mine).

[27] This account has been compiled, for the most part, from notes jotted down as I read the successive experimental studies from the Würzburg laboratory. It is, therefore, relevant only to the individual psychology of thought,—thinking, reading, writing, teaching,—and not to the intellectual processes at large; while, even so, it has in all probability been narrowed down by the consideration of the specific problems raised by the Würzburg school. However, it is with that school— with Marbe and Orth, Watt and Ach, Messer and Bühler —that the Lectures are mainly concerned.

[28] *Dict. Philos. Psych.*, ii., 1902, 515 f.—A great deal of confusion would be avoided if psychologists at large recognised the fact that the sensation of experimental psychology is a simple, meaningless (or, rather, non-meaningful) process, definable only by an enumeration of its attributes. Until this recognition is accorded, discussion between the experimentalists and the non-experimentalists (I apologise for the negative term!) must be largely a matter of beating the air. I have

tried to do my share towards clarity,—*e.g.*, in *Exp. Psych.*, I., ii., 1901, 3 f.; *Feeling and Attention*, 1908, Lect. i.; *Text-book*, 1909, 46 ff. But James has defined sensation as the (cognitively and chronologically) first thing in consciousness; the *Dictionary* offers a definition which it admits to be "not strictly psychological" and which ignores experimental usage; and psychology in general still shows the uncertainty which Bain deplored (Mill's *Analysis*, i., 65 ff.) as "causing serious embroilments in philosophical controversy." Experimental psychology has, of course, no exclusive rights in the word; but it has the right to define for itself, and to have its definition respected within its own universe of discourse. It is, for instance, axiomatic for the experimentalist that a sensation cannot function alone; at least two sensations must come together, if there is to be a meaning; the single element can do nothing more than go on; so far as cognition or function is concerned, *sentire semper idem, et non sentire, ad idem recidunt.*

[29] *Ibid.*, i., 1901, 80.

[30] A. Seth, *Man's Place in the Cosmos and Other Essays*, 1897, 47, 65. The addresses from which these quotations are taken contain some useful criticism; but I do not recommend them to the reader who wishes to acquaint himself with the aim and status of experimental psychology.

[31] H. Ebbinghaus, *Ueber das Gedächtnis*, 1885, 31 ff.

[32] In order to make my point clearly and sharply, I have here spoken as if modern psychology were descriptive only, and not descriptive and explanatory. Later Lectures furnish the necessary corrective: to

bring explanation into the present discussion would obscure the issue.

[33] W. Wundt, Ueber psychische Causalität und das Princip des psychophysischen Parallelismus, *Philos. Studien*, x., 1894, 123.

[34] Zur Lehre von den Gemüthsbewegungen, *ibid.*, vi., 1891, 389. Cf. 391: "Die Objecte der Psychologie sind sämmtlich Vorgänge, Ereignisse."

[35] *Princ. of Psych.*, i., 243 f. Woodworth reinterprets: "I do not understand the author of the 'Stream of Thought' to assert that feelings of relation must always be evanescent" (*Essays Philos. and Psychol.*, 1908, 494).

[36] *Ibid.*, 300. It is curious to note the differences in psychological attitude! Stout, commenting on this passage (which I have quoted with hearty approval), remarks: "Could anything be more perverse? Professor James is looking for his spectacles when he has them on. He is seeking for his own 'palpitating inward life,' the activity in which his very being consists, and he expects to find it in certain particulars, certain special contents of presentation," and so on (*Analyt. Psych.*, i., 1896, 162). But this—with allowance made for the caricature—is, I should suppose, precisely what every psychologist, as psychologist, must try and expect to do. On the other hand, Stout apparently approves James' account of the feelings of relation (218), which I have criticised. He and I, then, are opposed but consistent; and James can, accordingly, satisfy neither of us.

[37] *Analysis*, i., 1869, 90 f., 115.

[38] Bk. vi., ch. iv., §3.

[39] *Examination*, 1865, 286 f.; cf. the preceding chapter, on Inseparable Association, and editorial note in J. Mill's *Analysis*, i., 106 ff.

[40] *Treatise of Human Nature*, bk. i., pt. i., §4.

[41] So Bühler, 328. Cf. F. H. Bradley, *The Principles of Logic*, 1883, 320 f.; W. James, *Princ. of Psych.*, i., 1890, 161; G. F. Stout, *A Manual of Psych.*, 1899, 110 ff.; C. Stumpf, *Ueber d. psychol. Ursprung d. Raumvorstellung*, 1873, 103 ff.; *Tonpsychologie*, ii., 1890, 208 ff. (see other refs. in Index); W. Wundt, *Physiol. Psych.*, ii., 1902, 500 f., 684 (see refs. under *Resultante* in Index).

[42] D. Hartley, *Observations on Man*, [1749] pt. i., ch. i., §2, prop. xii., cor. 1 (ed. of 1810, i., 78).

[43] See i., 205.

[44] *Analysis*, ii., 1869, 190 f.

[45] See, *e.g.*, P. Flechsig, Ueber die Associationscentren des menschlichen Gehirns, and the following discussion, in *Dritter Internationaler Congress f. Psychologie*, 1897, 49 ff.

[46] See, *e.g.*, H. Münsterberg, *Grundzüge der Psychologie*, i., 1900, 307 ff.

[47] W. Wundt, Ueber die Definition der Psychologie, *Philos. Studien*, xii., 1895, 51 ff.

NOTES TO LECTURE II

[1] R. F. A. Hoernlé, Image, Idea and Meaning, *Mind*, N. S., xvi., 1907, 82 f. The writer adds that James' "account is wholly untrue as regards our ordinary consciousness of meaning. For what normally occupies the focus of attention is the meaning, the objective reference, whereas *the sign forms the fringe*, of which we have but a more or less shadowy consciousness. Professor James exactly reverses the true state of affairs, for according to his theory, the sign should occupy the centre of attention, and the meaning form the vague background." The fringe-terminology is, no doubt, apt to set up misleading associations (G. F. Stout, *Analytic Psych.*, i., 1896, 93). But, as I have tried to show in my *Feeling and Attention*, 239 ff., image and fringe are, for James, both alike in the focus of attention: fringe is not to be rendered as "vague background."

[2] F. Brentano, *Psychologie vom empirischen Standpunkte*, i., 1874, bk. ii., ch. v. (summary, p. 255).

[3] *Ibid.*, 115 f.; cf. 127, 260. Brentano has other criteria, but these are of secondary importance. Cf. A. Höfler, *Psychologie*, 1897, 2 ff.

[4] *Ibid.*, 103 f.

[5] *Lectures on Metaphysics*, ii., 432 (Lect. xlii).

[6] *Op. cit.*, 117 f.

[7] *Ibid.*, 167.

[8] O. Külpe, *Outlines of Psychology*, 1909, 227 f.

[9] G. T. Ladd, *Psychology, Descriptive and Explanatory*, 1894, 181.

[10] *Physiol. Psych.*, iii., 1903, 112 ff., 121 f., 332, 514 f., 552 ff., 625; *Grundriss d. Psych.*, 1905, 262 (Engl., 1907, 243); etc.

[11] Cf. T. Nakashima, Contributions to the Study of the Affective Processes, *Amer. Journ. Psych.*, xx., 1909, 181 f., 193.

[12] Brentano, *op. cit.*, 261, 264.

[13] *Ibid.*, 161.   "Mit unmittelbarer Evidenz zeigt uns die innere Wahrnehmung dass das Hören einen von ihm selbst verschiedenen Inhalt hat"; "eine Meinung, die so deutlich der inneren Erfahrung und dem Urtheile jedes Unbefangenen widerspricht."

[14] *Ibid.*, 162.   Brentano refers to A. Bain, *Mental Science*, 1872, 199 (bk. ii., ch. vii., Perception of a Material World, no. 4): "In purely passive feeling, as in those of our sensations that do not call forth our muscular energies, we are not perceiving matter. . . . The feeling of warmth, as in the bath, is an example. . . . All our senses may yield similar experiences, if we resign ourselves to their purely sensible or passive side." The same doctrine of 'passive sensibility' may be found in the notes to J. Mill's *Analysis*, i., 5 f., 35; ii., 149. Brentano also refers, in general terms, to J. S. Mill's *Examination* (I suppose, to chs. xi. and xii.) and to his notes in the *Analysis* (I suppose, to such notes as that in i., 229 ff.). I have preferred to take the obvious illustration from J. Mill himself: *Analysis*, i., 224 f. (cf. 16 ff.).

It should be added, by way of caution, that the criticism of associationism in Lecture I. holds of all the passages here cited; we are taking Brentano's argument at its face-value.

[15] *Examination,* 212. The criticism passed upon Brentano in the foot-note is supported by the treatment of memory and expectation in S. Witasek's *Grundlinien der Psychologie,* 1908. See 290: "noch deutlicher als an der Wahrnehmung ist an der Erinnerung die wesentliche Mitwirkung des *Urteilsaktes* ersichtlich"; and 317: "Ueberraschung und Erwartung . . . sind bestimmte eigentümliche Arten des Eintritts, der Vorbereitung, des Ablaufs von *Urteilen*" (italics mine).

[16] *Op. cit.,* 73 ff.

[17] In a review of Brentano's *Psychologie* (*Mind,* O. S., i., 1876, 122), R. Flint remarks: "As regards conception [Flint's translation of *Vorstellung*], our author is unfortunate in his language. His use of the term *Vorstellung* is extremely vague, confused, and self-contradictory. It is wider and looser even than Herbart's or Lotze's. In fact, the term, as employed by him, is not only incapable of accurate translation into English or any other language, but corresponds to no generic fact, no peculiar faculty, and no distinctive province of mind." These statements are, I think, justified by the facts; and the reason for the looseness of usage is, surely, that Brentano's *Vorstellung* is the direct descendant of the *vis repræsentativa* of the faculty psychologists. More than that: while much psychological water has flowed under the bridges since 1874, and while Witasek is accordingly clearer and closer in definition than was his master, I believe that the primacy of ideation in the *Grundlinien* is an after-effect of the same faculty influence.

[18] *Ibid.,* 81.

[19] *Ibid.,* 6 f.

[20] *Ibid.*, 76.

[21] *Ibid.*, 318 f.

[22] *Ibid.*, 281.

[23] *Ibid.*, 280-287. Even if we concede that Witasek's analyses are phenomenologically correct, it would still remain true that phenomenology is not psychology. Science implies attitude, standpoint, consistent adhesion to a special and voluntarily selected aspect of phenomena: cf. my *Text-book of Psych.*, 1909, §1.

[24] Brentano's psychology, despite its unfinished condition (vol. i. contains but two of the proposed six books), has exerted a powerful and wide-spread influence. The tracing of this influence lies beside my present purpose: let the space that I have devoted to act and content bear witness to my appreciation of it! I note here only a few typical criticisms. That Brentano's psychology is a psychology of reflection has been urged in various connections: so, *e.g.*, by Wundt, *Physiol. Psych.*, iii., 1903, 234 f., 240, and by F. Jodl, *Lehrbuch d. Pysch.*, 1896, 180 (in i., 1903, 211 the reference to Brentano is omitted). His principle of classification is rejected by J. Rehmke, *Lehrbuch d. allg. Psych.*, 1894, 349 ff., and by W. Jerusalem, *Die Urteilsfunction, eine psychologische und erkenntnis-kritische Untersuchung*, 1895, 4 ff.,—a book which takes constant account of Brentano's doctrine of judgment, and cites authorities for and against. In particular, Brentano's identification of feeling and will is criticised by C. von Ehrenfels, Ueber Fühlen und Wollen: eine psychologische Studie, *Sitzungsber. d. philos.-hist. Cl. d. Wiener Akad.*, cxiv., Heft 2, 1887, §5, and by Rehmke, *op. cit.*, 363 ff.; his distinction of idea and

judgment is criticised by Ebbinghaus, *Grundzüge*, i., 1905, 183.

These general references must suffice. Lest, however, I should seem to have overestimated the part played in Brentano's thinking by the doctrine of intentional in- existence, I quote the relevant passages from some contemporary reviews of his work. "The general im- pression which this chapter leaves on the mind of the reviewer is that a considerable number of the particular criticisms are just, but that the discussion as a whole is not successful, because these two essential questions are uninvestigated, *viz.*: Are perceptions not so in- separable from the act of perceiving as to be, in some measure at least, if not entirely, *psychical* phenomena? and, Are there really any such phenomena as those which our author frequently speaks of, any *'physical* phenomena in the phantasy'?" (R. Flint, in *Mind*, O. S., i., 1876, 120.) "Von Anfang an begrenzt er willkürlich das Gebiet des Psychischen, indem er Töne, Farben, Geruch, Figur u. s. w. dem Physischen zuweist. Wohlgemerkt der Act des Sehens, Hörens u. s. w. sowie die Phantasievorstellung ist psychisch, das Gesehene, Gehörte, Empfundene, Vorgestellte ist physisch. Offen- bar die grösste Willkür! Was ist denn die Farbe, der Ton, sobald man vom psychischen Moment absieht? Doch etwas ganz Anderes als Farbe und Ton, nämlich Molecularschwingung. . . . Man sieht, das Ganze ist ein unfruchtbarer Wortkram, . . . Alles gestützt auf die ganz unhaltbare Unterscheidung des Psychi- schen und des Physischen" (A. Horwicz, in *Philos. Monatshefte*, x., 1874, 269 f.). "Fragen wir danach, so wird sich doch wohl kaum eine andere Antwort geben lassen als: der Unterschied zwischen dem 'Act des Vorstellens' und 'dem, was vorgestellt wird,' also zwischen dem Act des Sehens und der gesehenen Farbe bestehe darin, dass das Vorstellen diejenige Thätigkeit sey, welche die Vorstellung mit ihrem Inhalt (dem vorgestellten Object) erzeugt. Dann aber folgt unabweislich: ist das Vorstellen eine psychische Thätigkeit, so ist nothwendig auch das vorgestellte Object ein psychisches Erzeugniss und mithin ein psychisches Phänomen. . . . Ja, dem vorgestellten Object wird zunächst und vorzugsweise der Name: psychisches Phänomen beigelegt werden müssen. Denn es ist unbestreitbare Thatsache, dass das vorgestellte Object zunächst und unmittelbar erscheint, der Act des Vorstellens dagegen nur mittelbar, mit Hilfe des erscheinenden Objects und von ihm aus, zur Erscheinung (zum Bewusstseyn) gelangt" (H. Ulrici, in *Zeits. f. Philos. u. philos. Kritik*, N. F. lxvii., 1875, 293 f.). I have not purposely picked out the unfavourable notices; but, so far as I have read, the appreciative reviews (*e.g.*, J. Rehmke, *Philos. Monatshefte*, xi., 1875, 113 ff.) simply postpone their criticism till the appearance of the second volume; and the second volume has not appeared.

[25] I therefore subscribe to Külpe's statement: "es giebt keine Thätigkeit des Empfindens oder Vorstellens oder Wahrnehmens, die neben dem Wahrgenommenen, Vorgestellten, Empfundenen eine besondere Existenz hätte" (Das Ich und die Aussenwelt, i., *Philos. Studien*, vii., 1892, 405; cf. *Outlines of Psych.*, 1909, 25 f.). But I think, at the same time, that the logical or phenomenological dualism is a distorted reflection of psychological fact.

G. Spiller (*The Mind of Man*, 1902, 135) remarks: "to me this distinction [between act and content of presentation] appears untenable, as would be the suggestion that one could distinguish between the act of a stone falling and the stone which is falling. . . . An act of presentation . . . is something presented. It is a misfortune for psychology that men with anti-scientific interests like Brentano profess to be psychologists, and champion opinions on the subject that have no real psychological value." I subscribe, again, to the factual criticism, but I should be sorry to lose anything that Brentano has written; I know of no modern psychologist whose work is more challenging, insistent, thought-compelling.

²⁶ G. F. Stout, *A Manual of Psych.*, 1899, 56 f. Stout's views on classification are set forth in three works: the *Analytic Psych.*, 1896; the *Manual*,* and *The Groundwork of Psych.*, 1903. I must go into some little detail regarding them.

(1) In the *Manual*, as the quotation shows, knowing, feeling and striving are the ultimate modes of being conscious of an object, and human consciousness is normally concerned with some object. The 'normally' is explained by the following sentence: "In waking life, we are usually, and perhaps always, perceiving something or thinking about something." Why should there be any doubt? Apparently, because those modifica-

---

* I learn from *Mind*, N. S. x., 1901, 545 that a second edition of this work appeared in 1901. The American publishers, however, are still supplying the edition of 1899, from which I am accordingly obliged to quote. I merely note the statement (547) that Stout "no longer identifies subconsciousness with 'sentience' "; I cannot tell how it is to be interpreted.

tions of consciousness which are capable of fulfilling the presentative function may exist even when they are not the means of cognising objects; there is, at any given moment, much material of experience which is to that extent without objective reference (68 f.). Cognition, as modification of consciousness, may be out of function, and may thus become sentience or subconsciousness. There is, then, the bare possibility that our consciousness may be objectless, and we ourselves merely sentient. Altogether objectless? What of the qualifying 'to that extent'? This is explained in *Analyt. Psych.*, i., 48 f. (quoted in the *Manual*). "They [*i.e.*, the modifications of consciousness just referred to] may exist as possible material for discriminative thinking without being actually utilised *to the full extent* in which they are susceptible of being utilised." "The essential point is the antithesis between the detailed determinateness of presentation [*i.e.*, of the presented objects] and the *comparative* indeterminateness of discriminative thinking" (italics mine). The meaning seems to be that sentience stands to cognition or knowing as inattentive, diffused and obscure apprehension stands to attentive, individual and clear apprehension. Cf. *A. P.*, 180: "the distinction between attention and inattention is . . . coincident with the distinction between noetic and anoetic experience."

The difference, therefore, appears to be a difference of degree. "We have no sufficient ground for asserting that any experience of a normal human being is so completely anoetic that it has no objective reference whatever"; "the indefinite objective reference has for its vehicle a single massive sentience" (*A. P.*, 180 f.).

Yet we read in *A. P.*, 50 that "thought and sentience are
fundamentally distinct mental functions"; and this
'thought' is identical with the cognition of the *Manual*
(69). Hence the difference must, at the same time, be
a difference in kind! So, in the *Manual* itself, we find
that sensation can exist "without cognitive function";
we may "have a variation in the sense-experience which
makes *no difference to cognition*" (120; italics mine).
Sensations "may exist as possible material for perceptual consciousness, without being actually utilised"
(130). The corresponding passage in *A. P.*, 48 reads,
as we have seen, "without being actually utilised to the
full extent in which they are susceptible of being utilised"; but the qualification, retained in the earlier
quotation of *Manual* 69, is now omitted. Cf. the
Groundwork, 55: nothing is said here of sentience or
subconsciousness or anoetic experience; but the objects
of the "outlying field of inattention" are "*in no way*
developed in consciousness" and "do not form part of a
stream of thought or train of ideas" (italics mine). So
the *A. P.*, 113: "Agreeable and disagreeable experiences
may exist *apart from objective reference*" (italics mine).
And even the passage just quoted (180 f.) qualifies its
statement by referring to the 'normal' human being, and
goes on to say that the mass of sensations and imagery
"which constitute the field of inattention at any moment
occupy this position because they do not refer to the
. . . discriminated object which specially occupies
our thoughts. Nevertheless, they *may* mediate an in-
determine awareness" (italics mine). May? But do
they?—that is, do they always? Stout seems to vacil-

late between the answers Yes and No. I cannot make
the passages consistent.

(2) I think, however, that I can see a reason for
inconsistency. Cognition, as functionless modification
of consciousness, becomes sentience. Is there, now, anything that stands to feeling and striving as sentience
stands to knowing? "In a merely anoetic experience
. . . the mere experience of struggle or effort, activity
free or impeded, may still remain" (*A. P.*, 113). There
is "conation in some form or degree," some amount of
felt mental activity, even when "in a state of delicious
languor I enjoy the organic sensations produced by a
warm bath" (*A. P.*, 160 f., 170 ff.; *Manual*, 67 f.).
We have, then, an objectless (or practically objectless)
conation or striving. So with feeling. "Agreeable and
disagreeable experiences may exist apart from objective reference. My consciousness may be agreeably toned
by organic sensations of which I take no note" (*A. P.*,
113); "the presumption appears to be that our total
consciousness is never [*i.e.*, whether noetic or anoetic]
entirely neutral" (*Manual*, 62). We have an objectless
(or practically objectless) feeling.

Very well! But the basis of Stout's classification of
mental phenomena is "the ways in which our consciousness is related tó its object" (*Manual*, 56), "the ultimately distinct modes of being conscious of an object"
(*Groundwork*, 18), "the attitude or posture of consciousness towards objects" (*A. P.*, 40 ff.). If, then, he admits a pure sentience, a wholly objectless feeling, a wholly
objectless conation, he is in a dilemma: either these three
modes of mental function are one and indistinguishable,
a matrix of experience lying behind and beyond the

possibility of classification; or, the three modes being already distinguishable, his principle of classification breaks down. Stout is led (I imagine, by his own introspection) to recognise the objectless sentience of the conscious margin and the objectless character of much feeling-experience, and is also bound by his doctrine of mental activity to read a conative factor into every sort and kind of consciousness. Now the difference in feeling and conation, as between the noetic and the anoetic consciousnesses, is obviously a difference only of degree; feeling is still recognisable in anoesis as feeling, conation as conation; we are, in so far, upon the second horn of the dilemma. Rather than give up his principle of classification, however, Stout qualifies his account of anoetic experience: consciousness "usually and perhaps always" refers to an object; the modifications of the marginal consciousness are not utilised "to the full extent," but nevertheless "may mediate an indeterminate awareness":—passages of this nature, which save the principle, alternate with the passages which make thought and sentience "fundamentally distinct," and regard the marginal objects as "in no way developed in consciousness."

The inconsistency, therefore, appears to be due, roughly, to the conflict between introspection (reinforced by the doctrine of conation) and preconceived ideas of the nature and function of consciousness. I cannot accept Stout's doctrine of mental activity. But the introspective testimony to sentience and objectless feeling seems to me to invalidate the principle of objective reference.

(3) The principle itself has led, in Stout's hands, to varying results. Thus, in the *A. P.*, we have:

I. Cognition
   a. Sentience
   b. Simple apprehension
   c. Belief or judgment

These "three fundamental modes of consciousness" are "combined in every complete cognitive act as integral constituents of it" (115). We have already discussed the possibility of a purely objectless sentience.

II. Volition
   a. Feeling
   b. Conation.

"Every mental attitude which partakes of the nature of volition includes two fundamentally distinct modes of reference to an object,—(1) being pleased or displeased with it or with its absence, and (2) striving after it or striving to avoid it,—desire or aversion" (115 f.).

In the *Manual* we find (56 ff.):

I. Ultimate modes of being conscious of an object
   a. Cognitive attitude or knowing
   b. Feeling-attitude or feeling
   c. Conative attitude or striving
II. Experience not at the moment contributing to the cognitive function of consciousness
   d. Sentience or Sub-Consciousness.

Finally, we have in the *Groundwork* (19) the schema:

Cognition		Interest	
Simple Apprehension	Judgment	Conation	Feeling-attitude

Sentience is not named; it appears only as a form of relative inattention (54 f.).

It may be freely admitted that a classification is,

primarily, a matter of convenience, and that a satisfactory classification of mental phenomena, on any principle, is not easy. It is again clear, however, that 'reference to an object' is not an unerring or unequivocal guide to grouping.

[27] *Analyt. Psych.*, i., 41, 46.

[28] *Grundlinien d. Psych.*, 3; cf. 5 f.

[29] *Ibid.*, 12.

[30] So I understand the passages in *A. P.*, 40 ff., 46 f., 58 ff., 61 ff.; *Manual*, 56 ff., 122 ff. Thus, sensation is distinguished from image, not by any difference in act, but by "peculiar intensity, steadiness, and other distinctive characters" (*Manual*, 119), *i.e.*, by attributes of the total mental process. Or again, sentience passes into thought, not by the supervention of an act of apprehension upon a bare content, but by a gradual process of transfusion, one of whose "most prominent forms is the progress in delicacy of discrimination" (*A. P.*, 58); the total mental process is transformed in the passage. Difficulty arises, I think, only if we take Stout to recognise the occasional existence of a wholly functionless sentience, or a wholly objectless feeling and striving.

[31] Bühler, 354 f.

[32] *Op. cit.*, 3 f. Cf. 5: "mit dem Erleben einer psychischen Tatsache ist uns in zweifachem Sinne etwas 'gegeben': direkt und unmittelbar die psychische Tatsache selbst, mittelbar und in übertragenem Sinne eben das, worauf sie gerichtet ist"; and 6: "unser Vorstellen ist so beschaffen, dass es uns *Dinge* zur Vorstellung bringt." This transitive character is apparent to a direct observation of mental phenomena themselves, *i.e.*, **to**

introspection; direct observation of physical phenomena, inspection, reveals nothing of the sort (4).

I take Bühler and Witasek as typical representatives, in a professedly psychological context, of the opposing views with regard to mental transcendence; I am, however, not further concerned with that function, considered either psychologically or epistemologically. The interested reader may refer to a series of papers by F. J. E. Woodbridge, in *Congress of Arts and Science*, i., 1905; *Studies in Philosophy and Psychology* (Garman Commemorative Volume), 1906; *Essays Philosophical and Psychological* (in honour of W. James), 1908; *Journ. Philos. Psych. Sci. Meth.*, ii., 1905; to articles by other hands in the same *Journ.*; and to the papers by R. B. Perry, F. Arnold, S. S. Colvin and others in recent volumes of the *Psych. Review.* The annual bibliographies will supply further references.

[33] Stout, *Analyt. Psych.*, i., 49; *Manual*, 70.

[34] See references in Note 14 above. Cf. also *The Senses and the Intellect*, 1868, 364 ff.; *The Emotions and the Will*, 1880, 574 ff.

[35] See Note 26 above.

[36] Ueber die Objectívirung und Subjectívirung von Sinneseindrücken, *Philos. Studien*, xix., 1902, 508 ff. Similar results, mentioned in my *Text-book*, 1909, §61, will shortly be published in the *Amer. Journ. Psych.* by M. C. West.

[37] Messer, 69.

[38] *Op. cit.*, 116.

[39] *Op. cit.*, 4.

[40] ii., 1902, 250 f.

[41] G. H. T. Eimer, *On Orthogenesis*, 1898, 2, 22, 21;

the address was delivered in 1895. See also *Organic Evolution as the Result of the Inheritance of Acquired Characters according to the Laws of Organic Growth,* 1890, Appendix, 431: "[my] conclusion . . . recognises a perfectly definite direction in the evolution and continuous modification of organisms, which even down to the smallest detail is prescribed by the material composition (constitution) of the body" (from an address delivered in 1883); and 4, 20, etc., etc.

[42] ii., 251.

[43] Witasek terms the relation an "inneres Bezogensein, Gerichtetsein, Hinweisen auf ein anderes" (*op. cit.,* 4).

[44] Perhaps I am unduly afraid of a word. Huxley, who wrote in 1864 that "that which struck the present writer most forcibly on his first perusal of the 'Origin of Species' was the conviction that Teleology, as commonly understood, had received its deathblow at Mr. Darwin's hands" (Criticisms on "The Origin of Species," in *Lay Sermons, Addresses and Reviews,* 1887, 261 f.)—that same Huxley wrote in 1869 that "there is a wider Teleology, which is not touched by the doctrine of Evolution, but is actually based upon the fundamental proposition of Evolution. That proposition is, that the whole world, living and not living, is the result of the mutual interaction, according to definite laws, of the forces possessed by the molecules of which the primitive nebulosity of the universe was composed" (The Genealogy of Animals, in *Critiques and Addresses,* 1883, 305). I suppose that this 'wider teleology' is, at bottom, identical with what I have called organisation. Jodl, again, commenting upon the sentence: "es besteht ein teleologischer Zusammenhang zwischen Vermögen und Reiz" (*Lehrbuch,*

1896, 185), writes: "der Sinn dieses Ausdruckes kann
auf dem Boden unserer heutigen Weltanschauung nicht
zweifelhaft sein, welche die Teleologie nur als Ergebniss
des gesetzmässigen Zusammenwirkens der Naturkräfte,
der Anpassung vorhandener Formen und Combinationen
an die umgebenden Medien, der Umbildung des Beste-
henden durch die Summation kleinster Wirkungen und
durch die Auslese der günstigen, den Bestand und die
Leistung einer Combination sichernden, Abänderungen
erklärt. Die empfindenden Organe sind nicht von irgend
einer zwecksetzenden Thätigkeit zur Aufnahme bestimmter Reize eingerichtet; . . . die Welt der physi-
kalisch-chemischen Reize hat sich durch fortgesetzte
Einwirkung auf das Protoplasma im Zusammenhang
der organischen Entwicklung die Organe, welche diesen
Reizen entsprechen und eine Abbildung derselben ermog-
lichen, selbst geschaffen."* I suppose that, in principle,
this view of teleology is also very like my own view of
organisation. Nevertheless, I have a rooted temperamental aversion to the word teleology and to its
idea,—a constitutional fear of "mistaking the mere tick-
ing of the clock for its function." I have, similarly, an
aversion to the term 'concept,' a constitutional fear
of hypostatising a mental construction. There is, perhaps, some connection between these temperamental
reactions and the habit of thinking in visual schemata,
described in Lecture I.

[45] *Op. cit.*, 4.

[46] We are all too apt to speak of the 'physical organ-

* The sentences immediately following this quotation are modified in i., 1903, 219; and in both editions the initial statements are
qualified by a reference to "die Spontaneität des Bewusstseins."

ism,' as if a human being were, as organism, complete
without mind; and then we are all too apt to parallel
the physical by a 'psychical organism,' as if there were
a perfect mental organisation apart from body. I have
argued against the latter view in *Text-book*, 1909, §9.
Cf. F. Jodl, *Lehrbuch d. Psych.*, 1896, 84 ff.; J. M.
Baldwin, Mind and Body from the Genetic Point of
View, *Psych. Review*, x., 1903, 242 ff.

NOTES TO LECTURE III

[1] W. Wundt, Ueber Ausfrageexperimente und über die Methoden zur Psychologie des Denkens, *Psychol. Studien*, iii., 1907, 334; cf. the account of the method, 302 ff., and ct. esp. Ach,* 21, 27 f. Bühler replies in an Antwort auf die von W. Wundt erhobenen Einwände gegen die Methode der Selbstbeobachtung an experimentell erzeugten Erlebnissen, *Arch. f. d. ges. Psych.*, xii., 1908, 93 ff. It will be observed that the title of this rejoinder neatly begs the whole question. Wundt returns to the fray in Kritische Nachlese zur Ausfragemethode, *ibid.*, xi., 1908, 445 ff. (issued later than the first part of vol. xii.). Bühler defends himself, briefly, in Zur Kritik der Denkexperimente, *Zeits. f. Psych.*, li., 1909, 108 f.

Marbe, who in his Beiträge zur Logik und ihren Grenzwissenschaften (*Vjs. f. wiss. Philos. u. Soziol.*, xxx., 1906, 465 ff.) had already protested against Wundt's comments in the *Physiol. Psych.*, iii., 1903, 579 ff., also takes a hand in the present controversy: W. Wundts Stellung zu meiner Theorie der stroboskopischen Erscheinungen und zur systematischen Selbstwahrnehmung, *Zeits. f. Psych.*, xlvi., 1908, 352 ff. Wundt barely notices his strictures in the Kritische Nachlese, 445. The discussion, throughout, strikes the disinterested observer as too warm for either comfort or dignity.

[2] Marbe, 15.   [3] *Ibid.*, 9 f.   [4] *Ibid.*, 16.

*See below, Note 13.

[5] Marbe made two principal series of experiments. The first is aimed at the psychology of *Urteilsvorstellungen, Urteilsgebärden, Urteilsworte, Urteilssätze* (15 ff.), the second at that of the *Verstehen und Beurteilen der Urteile* (ideas, gestures, words and phrases, propositions: 58 ff.). It is not necessary here to treat the series separately.

[6] Binet, 10.   [7] *Ibid.*, 2, 9, 301.

[8] *Ibid.*, 21 f.   [9] *Ibid.*, 306 ff.

[10] "Les recherches que j'ai pu faire sur ces deux enfants . . . se sont espacées sur trois ans. Elles s'y ont prêtées avec beaucoup de bonne grâce, sans timidité, ni fou rire; elles ont toujours compris qu'il s'agissait d'une chose sérieuse, et elles étaient persuadées que la moindre erreur pouvait me causer un préjudice des plus graves. Plût au ciel que les adultes qui servent de sujets aux psychologues eussent toujours une attitude aussi bonne!" *Ibid.*, 10. Cf. 51, 82, 167, 308.

[11] Watt, 289 f. Cf. F. Schumann, *Bericht über d. I. Kongress f. exper. Psych.*, 1904, 124.

[12] *Ibid.*, 316 f.

[13] N. Ach, *Ueber die Willenstätigkeit und das Denken: eine experimentelle Untersuchung mit einem Anhange über das Hippsche Chronoskop,** 1905. Ach's experimental work was begun in 1900, and a first draught of his results was submitted to the Göttingen faculty as *Habilitationsschrift* in 1902, but apparently was not published. A brief abstract, printed in Schumann, *Bericht*, etc., 80 ff., mentions the method of "systematische experimentelle Selbstbeobachtung." The expression is, I think, needlessly clumsy, since an

---

* Cited, in the following Notes, as 'Ach.'

experimental procedure is *ex vi definitionis* a systematic
procedure.

[14] Ach, 8 ff. I have no quarrel with Ach on the score
of fact; but I must dissent from his theory of introspection. "Dass die Selbstbeobachtung auf das Erlebnis,
so lange dasselbe sich nicht öfters wiederholt hat, einen
störenden Einfluss ausübt, davon konnte ich mich bei
meinen Untersuchungen vielfach überzeugen. Dass das
Erlebnis während seines Gegebenseins in der Regel nicht
beobachtet werden kann, hat seinen Grund darin, dass
sich . . . determinierende Tendenzen [see Note 49 be-
low] verschiedenen Inhaltes, die sich auf dasselbe Erlebnis beziehen, gegenseitig ausschliessen. Die Determinierung kann nur in *einer* bestimmten Richtung
erfolgen. Diese Richtung ist aber durch den Verlauf
des Erlebnisses selbst gegeben. Es kann also während
des Erlebens nicht noch eine weitere Determinierung z.
B. eine Selbstbeobachtung stattfinden, die eine andere
Richtung der Aufmerksamkeit—eine Richtung wie sie
durch das Verhalten des Subjektes zum Objekt char-
akterisiert ist—in sich schliesst" (9 f.). But why drag
in subject and object? The fact is, simply, that when
an experience is in progress you cannot (unless the
experience moves very slowly, or is very habitual, or
you yourself are very highly practised) take note of
it, find forms of verbal expression for it, report upon
it; the experience will not wait for you. And what holds
of inner holds under like conditions, in precisely the
same way, of outer experience; there are many observations in microscopy, in natural history, that you cannot
report, by words or by drawings, while they are in
course; all that you can do is to live them attentively,

and then recover them in the memory after-image.
The introspective determination is twofold; you are to
attend and you are to report. But then the inspective
determination, the instruction given for observation in
natural science, is also twofold; you are to attend and
you are to report. There is absolutely no difference in
principle between introspection and inspection; whether
you are able to attend and to report simultaneously (or,
rather, while the observation is going on) depends, in
both cases, upon the circumstances of the moment. I
have tried to make the point clear in my *Feeling and
Attention*, 1908, 174 ff.; *Text-book*, 1909, §6. Störring,
in his *Vorlesungen über Psychopathologie* (1900, 5 ff.;
Eng., 1907, 3 ff.), takes practically the same ground,
although he does not distinguish between attention and
report; and Meumann (*Exper. Pädagogik*, i., 1907, 14)
expresses agreement with Störring. Nevertheless, in
Germany the Kantian tradition dies hard; and in our
own psychology John Mill's reply to Comte (James,
Princ., i., 188 f.), while it saved the situation on the
practical side, naturally tended to overemphasize the
part played by memory or 'reflection.'

I agree with Ach that introspection of the thought-
processes is extremely difficult (16 f., 41, 215), and I do
not question the advantage of his method (19 f.).* But
I contend that the disturbances ascribed to *Selbstbeobachtung* (22, 37) are not intrinsic to introspection.
They are due to the observer's effort, in a case where
experience is both complex and fleeting, to take full
mental notes, as he goes along, without losing the

---

* Cf. Messer, 15 f.; Störring, *Arch. f. d. ges. Psych.*, xi., 1908,
29 f.

experience itself,—to translate adequately into words, for subsequent report, a consciousness that is moving, changing, with great rapidity, and that will not stand still to be described. Given a simpler experience, a slower movement of consciousness, and it would be altogether possible for report to keep even pace with attention.

The fact of disturbance is attested by Messer (20): "kommt es . . . zu einer eigentlichen Selbstbeobachtung während des Erlebnisses, so wirkt diese störend" (cf. Störring, *Arch. f. d. ges. Psych.*, xi., 1908, 3, 92; *ibid.*, xiv., 1909, 1 f.). Yet one of Messer's observers writes: "bei den Aussagen wird das Erlebte nicht immer reproduziert, aber es kommt vielfach dazu. Eigentümlich ist dies: wo derartige Aussagen sich nicht mit dem Erlebten bereit gestellt haben, da wissen wir nichts davon" (16). Messer himself generalises this remark (21), and refers the 'Bereitschaft der Aussagen' to the 'Wirksamkeit der Aufgabe, Protokoll zu geben.' It is, indeed, generally acknowledged that introspection is advantaged by the purpose to introspect (Messer, 20 f.; Binet, 92; Ach, 11, 19). I cannot but think that the getting ready of the verbal expression is a mental note-taking, of a simple and schematic sort, and that in his account of it Messer has really furnished an argument against his own and Ach's position.

[15] The term is Woodworth's: *Journ. Philos. Psych. Sci. Meth.*, iv., 1907, 170.

[16] Ach, 11; Fechner, *Elem. d. Psychophysik*, ii., xliv., b (1860, 1889, 491 ff.). Müller and Pilzecker (*Exper. Beiträge zur Lehre vom Gedächtniss*, 1900, 58 f.) refer only to Fechner's "Phantome des sogennanten Sinnen-

gedächtnisses" (498 ff.), which they name "Wider-
holungsempfindungen." There seems, however, to be
no reason why Fechner's term 'memory after-image'
should not cover Ach's phenomena of perseveration.

For a general account of the part played in recent
work by the 'perseverative tendencies,' see Watt, *Arch.
f. d. ges. Psych.*, vii., 1906, Literaturbericht, 17 ff.;
and cf. Watt, 341 ff.; Messer, 17, 20, 63, 66; Wreschner, 11 ff., 237 ff.

[17] Ach, 17 f.; Dürr, *Zeits. f. Psych.*, xlix., 1908, 327.

[18] *Grundriss d. Psych.*, 421; *Outlines*, 1909, 407.

[19] See *Philos. Studien*, x., 1894, 498; *Logik*, ii., 2,
1895, 226; *Physiol. Psych.*, iii., 1903, 305, 383, 452.

[20] Messer, 4, 22 ff., 108 f. The use of free associations had been criticised by Watt, 296 ff., on the ground
that the results would be indefinite, and the discrimination of factors and influences difficult or impossible.
Watt's objection that "es scheint kaum möglich, einen
Bewußtseinszustand vorzubereiten, in dem jedes Richten
der Aufmerksamkeit auf irgend etwas unterdrückt wird"
is, however, transformed by Messer into a merit of the
method: "[es ist] sehr häufig zu konstatieren, dass sich
die Vp. . . . unwillkürlich eine speziellere Aufgabe
stellten,—was methodisch recht beachtenswert ist." Cf.
Binet, 54 f.; Ach's account of determinate abstraction
(successive form), 240 ff.; P. Bovet, *Arch. de psych.*,
viii., 1908, 14, 19; Wreschner, 125 ff., 145, 480, 491;
E. Meumann, *Vorlesungen z. Einführung in d. exper.
Pädagogik*, i., 1907, 213.

This specialisation of the *Aufgabe* may be brought
into connection with the specialisation of verbal meaning. "[Es] findet unter Umständen eine Präzisierung,

eine Einschränkung des Sinnes [des Reizwortes] statt,
die weder durch das Reizwort, noch etwa durch die
Aufgabe bedingt ist, sondern sich wohl aus dem in der
allgemeinen Konstellation begründeten Vorherrschen
bestimmter Reproduktionstendenzen erklärt" (Messer,
81 f.; cf. Wreschner, 148 ff., 480). It seems also to
be related to the specialisation of the visual image which
accompanies and partly expresses a thought: Binet,
85 f.; Watt, 369; Messer, 88; Wreschner, 180 ff. At
any rate, this phenomenon of specialisation, of partial
expression, is to be distinguished from the occurrence
of incongruous or wholly irrelevant visual images.

I have on occasion been tempted to think, further,
that these various types of specialisation—possibly the
various phases of the psychology of *Aufgabe* at large—
have something to do with Royce's problem of the 'in-
hibitory consciousness' (Recent Logical Inquiries and
their Psychological Bearings, *Psychol. Review*, ix., 1902,
131, 133 ff.). Royce, however, assumes that our
"motor acts," our "positive tendencies and inhibitions"
must, in "live thinking," come to consciousness; "our
abstract ideas are products of . . . an organised union
of negative and positive tendencies"; and we can understand the psychology of thinking "only in case we understand *when, how far, and under what conditions,
inhibition becomes a conscious process.*" The psychology
of *Aufgabe* has tended rather to emphasise the unconscious direction and determination of consciousness. I
make the suggestion for what it is worth; I am not at
all sure that I have understood Royce.

[21] *Ibid.*, 4 ff. On "begriffliches und gegenständliches
Denken," see esp. 148 ff. The distinction is criticised by

Bühler, Remarques sur les problèmes de la psychologie de la pensée, *Archives de Psych.*, vi., 1907, 383 f.; defended by Messer, Bemerkungen zu meinen 'Experimentell-psychologischen Untersuchungen über das Denken,' *Arch. f. d. ges. Psych.*, x., 1907, 419 ff.; and relegated by Bühler to epistemology, Ueber Gedankenzusammenhänge, *ibid.*, xii., 1908, 12. Bovet (*Arch. de Psych.*, viii., 1908, 29) ascribes it to individual difference; von Aster (*Zeits. f. Psych.*, xlix., 1908, 97, 100 f.) thinks that 'begriffliches Denken' is a matter of direct impression ('Uebergangserlebnis': see Lecture IV., Note 66) and that 'gegenständliches Denken' involves the comparison of attitudes or images. Wreschner has a new distinction, that of 'Vorstellungen schlechthin' and of 'Zentral erregte Empfindungen' (6 f.).

[22] A statement of this sort can rest on nothing more tangible than general impression. Watt's paper seems to me to bear all the marks of an unitary conception. Ach's work is admittedly incomplete (v.) and the "und das Denken" of the title is an afterthought (vi.); but the work itself is organic, and the inclusion of thought is logically sanctioned by the whole trend of the investigation.

Bühler writes (*Archives*, 377): "Messer a interprété [son] matériel en logicien. . . . Cela fait paraître, d'un côté, ses recherches très étendues. . . . Mais d'un autre côté ça leur donne un certain air d'incohérence, car les résultats obtenus ne sont pas plus rattachés entre eux que les questions auxquelles ils doivent répondre." Cf. 386, and Bühler, 303.

[23] Messer, 12; so Bühler, 308.   [24] Bühler, 300 ff.
[25] *Ibid.*, 306, 309. Cf. Binet, 300 f. [26] *Ibid.*, 305.

[27] R. S. Woodworth, Imageless Thought, *Journ. Philos. Psych. Sci. Meth.*, iii., 1906, 703 f.

[28] Ueber Gedankenerinnerungen, *Arch. f. d. ges. Psych.*, xii., 1908, 24 ff. On the method of right associates, see G. E. Müller and A. Pilzecker, *Exper. Beiträge zur Lehre vom Gedächtniss*, 1900.

[29] Wundt, *Psych. Studien*, iii., 1907, 305 ; Dürr, *Zeits. f. Psych.*, xlix., 1908, 330.

[30] G. Störring, Experimentelle Untersuchungen über einfache Schlussprozesse, *Arch. f. d. ges. Psych.*, xi., 1908, 1 ff. The illustrations occur on pp. 7, 126. See also Experimentelle und psychopathologische Untersuchungen über das Bewusstsein der Gültigkeit, *ibid.*, xiv., 1909, 1 ff.

[31] Woodworth, The Consciousness of Relation, in *Essays Philosophical and Psychological*, 1908, 489 ff.

[32] There is a certain fatality about these dates. Ach, publishing in 1905, brings his references only "bis zum Jahre 1904" (vi.); Watt's dissertation, published in the *Archiv* for January, 1905, was current in separate form late in 1904, and is dated 1904. Messer's manuscript went to the printer in May, 1906; but he says that Ach's book "wurde mir erst bekannt als die Verarbeitung meines Materials schon fast ganz . beendet war" (11)—too late, therefore, to influence his perspective; Ach's work is referred to only in foot-notes. Wreschner, again, performed his experiments in the years 1900-1903 (Wreschner, 21).

[33] *Analyt. Psych.*, i., 85 f. Cf. *Manual*, 394 ff.; 248 ff.; *Groundwork*, 104 ff.

[34] J. R. Angell, Thought and Imagery, *Philos. Rev.*, vi., 1897, 648 f. Cf. *ibid.*, 534 f.

[35] *Ibid.*, vii., 1898, 74 f.

[36] A. Mayer und J. Orth, Zur qualitativen Untersuchung der Association. *Zeits. f. Psych. u. Physiol. d. Sinnesorg.*, xxvi., 1901, 1 ff., esp. 5 f.

[37] I give some illustrative references to Marbe's work. The observers were Külpe, Mayer, Orth, Pfister and Roetteken. Doubt, K p. 18, O p. 88; uneasiness, R 38; difficulty, K 21; uncertainty, R 30; effort, R 27; hesitation, K 29; vacillation, R 18; incapacity, M 81; ignorance, K 65; certainty, R 30; assent, O 87, M 88; conviction of right or wrong judgment, R 18, R 36, K 39.

Surprise appears as emotion, K 70, 71, and as *Bewusstseinslage*, O 87; wonder as emotion, K 79, M 80; astonishment, R 85; expectation, K 71, K 79, O 81 (as *Bewusstseinslage*, K 65); curiosity, O 80.

Remembrance of instructions, R 18; of answering in sentences, K 37; of past conversations, P 87; nonsense has come before, O 88; sense or nonsense is coming, O 88, 89; division leaves no remainder, K 35. Cf. also unnaturalness of form of answer, K 37; must compare, K 60; must calculate, K 79; that is too big, K 66; that is wrong, R 66; is it winter now? M 80; range of meaning of word lock (of hair), P 87.

The *Bewusstseinslagen* are reported sometimes with, sometimes without an affective concomitant: see, *e.g.*, the reports of R and P, 85-87. Associative arousal, K 23; part played in associative consciousness, R 24; attended to, R 24; forgotten, R 31.

Indefinite or indescribable forms, *e.g.*, K 35, R 74, P 85, 86.

[38] H. Höffding, *Psych. in Umrissen*, 1887, 152 f.; 1893, 163: Ueber Wiederkennen, etc., *Vjs. f. wiss. Philos.*, xiii., 1889, 427: Zur Theorie des Wiedererkennens, *Philos. Studien*, viii., 1893, 94. Cf. W. Wundt, *ibid.*, vii., 1892, 33; *Physiol. Psych.*, iii., 1903, 536; Ach, 236.

Ach refers also to J. Volkelt's *Erinnerungsgewissheit*: Beiträge zur Analyse des Bewusstseins, *Zeits. f. Philos. u. philos. Kritik*, cxviii. (1), 1 ff. In a characteristic review of this article (*Zeits. f. Psych. u. Physiol. d. Sinnesorg.*, xxix., 1902, 142 ff.), Witasek remarks: "Bei manchem der Ergebnisse hat man fürs Erste freilich den Eindruck, dass es weniger aus den Thatsachen herausanalysirt als vielmehr in diese hineindedcirt ist," and transforms Volkelt's 'Gewissheit' into 'Evidenz des Urtheils,'—*Evidenz* meaning 'psychisch-actuelle Ueberzeugungs-Berechtigung.' Cf. the account of Witasek's psychology of judgment in Lecture II. above.

Ach mentions, further, F. Schumann's 'Nebeneindrücke der Spannung der Ewartung' and 'der Ueberraschung' (*Zeits. f. Psych. u. Physiol. d. Sinnesorg.*, iv., 1892, 2, etc.), and the 'absolute impression' of the metric methods of psychophysics (L. J. Martin u. G. E. Müller, *Zur Analyse d. Unterschiedsempfindlichkeit*, 1899, 43).

[39] See, *e.g.*, *Physiol. Psych.*, ii., 1893, 501, 521; iii., 1903, 121 f., 625. I suppose that neither Orth's nor Ach's list of references is meant to be more than suggestive. It would be easy to add others; but I doubt if anything is to be gained by bracketing together a

number of experiences which obviously await analysis, and which are very differently placed in different systems.

[40] J. Orth, *Gefühl und Bewusstseinslage, eine kritisch-experimentelle Studie*, 1903, esp. 69-75, 130. I am not able to gather anything new from Orth's tables. Cf. Ach, 238 f., and ct. von Aster, *Zeits. f. Psych.*, xlix., 1908, 104 ff.

[41] Ach, 210, 215, 238. On previous use of the term *Bewusstheit*, see note, 239.

[42] *Ibid.*, 11, 211. The *Bewusstheit* may be attended to, as if it were a *Wahrnehmungsinhalt;* 211, 214.

[43] *Ibid.*, 213.

[44] *Ibid.*, 217 f.

[45] *Ibid.*, 96 f., 212 f., 219. Cf. the discussion of contributory factors, 220.

[46] *Ibid.*, 230, 235.

[47] *Ibid.*, 232, 235. Cf. Watt, 368 f.; E. Claparède, *L'association des idées*, 1903, 228 ff.

[48] *Ibid.*, 235 ff.

[49] The 'determining tendencies' are placed by Ach alongside of the perseverative and associative tendencies to reproduction (187, 195, 247), and are defined as follows (187): "Unter den determinierenden Tendenzen sind Wirkungen zu verstehen, welche von einem eigenartigen Vorstellungsinhalte der Zielvorstellung ausgehen und eine Determinierung im Sinne oder gemäss der Bedeutung dieser Zielvorstellung nach sich ziehen." Cf. 224 f.: "Es ist . . . die Regel, dass die wirksame Zielvorstellung beim Auftreten der konkreten Bezugsvorstellung als solche nicht im Bewusstsein erscheint, aber trotzdem einen bestimmenden Einfluss ausübt. In dieser eigentümlichen Wirksamkeit sehen wir neben den früher

angegebenen Merkmalen ein charakteristisches Zeichen für die Determinierung, und diese eigenartigen von der Zielvorstellung ausgehenden, sich auf die Bezugsvorstellung beziehenden Wirkungen bezeichnen wir als die determinierenden Tendenzen." Or again (228): "[Die] im Unbewussten wirkenden, von der Bedeutung der Zielvorstellung ausgehenden, auf die kommende Bezugsvorstellung gerichteten Einstellungen, welche ein spontanes Auftreten der determinierten Vorstellung nach sich ziehen, bezeichnen wir als determinierende Tendenzen." The effects of these tendencies are described 196, 209 f., 222, 234.

⁵⁰ Messer, 184.   ⁵¹ *Ibid.*, 180.

⁵² *Ibid.*, 180 f.   ⁵³ *Ibid.*, 181 ff.

⁵⁴ *Ibid.*, 184 ff., 188.   Messer's terms are *Gedanken* and *Begriffe*. The latter are "die *Bsl* von der Bedeutung einzelner Worte oder Phrasen."

⁵⁵ *Ibid.*, 187.   ⁵⁶ *Ibid.*, 84.

⁵⁷ Ach, 219.   ⁵⁸ Messer, 51.   Cf. 188 ff.

⁵⁹ *Ibid.*, 71 f., 83, 85.

⁶⁰ C. L. Taylor (Ueber das Verstehen von Worten und Sätzen, *Zeits. f. Psych.*, xl., 1905, 225 ff.) notes that both the imaginal representation of meaning and the attitude of 'understanding' tend to lapse as a printed text becomes familiar (241, 246).   More to our present point, however, is the fact that an observer, who finds visual ideas essential (229) or at any rate useful (235) in the solution of a given problem, drops these ideas and employs simply 'thoughts' and attitudes in the solution of further problems of the same kind (236).   It would be overhasty to suppose that the visual ideas formed, in these cases, the sole psychological representatives of

logical meaning; that state of affairs is possible, but not probable. Hence we may not either infer that the attitudes and the attitudinal constituents of the thoughts (these are described as "kompliziertere Gefüge von Bewusstseinslagen und Wortvorstellungen": 235) are vestigial derivatives of visual imagery; they might also derive, *e.g.*, from kinæsthetic complexes that had entered, along with the visual ideas, into the representation of meaning. In any event, the change from imagery to attitude, within the individual mind, appears to proceed rather by way of substitution and short cut than by way of gradual reduction,—though there may, doubtless, be individual differences (cf. Stout, *Analytic Psych.*, i., 83 f.). The point is taken up in Lecture V.

It is a fortunate chance that my colleague, Dr. L. R. Geissler, has—like Ach (216)—"eine ausgesprochene Veranlagung in Bewusstheiten zu denken," so that we may hope presently to throw some light upon the problem set in the text. So far, I can report only that the assimilation of a new idea, or the understanding of a novel term, is for Dr. Geissler a definitely imaginal experience, but that with growing familiarity the images very quickly lapse, and are replaced by an awareness which (though we have as yet had no opportunity to attempt its complete analysis) appears to be predominantly kinæsthetic in composition.

[61] Binet, 82.

NOTES TO LECTURE IV

[1] References are given in Notes ii., viii., pp. 239, 246, of Veitch's translation of *The Meditations, and Selections from the Principles, of René Descartes*, reprint of 1901. Add *Med.*, iii., p. 45. The letters here quoted will be found in *Œuvres*, ed. C. Adam et P. Tannery, iii., 1899, 395, 691 f.

[2] "Thought is impossible without an image," *On Memory and Recollection*, 449 b, *sub fin.* (W. A. Hammond, *Aristotle's Psychology*, 1902, 197. Cf. 6, 106, 123).

[3] Marbe, 9 f., 15, 44. The phrasing of this result is Marbe's.

[4] *Ibid.*, 43.   [5] *Ibid.*, 90.

[6] *Ibid.*, 52.   [7] *Ibid.*, 52 f.

[8] *Ibid.*, 91.

[9] *Ibid.*, 92. Messer seeks to effect a reconciliation between Ach and Marbe; the latter's 'Wissen' is "lediglich eine Disposition" (207).

[10] *Ibid.*, 92.

[11] *Ibid.*, 52: "in den Protokollen unserer Versuche von einer derartigen Absicht nichts nachgewiesen wurde."

[12] Watt, 412.

[13] *Ibid.*, 413. The influence of the *Aufgabe* is also plainly apparent in O. Külpe's Versuche über Abstraktion (*Bericht über d. I. Kongress f. exper. Psych.*, 1904, 56 ff.), published in the same year: cf. Watt, 426; Ach, 239 f.; Störring, *Arch. f. d. ges. Psych.*, xi., 1908, 7 f.; Wreschner, 493 f., etc.; E. Meumann, Ueber

Assoziationsexperimente mit Beeinflussung der Repro-
duktionszeit, *Arch. f. d. ges. Psych.*, ix., 1907, 117 ff.
(answered by Messer, *ibid.*, x., 1907, 409 ff.).   For
further references see Watt, *Arch. f. d. ges. Psych.*, vii.,
1906, Literaturbericht, 25 ff.

[14] *Ibid.*, 413.   [15] *Ibid.*, 410.

[16] Marbe, 54: "doch irgend welche Absichtlichkeit im
Bewusstsein des Erlebenden nicht nachweisbar zu sein
braucht."

[17] Watt, 346.   [18] *Ibid.*, 416.

[19] *Ibid.*, 300.   Note the lapse into phenomenology,
as soon as a mental formation is mentioned which the
writer has not himself analysed!   "In einem Zustand der
Erwartung, die von mehr oder weniger lebhaften Span-
nungsempfindungen begleitet wird"—so the phrase runs.
But why 'accompanied'?   May not the kinæsthesis be
an integral constituent of the expectation?   Cf. a forthcoming paper on Expectation by W. H. Pyle, in the
Amer. Journ. Psych.

[20] Messer, 7 f.   Cf. 108 f., 126, 208 f.

[21] *Ibid.*, 109 f.   It may be questioned whether this
"Aufgabe, das Seiende zu erkennen" is not, in reality,
of an instinctive nature;—whether the *Einstellung* which
underlies it is not a matter of racial heritage.   The
psychophysical organism has, after all, been developed,
throughout the course of evolution, in interaction with
its natural environment.   If this hypothesis is sound,
the *Aufgabe* need never come to consciousness: not because it is "ganz gewöhnlich und selbstverständlich"—
for what is customary now must once have been novel
and unaccustomed; but rather because instinctive attitudes are normally and intrinsically unconscious.

The Feeling of Reality.—There are, however, explicit 'feelings' of reality and unreality; there are times when we say, quite naturally, 'How real it all was!' or 'The whole thing struck me as unreal.' What is the systematic position of these 'feelings'?

Calkins (*An Introd. to Psych.*, 1901 or 1905, 124 ff.) recognises 'feelings of realness' as a sub-group of the 'attributive elements of consciousness.' The feeling of realness or consciousness of reality (126) can best be illustrated by a contrast of memory with imagination; there is an elementary experience, 'embedded' in the memory-image, which is utterly lacking to images of imagination. It resembles affection in that "it is always realised as belonging to some element or complex of elements" and "is not always present" in consciousness. It has, however, no simple opposite, as pleasantness has an opposite in unpleasantness (113 ff.); for the "feeling of the not-real is evidently a composite of the consciousness of opposition [a probably elemental relational experience: 131] and the consciousness of reality" (126). Whether it evinces a qualitative variety we are not told; the section-heading speaks of 'the feelings,' the text of 'the feeling' of realness.

In support of the elementary character of the feeling of realness, the writer appeals, first, to John Mill's note in *Analysis*, i., 1869, 412. Mill here raises the question "what is the difference to our minds between thinking of a reality, and representing to ourselves an imaginary picture," and decides that "the distinction is ultimate and primordial." The following discussion (413) is not very clear; but I do not find that Mill ascribes the difference to any feeling of realness that is 'embedded' in memory, or that may 'attach' to an image (Calkins, 187); he seems rather to regard imagination and belief (memory or expectation) as coördinate mental functions, differing in what Brentano would term their 'act.' Later, however, he writes (423) that "there is in the remembrance of a real fact, as distinguished from that of a thought, an element" which is other than a difference between ideas. This 'element,' then, might be considered as a feeling of realness superadded upon or attached to mere imagination. But then Mill terms it belief: "this element, howsoever we define it, constitutes Belief": whereas Calkins defines belief as "an idea distinguished both by the feeling of realness and by the [relational] feeling of congruence" (305). James, too, identifies the 'sense of reality' with 'belief' (*Princ.*, ii., 283 ff.).

The reference to Baldwin's *Handbook of Psych.*: *Feeling and Will*, 1891, 155, is erroneous. The feeling which there "cannot be explained, any more than any other feeling; it must be felt" is not the reality-feeling —which is discussed 148 ff.—but belief. Baldwin, of course, posits a reality-feeling. "Two different sorts of feeling may be denoted by the terms *reality-feeling* and *belief*. . . . To the mind of the writer this distinction is a fundamental and vital one" (149). Calkins' feeling of realness is, however, not identical with Baldwin's reality-feeling. It is rather—as is shown by the instances given (C., 124; B., 152 f.), and by the fact that the reality-feeling is correlated with an equally simple and original unreality-feeling (B., 151)—a blend of Baldwin's reality-feeling and belief.

But there is a wider difference between Calkins' position and that of the three psychologists to whom she refers. I can best express it by using the terminology —which of late has been somewhat abused—of structure and function.* The feeling of realness is, for Calkins, an element of mental structure. Mill and James and Baldwin speak the language of function. How else could Baldwin write that "the feeling of reality is simply consciousness itself" (154), or James describe belief as "the psychic attitude in which our mind stands towards the proposition taken as a whole" (287)? We have, accordingly, to consider whether Calkins is justified in ranking the feeling or feelings of reality among the "structural elements of consciousness" (17).

I have already said that the existence of 'feelings of reality' is beyond question. We have them when we

---

* James writes, in 1907: "We habitually hear much nowadays of the difference between structural and functional psychology. I am not sure that I understand the difference" (*Philos. Rev.*, xvi., 1). And yet James coined the terms, so lately as 1884, and uses them in his *Principles*, so lately as 1890! "[There are] two *aspects*," he says, "in which all mental facts without exception may be taken; their structural aspect, as being subjective, and their functional aspect, as being cognitions. In the former aspect, the highest as well as the lowest is a feeling, a peculiarly tinged segment of the stream. This tingeing is its sensitive body, the *wie ihm zu Muthe ist,* the way it feels whilst passing. In the latter aspect, the lowest mental fact as well as the highest grasps some bit of universal truth as its content, even though that truth were as relationless as a bare unlocalised and undated quality of pain. From the cognitive point of view, all mental facts are intellections. From the subjective point of view all are feelings" (*Mind,* O. S., ix., 1884, 18 f.; *Princ.,* i., 478). There are probably a good many psychologists who would object to the identification of mental function with the function of cognition; but apart from this—which is, after all, only an accident, due to the context in which James is writing—the distinction is perfectly clear and genuine.

find that the brooch we have picked up is real gold, and
the table we have spied in the second-hand store real
mahogany; we have them when, after ploughing through
the introductory pages, we come to the real point of a
scientific paper; we have them, in very uncanny form,
if we happen to be alone in a room full of waxwork
figures. We say—and feel—that Colonel Newcome and
Mr. Micawber, Becky Sharp and Dora, are more real
than half the people of our acquaintance. We often
get a particularly keen sense of the reality of the third
dimension from perspective figures.* An unexpected
meeting with a friend; the express recognition of a half-
heard sound as that of the fire alarm; the taking of a
'day off'; the first hint of the possibilities of a theory:
all these experiences, and a hundred others, give us the
feeling of reality. And there are counter-feelings of
unreality, over and above that special feeling of unreality which comes in states of lassitude and fatigue, when
the world of men and things is as shadowy and insub-
stantial as the world of the Lotos-eaters. There are,
indeed, as many feelings of reality and of unreality as
there are distinguishable meanings of the words real
and unreal.

But elementary feelings? elemental experiences?
Surely not: surely, on the contrary, a very heterogeneous
group of complex formations, every one of which demands its own analysis. We have feelings of reality
as we have feelings of utility, feelings of superiority,
feelings of amity: as, in the sphere of the concrete, we
have feelings of tables and chairs, horses and carts,

* Wundt, *Völkerpsychologie: Mythus und Religion*, ii., 1, 1905,
44.

books and papers. If we are to classify mental processes
as feelings 'of' anything, we can multiply our elements
ad infinitum.* But, for a psychology of structure, that
'of' which we have the feeling is irrelevant. The psychological datum is the feeling itself, the feeling as felt;
and the business of psychology, as a descriptive science,
is to analyse the conscious representation of meaning—
in the present case, the representation of the meaning
'real'—which the feeling is or contains. It seems to me
(though I speak with reserve, as I have not yet carried
the question into the laboratory) that the feelings of
reality are always of an emotive character, implying
affective process in connection with kinæsthetic or other
organic sensations, and running their course under the
influence of an *Aufgabe* or *Einstellung*. I am sure that,
in my own experience, they are complex.

Nevertheless, they might still include an unanalysable
core or residuum, a non-sensational and non-affective

* Woodworth, in his Non-Sensory Elements of Sense Perception
(*Journ. Philos. Psych. Sci. Meth.*, iv., 1907, 169 ff.), seems actually to accept this conclusion. "Each thing perceived, each size
and shape distinguished, probably we should add each relation
observed, has its own felt quality, which is not one of the qualities
of sensation." "The appropriate size qualities and distance qualities are clapped on to the sense presentation without the intermediary of sensorial imagery." "The thing quality must be
present if we are to have the consciousness of a thing or of
properties of a thing." The doctrine is, evidently, an extreme
form of Mach's doctrine of sensations and von Ehrenfels' doctrine
of *Gestaltqualitäten* (to which Woodworth refers, 171). It involves, among other things, that arithmetical treatment of psychology which Woodworth elsewhere (*Essays Philosophical and
Psychological*, 1908, 493) rightly rejects: see I. M. Bentley, The
Psych. of Mental Arrangement, *Amer. Journ. Psych.*, xiii., 1902,
276 ff. For a general criticism, with which I am in substantial
agreement, I may refer to Bentley, *loc. cit.*, 228 ff.

elementary process; and this core or residuum might be
their essential feature, as reality-feelings. I reply, first,
that I do not find it, although I know well enough what
the 'contrast' is between a memory-image of the Doge's
palace and a poetry image of the towers of Camelot.
And I reply, secondly, that—even if we grant its existence, in minds of a certain type—it cannot rank as a
mental element until it has been characterised as mental
content, defined in attributive terms. On this point I
take issue, not only with Calkins, but with James as well.
"Damit," says Messer, "dass gelegentlich unter besonderen Bedingungen die Erfassung der Bedeutung, das
Verstehen, als besonderes Erlebnis zu Bewusstsein kommt,
ist nun natürlich noch nicht gegeben, dass dies Erlebnis
genauer beschrieben oder analysiert werden kann" (77).
That is true, if it is a little obvious. "Die klare
Erkennung eines bestimmten psychischen Phänomens und
sein Unterscheiden von anderen psychischen Phänomenen
kann stattfinden," says Störring, "ohne dass deshalb
das Individuum in der Lage zu sein braucht, eine psychologische Beschreibung des betreffenden Phänomens
unter Angabe des Unterschieds von ähnlichen Phänomenen zu vollziehen. Mit anderen Worten: in vielen
Fällen wird von dem das psychische Phänomen erlebenden Individuum erkannt, dass es sich um das Phänomen
handelt, und es wird deutlich von ähnlichen Phänomenen
unterschieden, aber worin der Unterschied besteht, kann
nicht im einzelnen angegeben werden oder ist wenigstens
schwer angebbar" (*Arch. f. d. ges. Psych.*, xiv., 1909,
20). That also, if we take the general sense of the
passage, is true. Introspection demands conditions, and
demands observers. But if the *differentiae* are not speci-

fied, we have no right to count the experiences as
elemental. When James declares that "the challenge to
produce these psychoses [the transitive parts of the
stream of thought] . . . is as unfair as Zeno's treatment of the advocates of motion" (*Princ.*, i., 244), and
when Calkins postulates a mental element without men-
tioning its attributes,—without anything more than the
bare intimation that it will be found 'embedded' in the
memory-image if that is contrasted with a poetry image,
—these writers seem to me to miss the purpose and
to underestimate the responsibilities of psychology.
For the exhibition of psychoses, their analysis, the
discovery and formulation of their laws of connection,
all this is precisely the business of psychology:* and
indeed, it is but fair to say that James, having made his
disclaimer, addresses himself resolutely to the task dis-
claimed.† Moreover, the introduction of a new element
should, in the present state of psychology, be tentative
only, accompanied by references *con* as well as *pro*. Its
dogmatic assertion, in a text-book, absolves the student

* Bühler is within his rights when he says: "Zu verlangen:
Charakterisieren Sie mir dieses Wissen durch Angabe seiner
Intensität und seiner (Empfindungs-)Qualitäten, ist ebenso klug
als die Forderung: Charakterisieren Sie mir die räumliche Tiefe
durch Höhe und Breite" (361). But he is within his rights because he has 'produced'—by experimental procedure and to his
own satisfaction—mental processes which can be grouped neither
with ideas nor with feelings nor with attitudes. Marbe writes to
the point in *Zeits.*, xlvi., 1908, 353 f.

† I have pointed out, in Lect. I., the inconsistency between
James' treatment of the transitive feelings and his treatment of
the feeling of the central active self. I have referred, in the same
Lect., to my personal tendency to travel, under verbal guidance,
out of my visual schema, and so to involve myself in contradiction
and to become loose-ended in statement. It is not, I hope,

17

from any attempt at introspection in a direction where
first-hand judgment is imperatively needed;* its forth-
right acceptance, by the psychologist, gives an appearance of finality to chapters that are very far from
closed.†

[22] Messer, 209.

[23] Ach, 230 ff.   Cf. Watt, 368 ff.

[24] Watt, 429.

[25] *Ibid.*, 423.   Watt is at pains, throughout his thesis,
to take account of Wundt's opinions, and especially of
the Wundtian doctrine of apperception: *e.g.*, 321, 359 f.,

impertinent to remark that the passage in *Princ.*, i., 244 strikes
me as precisely analogous to one of my own verbal rushes; I am
speaking simply of mode of composition.   In my experience, the
verbal flow runs at a white heat; language becomes picturesque,
and full of metaphor; I achieve sentences that I am heartily
sorry to destroy.   I infer that James often writes in this way,
and that—having no visual schema—he lets his loose ends lie.

* The sole introspective mark which Calkins offers is that the
feeling of realness "is always realised as belonging to some element or complex of elements" (124).   This realisation is, however, a matter of 'reflective observation' (*ibid.*, and 132 f.); and,
since it attaches equally to the affections and to the feelings of
relation, it cannot serve here as *differentia*.   I come back to it in
Lect. V.

† Calkins' argument runs as follows: "It cannot be too often
repeated that an obstinately realised difference between one set
of psychic phenomena and another, even if the difference cannot
be analysed and explained, is nevertheless a sufficient reason for
distinguishing the experiences.   Now there certainly is a recognised
difference between the feelings of 'like,' 'more' and 'one,' and the
feelings of 'red,' 'warm' and 'pleasant'; and this difference in
itself suffices to mark these off as distinct groups of conscious
elements" (132).   The first sentence is correct; but the second
does not follow from it.   Realised differences must be rubricated
under the specific headings of their difference.   Thus a perception
is always and obstinately different from a volition; yet neither
perception nor volition is a conscious element.

400, 403 ff., 419, 421 ff. It is strange that he has
not sought to bring Wundt's psychology of judgment
into connection with his own theory of the *Aufgabe.*
Wundt writes as follows: "Meistens steht . . . die
ursprüngliche Gesammtvorstellung zuerst nur als ein
undeutlicher Complex einzelner Vorstellungen vor un-
serem Bewusstsein; die einzelnen Theile dieses Complexes
und die Art ihrer Verbindung treten dann erst bestimmter
während der Zerlegung hervor. Es kann so der Schein
entstehen, als wenn das Denken erst die Theile zusam-
mensuchte, die es in der successiven Gliederung der
Gesammtvorstellung an einander fügt. Nichtsdesto-
weniger ergibt es sich auch hier . . . dass das Ganze,
wenngleich in undeutlicher Form, früher appercipirt
werden musste, als seine Theile. Nur so erklärt sich
die bekannte Thatsache, dass wir ein verwickeltes Satz-
gefüge leicht ohne Störung zu Ende führen können.
Dies ware unmöglich, wenn nicht bei Beginn desselben
schon das Ganze vorgestellt würde. Der Vollzug der
Urtheilsfunction besteht daher, psychologisch betrachtet,
darin, dass wir die dunkeln Umrisse des Gesammtbildes
successiv deutlicher machen, so dass dann am Ende des
zusammengesetzten Denkactes auch das Ganze klarer
vor unserm Bewusstsein steht" (*Physiol. Psych.*, iii.,
1903, 575). Watt, now, has given us his equivalent of
the apperceptive activities; and it would seem that he
might, similarly, translate the *Gesammtvorstellung*—especially in view of its origin in Wundt's system—into
an *Aufgabe*-consciousness. One may grant that the
translation would be forced, and yet see that there is a
common element in the two theories. Watt, on the con-

trary, sets them in sharp opposition (412): ct. refs. in Lecture V., Note 31.

[26] Ach, 224.

[27] *Ibid.* "Ist die Absicht von guter Konzentration der Aufmerksamkeit begleitet, so besteht auch noch eine Zukunftsbeziehung insofern, als die Absicht auf die künftig eintretende konkrete Bezugsvorstellung gerichtet ist" (the 'concrete idea of object' is the perception of object, the presented stimulus). This 'relation to the future' is, apparently, a conscious process. We need not quarrel with its name, any more than we quarrel with the names 'idea of end' and 'idea of object,' so long as we realise that name does not in any way specify contents. It would, however, be wrong to imagine that there must be, in the *Absicht*, any conscious representation of futurity, of the temporal to-be or to-come. That is no more the case with purpose than it is with expectation.

[28] *Ibid.*, 193.

[29] *Ibid.*, 228. Ach, like Watt, operates with the concept of apperception: see, *e.g.*, 116 ff., 214, 225 ff.

[30] Marbe, 52.   [31] *Ibid.*, 53 f.

[32] Watt, 416.   [33] *Ibid.*, 410.

[34] Watt, 230; Messer, 111. Watt writes (411): "alles, was nur vermöge der eigenen Kraft von Reproduktions-tendenzen geschieht, ist noch nicht Urteil. Das sieht man deutlich an allen Gedächtnisversuchen und dergleichen"; and refers, apparently with approval, to Wundt, *Physiol. Psych.*, iii., 1903, 580, where a sharp distinction is drawn between associative and apperceptive processes. "Wird die Reproduktion," he goes on, "bis zu einem gewissen Grade aufdringlich, dann ist die Vp.

nicht mehr geneigt, das Erlebnis überhaupt als Urteil anzusehen." And he concludes: "was den Anteil des Faktors der blossen Reproduktion im Urteil betrifft, ist es eine notwendige Bedingung zum Zustandekommen eines Urteils, dass mehr als eine Reproduktion auf das betreffende Reizerlebnis folgen kann" (411 f.).

It is regrettable that Watt did not make experiments with free association. Suppose that such experiments are made, and that the observer does not specialise the *Aufgabe*. The results should, by hypothesis, be associations, not judgments: Messer (95) reports that one of his observers gave himself the express instruction "Sollst nicht assoziieren, sondern ein Urteil aussprechen." Yet, if they proceed from the *Aufgabe*, they must, according to Watt, be judgments. Aesthetic contemplation, too, seems to me, very definitely, to imply an *Einstellung*, which in turn implies and is conditioned upon a foregone *Aufgabe*. And since we have become interested in psychoanalysis, most of us, I fancy, find that our reveries and day-dreams, the free play of the reproductive imagination, are also determined by more or less remote *Aufgaben*. On this side, then, it is difficult to draw the dividing line, by Watt's definition, between judgment and non-judgment.

On the other side, of singly determined reproduction, there is also a difficulty. We have, say, the *Aufgabe* of memorising a set of nonsense-syllables. After a certain number of repetitions, the course of reproduction is determined. But with any less number of repetitions, it is possible "dass mehr als eine Reproduktion auf das betreffende Reizerlebniss folgen kann." The same thing holds, of course, of the memorising of sense-material.

Where does judgment end, and the play of reproductive tendencies begin?   Or is judgment involved at all? Moreover, if it is the *Aufdringlichkeit* of a response to stimulus that differentiates association from judgment, then has not Watt, in this *Aufdringlichkeit*, a second (even if a negative) psychological criterion of judgment?   There are, indeed, various connections in which Watt's analysis appears inadequate: see, *e.g.*, what is said of *Verwerfen*, 324, 340.

[35] Messer, 93.   Cf. Bühler, 331.

[36] *Ibid.*, 105.   In *Arch. f. d. ges. Psych.*, x., 1907, 416, Messer writes: *"Auf Grund der Angaben meiner Versuchspersonen* hatte ich (a. a. O. S. 105) das Urteilserlebnis bei Reaktionsversuchen so beschrieben" (italics mine); and in the following account of the instruction given to the observers, he makes no mention of the predicative relation.   Has he then forgotten the passage a. a. O. S. 93?

[37] *Ibid.*, 3 f.; Watt, 290.

[38] Messer, 105 ff.   The term *Beziehung* is here used in its active sense, so that in strictness *Beziehungserlebnis* should be translated 'feeling of relating,' and the phrase 'feeling of relation' should be reserved for the experiences discussed in Lecture V., Note 28.   The observers speak of an 'aktives Zusammenfassen' (99), and Messer himself of 'der Charakter der Aktivität beim Urteilsvollzug' (125).   Messer later attempts the analysis of 'bewusstes, aktives Beziehen' (195 ff.), and comes to nothing more definite than phenomena of attention ('Aufmerksamkeitszusammenhang,' 'gleichzeitiges aufmerksames Erfassen'),—the same phenomena that are

mentioned by his observers (105 f.) as characteristic of the predicative relation in particular.

The 'feeling of relation' is thus, for Messer, a *Bewusstseinslage*; the 'feeling of relating' is a matter of attention. The latter explanation, however, has its difficulties. Thus, in his discussion of 'bewusstes, aktives Beziehen,' Messer remarks: "freilich fehlt es dabei auch nicht an Fällen, bei denen die Beziehung ohne Zutun des Subjekts gewissermassen von selbst gegeben erscheint" (195). This may perhaps mean simply that the observer sometimes finds himself relating, slips into relating (under the conditions of the experiment) as a matter of course; the feeling of relating itself may still be a function of attention. More serious are the objections (198 f.) that the reference to attention does not account for all the various modes of relating, predicative and other, that come to the observer's consciousness; and that it is at least an open question whether simultaneous 'apprehension' by the attention necessarily rouses the feeling of relating.

If I may risk an opinion, on the basis of a limited number of rather casual introspections, I should say that these difficulties are not insuperable. Active attention is always 'voluntary' attention, that is, attention under *Aufgabe;* and the 'ideas' that are simultaneously apprehended by active attention are, under Messer's conditions, always meanings (51, 188; cf. *Arch. f. d. ges. Psych.,* x., 1907, 418). It might, then, be argued, with some plausibility, that the sets and adjustments of active attention form the conscious representation of 'relating': that differences of *Aufgabe* account for the various modes of this relating, and that the determinate apprehension of two meanings, their apprehension under a single *Aufgabe*, must arouse the relating consciousness. However, the question can be decided only by further experimental work.—

The slipperiness of terms is attested by Bühler's criticisms (Bühler, 346 [cf. 316] ; *Arch. de Psych.*, vi., 1907, 378) and by Messer's replies (*Arch. f. d. ges. Psych.*, x., 1907, 418 f.). It is inevitable, so long as the terms are common to psychology and to logic,—not to speak of the looseness of their ordinary, everyday use.

[39] *Ibid.*, 107 f.   [40] *Ibid.*, 112, 114.

[41] *Ibid.*, 109.   [42] *Ibid.*, 112.

[43] *Ibid.*, 113.

[44] *Ibid.*, 113. Messer is speaking of Ebbinghaus' memory-work. He does not, himself, raise the question of justification ; he simply says : "es ist daher charakteristisch, dass [dieser] Forschungszweig erst dann die entscheidende Wendung zu exakterer Gestaltung nahm, als H. Ebbinghaus . . . dazu griff, als Untersuchungsmaterial sinnlose Silben zu verwenden." The 'daher' follows from the bare fact of there being two "Wege der psychologischen Forschung" (112).

[45] *Ibid.*, 111. Cf. Ach's 'Einverständnis des Subjektes,' 230 ff.

[46] *Ibid.*, 111. Cf. P. Bovet, *Arch. de Psych.*, viii., 1908, 20.—Here I am interpreting. Messer does not say that the discovery of the 'eigenartiges Erlebnis' of volition or intention is due to the existential attitude of descriptive psychology ; indeed, the trend of his later remarks would seem to make that attitude, over against the judgment, inadequate and mistaken. But if you are to compare an *Urteil* with a *blosse Assoziation*, you must

compare them under the same conditions. To get a mere association, you must have the artificial idea-attitude, the attitude that makes the conscious contents as such the object of attention: I suppose, then, that in the comparison of judgment with association, for the discovery of a 'besondere Bewusstseinsqualität,' this attitude must be continued. Indeed, it seems to be implied in all of Messer's introspective work.

[47] *Ibid.*, 121.

[48] *Ibid.*, 115 ff., esp. 121. "Dass in diesem Bejahen und Verneinen, Anerkennen und Verwerfen ein Erlebnis spezifischer Art vorliegt, dass es jedenfalls von den 'Vorstellungen' zu unterscheiden ist, das dürfte das Berechtigte an Brentanos Urteilslehre sein."

[49] Ach, 209 f.

[50] Messer, 112. I have already, in Note 46, pointed out what I take to be Messer's inconsistency in this connection, and I refer to the 'stimulus error' (in connection with Bühler's results) in Note 64 below. What I say in the text has, of course, been said over and over again by the experimentalists. I quote the last author to come into my hands: "Unser gewöhnliches Leben bewegt sich in der Welt der Gegenstände; jeder Eindruck ist für uns nur Seite eines Gegenstandes. Das Experiment dagegen sucht mit reinen Eindrücken zu arbeiten" (O. Klemm, *Psychol. Studien*, v., 1909, 85).

[51] *Ibid.*, 121 f.

[52] *Ibid.*, 8 f., 10, 208.

[53] *Ibid.*, 209; cf. Bühler, *Arch. f. d. ges. Psych.*, xii., 1908, 5.

[54] *Ibid.*, 125 f., 126 f., 145 f.; cf. Bühler, *Arch. de Psych.*, vi., 1907, 379. Messer defends himself (*Arch.*

f. d. ges. Psych., x., 1907, 420 f.) by the statement that
" 'Erlebt' und 'Bemerkt' werden ist nicht dasselbe." But
what—for descriptive psychology—is an 'unbemerktes
Erlebnis'? Messer himself had previously applied the
law of growth and decay in a very different fashion:
see the ref. in Note 22 above.

[55] Bühler, 310.

[56] *Ibid.*, 310 f., 313 f., 347 f., 351 ff.

[57] *Ibid.*, 315 f.

[58] *Ibid.*, 317.

[59] Bühler, 315. Cf. von Aster, *Zeits. f. Psych.*, xlix.,
1908, 63. "Ich glaube [Bühler] nicht misszuverstehen,
wenn ich annehme, dass der Ausdruck 'zuständliche'
Erlebnisstrecke die Bewusstseinslage . . . gerade im
Gegensatz zu den Gedanken charakterisieren soll. Das
Zuständliche steht, scheint mir, hier entgegen dem In-
tentionalen, wenn wir diesen Husserlschen Ausdruck im
weitesten Sinn nehmen." Bühler, in fact, says very little;
and I doubt if he has thought out the distinction in the
way suggested.

[60] Watt, 430: instances occur 304, 324, 332, 339, etc.
The difficulty lies in such instances as day-dreaming.
If that type of consciousness is not determined by an
Aufgabe, how can the attitude be so determined?—for
day-dreaming is, at times, little more than a succession
of attitudes.

[61] Bühler, 318; cf. 321: "ich behaupte . . . dass
prinzipiell jeder Gegenstand vollständig ohne Anschau-
ungshilfen bestimmt gedacht (gemeint) werden kann."

[62] *Ibid.*, 361.

[63] *Ibid.*, 329, 330. Bühler is criticised in some detail
by Messer, *Arch. f. d. ges. Psych.*, x., 1907, 421 ff., and

by Dürr, *Zeits. f. Psych.*, xlix., 1908, 318 ff. Cf. also
Bovet, *Arch. de Psych.*, viii., 1908, 33 ff.

[64] On the stimulus-error see my *Exp. Psych.*, II., ii.,
1905, lxiii., etc. The name 'stimulus-error' is natural,
since the confusion lies, in terms of Fechnerian psychophysics, between 'sensation' and 'stimulus.' Intrinsically,
however, 'thing-error' or 'object-error' would be a better
phrase; what the naïve observer confuses with his mental
process is not the physical stimulus, but the thing of
common sense. The error itself is widespread and insidious. It is responsible, I believe, among other things,
for the current tendency to deny the attribute of intensity to the image.

[65] Bühler, 311.

[66] E. von Aster, Die psychologische Beobachtung und
experimentelle Untersuchung von Denkvorgängen, *Zeits.
f. Psych.*, xlix., 1908, 102; cf. 77. The writer himself
tentatively reduces the experiences that are characterisable as 'Bewusstsein von,' 'Wissen um,' to three types:
(1) "gefühlsbetonte Bewusstseinslagen, seien sie nun
direkt erlebte oder eingefühlte 'zuständliche Erlebnis-
strecken' "; (2) 'Uebergangserlebnisse,' that is, direct
impressions of sameness, difference, relation, in which a
comparison is not involved; and (3) "optische, akust-
ische, haptische u. s. w. Vorstellungsinhalte."

[67] *Ibid.*, 69, 71. Obvious instances of the substitution of *Kundgabe* for *Beschreibung* will be found in
E. D. Starbuck, *The Psychology of Religion; an Empirical Study of the Growth of Religious Consciousness*,
1899 (cf. J. H. Leuba, *Psychol. Review*, vii., 1900, 515).
A much subtler instance is afforded by W. H. Sheldon,
Analysis of Simple Apprehension, *Psychol. Review*, xvi.,

1909, 107 ff. Reference may be made also to Binet's list of characterising terms, 303; to various phrases employed by Störring's observers in their study of the 'Bewusstsein d. Gültigkeit' (*Arch. f. d. ges. Psych.*, xiv., 1909, 1 ff.); and to Ach's 'intentional' movement sensations (Ach, 40, 49 ff., 149 ff.; Messer, 59 f.). The sensations themselves are described, but the adjective 'intentional' is not descriptive; it is, however, introduced with the explicit statement that "eine genauere Analyse . . . war nicht möglich."

I may add that one of the principal difficulties in the way of a psychology of the *Aufgabe* itself lies in the fact that the problem, as given to the observer, must be couched in terms of information. The observer, responding to the informatory attitude of the experimenter, will naturally take up the same attitude to himself,—will repeat 'subordinate idea, superordinate idea, find a part,' etc., without effort to translate the instruction into descriptive terms.

[68] E. Dürr, Ueber die experimentelle Untersuchung der Denkvorgänge, *Zeits. f. Psych.*, xlix., 1908, 315, 323, etc. Dürr's own view is given as follows: "ich schliesse mich der Ansicht derjenigen an, die in dem Raumbewusstsein, im Zeitbewusstsein, im Bewusstsein von Gleichheit, Aehnlichkeit, Verschiedenheit oder (zusammengefasst) im Vergleichsbewusstsein und im Bewusstsein von Indentität und Einheit . . . ein . . . Plus anerkennen, welches im Vorstellungsleben neben den Empfindungen vorhanden ist. Und eben dieses Plus, von den Empfindungen abgelöst, scheint mir das Wesen des abstrakten Denkens auszumachen. Als zusammenfassender Name für dieses Plus scheint mir der Name

Beziehungsbewusstsein geeignet, wenn man dieses
Wort ohne Nebenbedeutung lediglich als Bezeichnung
für die betreffende Klasse von Bewusstseinstatsachen
gebraucht. Man muss sich dabei freilich sehr hüten, an
die Beziehungen zu denken, die wir neben den Dingen,
Eigenschaften und Zuständen als die vierte Klasse von
Denkobjekten zu betrachten gewöhnt sind. Durch das
Beziehungsbewusstsein erfassen wir nicht nur Beziehung-
en, sondern auch Dinge, Eigenschaften und Zustände"
(326).

[69] *Ibid.*, 316. In his reply to von Aster and Dürr
(*Zeits. f. Psych.*, li., 1909, 108 ff.), Bühler makes two
points which call for notice here. (1) He doubts whether
von Aster's *Kundgabe* is identical with Dürr's *sprach-
licher Ausdruck* (118; cf. *Bericht über d. III. Kongress
f. exp. Psych.*, 1909, 104). The identification is made
by von Aster (*ibid.*, xlix., 107) ; and it seems to me that
the *Kundgabe*, the *sprachliche Ausdruck*, and my own
reference to the stimulus-error all contain practically the
same criticism, though the form in which the criticism
is presented naturally varies with the standpoint and
preoccupation of the critic. (2) Bühler admits that his
observers' reports contain a large proportion of *Kundgabe* and *sprachliche Darstellung;* but he adds: "man
darf dabei auch nicht aus dem Auge verlieren, dass ich
vieles mitteilen musste, nur um den Zusammenhang
verständlich zu machen, in dem das stand, worauf es
gerade in dem Protokoll ankam" (118). He refers also
to his original article, 318: "es kommt darin [in the
reports quoted] jeweils nur auf den hervorgehobenen
Teil an, wir müssen aber hier die Protokolle ganz an-
führen, damit man sehen kann, in welchem Zusammen-

hang die anschauungslosen Gedanken aufgetreten sind."

The reply does not fit the criticism. It is, of course, precisely the 'anschauungslosen Gedanken' against which von Aster is arguing; it is the italicised part of the protocols that is in question; von Aster would not for a moment deny that true psychological description, true introspective detail is mixed in with the *Kundgabe*, where the report is not concerned with what Bühler interprets as the thought-element. Besides: if Bühler knew that his observers' reports were only in part descriptive, introspective, why did he not attempt to separate the essential from the inessential, the description from the connective intimation? Why does he fall, for instance, into an obvious confusion of the two in his reference to the range of consciousness (Bühler, 348)?

I agree with von Aster that the experimenters of the Würzburg school began with a descriptive problem; the *Bewusstseinslage* was, avowedly, introduced to save the situation in cases where introspective analysis, under the conditions of the experiment, was at fault. But the whole tendency of the work has been away from description, and towards *Kundgabe*. Watt (345) censures an observer for confining his introspective report to perception and sensation, idea, feeling and attitude; the effort at rubrication is likely to miss the transitory phases of consciousness. Watt, of course, was justified from his own point of view; he could rubricate for himself, after the report was handed in. Nevertheless, the call for a full description of a complex consciousness puts a premium on *Kundgabe*. The tendency becomes increasingly manifest in Messer and Ach; and is clearly realised in Bühler. Every one of Messer's attitudes

(181 ff.) and feelings (187) sets a problem to descriptive psychology.

[70] Binet, *e.g.*, 81 f.

[71] *Journ. Philos. Psych. Sci. Meth.*, iii., 1906, 704.

[72] *Essays Philos. and Psychol.*, 1908, 491 f., 499. I return to the question of the 'feelings of relation' in Lecture V.

[73] Messer, 51 ff.

[74] G. Störring, Experimentelle Untersuchungen über einfache Schlussprozesse, *Arch. f. d. ges. Psych.*, xi., 1908, 1 ff. Störring's interest is primarily logical; he wishes to ascertain whether inference necessarily implies spatial ideation, whether the conclusion is derived from the premises by a synthesis of the thoughts contained in the premises, etc.; though he also acknowledges the suggestion received from the Würzburg studies of concept and judgment (1 f.). The paper has no summary; nor is there any explicit reference in the text (save that to space, 77 f.) to the problems mentioned in the introduction: the reason is, perhaps, that the present investigation, with visual material, is to be supplemented by another, in which the premises are to be given in auditory form.

The article is difficult reading, since Störring describes his observers' 'operations' in logical terms, and throws the introspective reports into running narrative. I take a simple instance. "Hier tritt," says Störring, of a certain inference involving the relations 'larger' and 'smaller,' "hier tritt das Bewusstsein der nur repräsentativen Bedeutung dieser Lagebeziehungen sehr schön hervor." The introspective report, after characterising the observer's efforts at visual localisation, reads: "dabei wurde gedacht: je höher um so grösser" (55). This, then, is the consciousness of the merely representative significance of the positional relations. But what was 'dieser Gedanke'? Was it a series of words, or an attitude, or a complex of words and attitude? Or is the term 'thought' used in its popular meaning, without reflection upon its psychological significance?

In order to gain light upon this and similar questions, I have myself worked through a fairly large number of examples of the same sort as those used by Störring. Unfortunately, my tendency is towards a purely mechanical procedure (cf. Störring, e.g., 65, 72, 97, 107); I 'read off' the conclusion from the premisses, oftentimes without any special 'Auffassung' of the premisses themselves, very much as one factorises a familiar algebraical expression. Sometimes I get a visual schema, into which I 'throw' the terms of the premisses by movement of finger or eyes or head: even so, however, the conclusion shoots to a point, in verbal terms, almost before I am aware of the visual and kinæsthetic images. I may add that the placing of an 'earlier' to the left and of a 'later' to the right is, for me, as natural as the placing of a 'past' behind my back and a 'future' in front of me; so that if I come, without practice, to the major premiss "Process A later than process C," I instinctively throw C over to the other side of A,—I see the curve of the path, and feel the movement of throwing; though, with a little practice, this imagery disappears. I doubt if the localisation has anything to do with the left-to-right movements of reading (36 f.).

It is, however, not an easy matter to experiment on

oneself, and I should probably have had fuller consciousnesses had I been observing under Störring's instructions. A general appreciation of his work is hardly possible without this first-hand experience. I note only that he cannot at all mean to imply that the various forms of 'consciousness' appearing in (or inferred from) the introspective reports are to be regarded, off-hand, as ultimate and unanalysable; for he devotes a later paper to the special analysis of that "Bewusstsein absoluter Sicherheit" with which the observers in the present enquiry were enjoined to draw their conclusions (3: cf. Experimentelle und psychopathologische Untersuchungen über das Bewusstsein der Gültigkeit, *Arch. f. d. ges. Psych.*, xiv., 1909, 1 ff.).

NOTES TO LECTURE V

[1] W. C. Bagley, The Apperception of the Spoken Sentence, *Amer. Journ. Psych.*, xii., 1900, 80 ff., esp. 126. The admission made in the text has, of course, its obverse side; Stout's observers would, in all probability, have an anti-sensationalistic bias. Bagley, as a matter of fact, recognises the possibility of an effective apperception when the only discriminable contents of consciousness are verbal ideas (117), and also when the associated imagery is inconsistent with the meaning of the sentence (121). Taylor (*Zeits.*, xl., 1905, 228) brings this latter result into connection with Marbe's conclusions: he himself (239) adduces evidence of the irrelevant visual associates to which I have referred in Lecture I.

The marginal theory of meaning, which Bagley develops briefly in *Amer. Journ. Psych.* and more elaborately in *The Educative Process*, 1905, gives a consistently sensationalistic account of certain *Bewusstseinslagen* (Taylor, 248), which seems to fit the observed facts. That it has not been discussed by recent workers in the field of attitude may be ascribed, perhaps, to the difference of material: Bagley worked with auditory, the rest for the most part with visual stimuli. It is further possible that pattern and composition of the attitude vary even with variation of the experimental method, as employed upon the same sort of material: cf. Watt, 367 f.

[2] G. E. Müller and F. Schumann, Ueber die psychol.

Grundlagen der Vergleichung gehobener Gewichte, *Arch. f. d. ges. Physiol.*, xlv., 1889, 37 ff.

[3] Külpe, *Grundriss*, 1893, 422 f., 427 f., 428 f.; *Outlines*, 1909, 407 f., 412, 413 f.; Anfänge u. Aussichten d. exper. Psych., *Arch. f. Gesch. d. Philos.*, vi., 1893, 466. Cf. the discussion in Watt, 403 ff.; Ach, 156 ff.

[4] G. Martius, Ueber die muskuläre Reaction und die Aufmerksamkeit, *Philos. Studien*, vi., 1891, *e.g.*, 175 f.

[5] H. Münsterberg, *Beitr. z. experiment. Psych.*, i., 1899, *e.g.*, 75 f., 90, 168.

[6] L. Lange, Neue Experimente über d. Vorgang d. einfachen Reactionen auf Sinneseindrücke, *Philos. Studien*, iv., 1888, 487 ff. "(1) Es lassen sich einerseits Reactionen gewinnen, wenn man an den bevorstehenden Sinneseindruck *gar nicht denkt*, dagegen so lebhaft als möglich die Innervation der auszuführenden Reactionsbewegung vorbereitet. (2) Andererseits kann man, indem man jede vorbereitende Bewegungsinnervation *grundsätzlich vermeidet*, seine ganze vorbereitende Spannung dem zu erwartenden Sinneseindrucke zuwenden, wobei man sich aber gleichzeitig vornimmt, unmittelbar nach Auffassung des Eindruckes, ohne bei diesem unnöthig zu verweilen, den Impuls zur Bewegung folgen zu lassen. . . . Es versteht sich fast von selbst, dass man auch einen Mittelweg zwischen den beiden extremen Methoden einschlagen kann, indem man seine Spannung sozusagen nach irgend einem Theilverhältniss zwischen Hand und Ohr theilt. . . . Mit Rücksicht auf die extremen Methoden aber müssen wir uns eines immer gegenwärtig halten: der Spannungsgrad der Erwartung ist bei beiden vollkommen der nämliche und

nur die Richtung, nach welcher hin die Erwartung gespannt ist, eine verschiedene." And again (510): "Die musculäre Reaction . . . stellt . . . eine unwill-kürliche, reflectorische Bewegung dar, allerdings eine solche, die unter dem nachwirkenden Einflusse eines *vorangegangenen* Willensimpulses erfolgt." This is admirably clear; and Ach remarks, with truth, that "L. Lange hat durch seine Beobachtung, dass die Dauer der Reaktionsversuche in enger Beziehung zur vor-bereitenden Aufmerksamkeitsspannung steht, wohl mehr zur Erforschung dieses Gebietes beigetragen als sämt-liche vorhergehenden Untersuchungen zusammen ge-nommen" (Ach, 6 f.).

[7] *Leviathan*, pt. i., ch. iii. (*Works*, ed. Molesworth, iii., 1839, 12 ff.). Cf. *Human Nature*, ch. iv. (iv., 1840, 14); *Physics*, ch. xxv. (i., 1839, 398).

[8] J. Volkelt, Psychologische Streitfragen, i. Selbst-beobachtung und psychol. Analyse, *Zeits. f. Philos. u. philos. Kritik*, N. F. xc., 1887, 11. Much of the earlier part of this paper, and much of Wundt's controversial reply to it (Selbstbeobachtung und innere Wahrnehm-ung, *Philos. Studien*, iv., 1888, 292 ff.), are written in the very spirit of an *Aufgabe*-psychology. I have already indicated my position on the general question, in Lecture III., Note 14 above.

[9] I venture to suggest that there is a danger, in some fields of current psychological investigation, that the extreme difficulty of introspection be lost sight of. No one who knows anything of the history of psychology needs to be reminded of this difficulty; it has been dis-cussed, and it has been illustrated, over and over and over again. Yet there are recent writers who take a

light-hearted appeal to introspection,—as if vexed questions could be settled out of hand, as if there were
nothing to do but to 'look into consciousness,' as if
introspective attitude and introspective capacity were
the common property of anyone who cares to exercise
them.   Now, in the first place, there are very different
degrees of introspective ability.   Whether it is ever
entirely lacking, as musical ability may be entirely
lacking, I do not know; the historical instances are
equivocal; Comte, *e.g.*, may have had it, in some measure, and have lost it by his preoccupation with other
methods.   But there is no doubt that the introspective
talent or the introspective gift differs enormously in
different individuals.   In the second place, the ability,
in whatever degree it is present, must be trained by long
and arduous practice, if the results of introspection are
to be valid.   And even so, the introspective observer is
still, to some extent, at the mercy of circumstances.
"On peut," remarks Binet (155), "pendant une année,
analyser assidument la structure d'un esprit sans s'aper-
cevoir d'une propriété mentale de prime importance, que
l'échange fortuit d'une question et d'une réponse suffit
à découvrir en moins d'une minute."   Yes! and, in the
same way, one may live on good psychological terms
with one's own mind for a great many years, and fail
to see something that—when the psychological moment
arrives—stares one in the face.   Here, indeed, lies a
principal reason for the cultivation of a permanent
introspective habit.   If one is, always and everywhere,
on the alert for psychological observation, chance will
throw things in one's way that the special procedure of
laboratory experiments may very possibly miss.

I have, personally, a profound confidence in introspection, and I try to encourage a like confidence in
my students. I believe that a great many psychological
controversies might be laid to rest if the protagonists
could get together, for half a year, and work the issue
out under test conditions. We are now, as I have remarked earlier in this book, sacrificing literary form in
order to make a clean breast of our methods and introspective results; but nothing in the way of a printed
report can, after all, take the place of common work
and the conversational interchange of ideas. Psychology is here at a great disadvantage, as compared
with the sciences of external nature, since physical
apparatus and biological specimens may be shipped
from place to place unaccompanied by their owners.
At the same time, and with all this confidence, I have no
respect for introspective authority. I have just referred
to the lessons that we may learn from the history of
psychology. There are plenty of similar lessons to be
learned from individual experience. Again and again
I have been honestly sure of an introspective result, only
to find that a more refined enquiry, or the shift of the
angle of observation, convicts me of error. It is a certain consolation to note that precisely the same thing—
despite the advantages of objectivity—holds of observation in the natural sciences; the history of the micro-
scope, for instance, and the present status of nerve
histology, tell a like story.

While, therefore, the introspective data of any given
period represent, on the whole, the facts of mind so far
as examined, we have to remember, first, that the
exploration is still partial only, and secondly, that in a

new field we are all of us liable to make mistakes. Above all, we have to remember that intrinsic difficulty of introspection to which I made reference at the outset. The hypothesis of fraud (if I may borrow a phrase from the students of Psychical Research) is excluded; we mean to be honest. And there are plenty of established results, let us say, in the sphere of sensation. Nevertheless, do we agree as regards the qualities of organic sensation? or as regards the 'effect of attention' upon the intensity of sensation? or even as regards the psychological simplicity of colours?

So the present discussion between the representatives of sensationalism and intellectualism, in the realm of thought, must continue for a long time, before anything like a settlement can be expected. No single investigation, still less any authoritative pronouncement, can solve or dismiss the problem. We must patiently accumulate and examine evidence, making what allowance we may for systematic and controversial bias on both sides, and sharpening our wits for the discovery of positive sources of error. There is no need to hurry; there is every need to take the work seriously. Psychology has been in somewhat of a hurry to reform the doctrine of feeling; but we now see that years of laboratory research and a great many doctorate theses will be required before we are able to form a decisive judgment. Psychology and the psychologising philosophers are, similarly, in somewhat of a hurry to accept the unanalysable attitudes and the thought-elements of a transfigured intellectualism. They may prove to be in the right, as the champions of a multidimensional feeling may be in the right. But they have not yet made out their case; and introspection will be as slow as any other court of appeal in rendering a final verdict. Meanwhile, it is the part of wisdom to accept a working hypothesis, and to push it as far as it will go; but to be clear that it is nothing more than a working hypothesis, and to keep an open mind for the facts that will not fit it. And it is the part, not so much of psychological wisdom as of sheer psychological sanity, to realise the natural and inevitable difficulties of psychological observation.

[10] R. S. Woodworth, in *Essays Philos. and Psychol.*, 1908, 502 ff. James Angell, reviewing Woodworth's article in the *Studies in Philos. and Psych.* (1906) dedicated to C. E. Garman, declares that "the 'naked thought' concept is a logical abstraction finding no real psychological basis in a careful examination of consciousness" (*Journ. Philos. Psych. Sci. Meth.*, iii., 1906, 641). Woodworth replies (*ibid.*, 702) that a position like Angell's is much more likely than his own "to owe its acceptance to logical deduction."

Bühler thinks that the formulation of the problem, in the work both of Marbe and of Messer, betrays its "logische Herkunft" (303). He further believes that "die Gesichtspunkte [der] Unterscheidung [des direkten und indirekten Meinens], die schon der Wattschen Arbeit ihrer ganzen Anlage nach zu grunde liegen, sind ursprünglich aus erkenntnistheoretischen Erwägungen hervorgegangen"; and that Messer is similarly contaminated (359). "Messer a obtenu un important matériel d'observation. . . . Malheureusement, Messer a interpreté ce matériel en logicien. . . . Il y a un fait spécifique de jugement, et, ce fait, [Messer] le conçoit, en s'appuyant évidemment sur les définitions logiques de B. Erdmann, comme la prise de conscience d'une relation prédicative" (*Arch. de psych.*, vi., 1907, 377).

Messer is at no great pains to deny this impeachment, though he pleads that he has, on the whole, kept his logic separate from his psychology (*Arch. f. d. ges. Psych.*, x., 1907, 419 ff.) Nor does he retort on Bühler, except in the assumption that Bühler is influenced by Husserl's and Külpe's epistemology (*ibid.*, 421 ff.). That, indeed, is obvious; and the charge becomes explicit in von Aster's remark that Bühler's "Experimente sind gewissermassen ein mehr oder minder absichtlicher Versuch, Husserls Phänomenologie experimentell zu prüfen bzw. zu bestätigen" (*Zeits. f. Psych.*, xlix., 1908, 62). Dürr suggests that Bühler has commingled *metaphysics* and psychology: *Zeits. f. Psych.*, xlix., 1908, 319 f.

Ach (Vorwort, vi.) expressly reserves the epistemological implications of his work for a later discussion.

[11] Cf. Wundt's discussion of panoramic and stereoscopic vision, *Princ. of Physiol. Psych.*, i., 1904, 299 ff.; and the discussion of his genetic theory of tactual and visual space perception, *Grundzüge d. physiol. Psych.*, ii., 1902, 489 ff., 668 ff. See also Stumpf, *Tonpsych.*, ii., 1890, 215 ff.; C. Stumpf and M. Meyer, *Zeits. f. Psych. u. Physiol. d. Sinnesorgane*, xviii., 1898, 394 (feeling for the purity of musical intervals); C. Stumpf, *Zeits. f. Psych.*, xliv., 1906, 44 ff. (sense-feelings); etc. I have touched on this topic in *Exp. Psych.*, I., ii., 1901, 228 ff.

[12] *Feeling and Attention*, 1908, 291 f.; *Text-book*, i., 1909, 260 f.

[13] A great deal has been written, of late years, against psychological analysis. Consciousness, we are told in effect, is a living continuum; but the analyst kills, in order to make his dissection; and, after killing and dissecting, he is unable to restore the life that he has taken, to show consciousness in its original integrity. The argument, if it were taken seriously, would apply to biology as well as to psychology, and would banish the muscle-nerve preparation and the microtome from the biological laboratory. But, indeed, it rests only upon misunderstanding,—a misunderstanding due in part to temperamental reaction, in part to the pressure of history and tradition. When the physiologist describes a tissue as 'composed' of muscle fibres or nerve cells, nobody takes him to mean that the fibres and cells existed first, in isolation, and that they were presently brought together, by some law of organic growth, to constitute the tissue. What grew was the tissue itself, which the physiologist now finds, in his *post mortem* examination, to consist of the cells or the fibres. It is worth while to trace the laws of growth; it is also worth while to know the constitution of the tissue; knowledge of the one may very well help towards a knowledge of the other; but the two aims are different, and do not cross. Yet the analytical psychologist is supposed to generate his mind by allowing sensations to fuse and colligate,—precisely as the physiologist might be supposed to generate his muscle by allowing fibres to 'constitute.' Fusion and the rest are patterns of consciousness, recognisable precisely as you recognise a preparation under the miscroscope as a tissue-pattern, and say 'That's liver' or 'That's the optic nerve.' To charge

the analytical psychologist with deriving mind from the interconnection of sensations,—and how often and how recklessly has not that charge been made!—is sheerly to misunderstand the purpose of analysis in the hands of those who use it.

The scientific legitimacy of the analytical attitude is beyond question. Whether the results of analysis, in the sphere of mind, are of 'value' is another question, and a question whose answer depends on what one is disposed to consider valuable. What is psychology 'for'? If the object of the psychologist is to know mind, to understand mind, then it seems to me—in view of the overwhelming complexity of mind in the concrete—that the only thing he can do is to pull mind to pieces, and to scrutinise the bits as minutely as possible and from all possible points of view. His results, in synthetic reconstruction, give him the same sort of intelligent grip upon mind that the analytical results of the physiologist give him upon the living body. To approach the study of mind without analysis would, indeed, be nothing less than ridiculous. And in fact no one does it. I pointed out some years ago that the teacher who opens a course in experimental psychology with an exercise in association of ideas, in order to start out from the 'real mind,' falls entirely short of his intention. An association is just as 'unreal' as a sensation, just as much an abstraction, known by the same sort of analysis (*Exp. Psych.*, I., ii., 3). It may be preferred for pedagogical reasons, and these may be sound or unsound; it certainly is not the real mind. Even the integrative psychologists can, after all, trace out only one mental aspect or one mental function at a time. Just as we study separately the embryology of the nervous system, the vascular system, the digestive system, so must we study, in the light of analysis and in analytical terms, the genesis of mind.

I have assumed that a result is of 'value' in psychology in so far as it helps us to an understanding of mind. On this assumption, analysis is not only valuable, but also indispensable to psychology. I do not say that A's particular bit of analysis is more valuable than B's effort at imaginative reconstruction, or than C's flash of inspiration or happy thought. Estimations of that sort are waste of time. I do say that many of the current arguments against psychological 'atomism' show a woeful misunderstanding of scientific method; and that much of the current depreciation of analytical results shows a like misunderstanding of the aim of scientific psychology.

All this has been better said by Ebbinghaus, in *Psych.*, i., 1905, 179 ff. But, if Ebbinghaus' statements are to be discounted for their experimental bias, the reader may be referred to the opening paragraphs of Jodl's *Psych.* The application to the special case is made by Watt (418). After asserting that we have before us, in consciousness, a continuity with varying emphasis, Watt goes on: "Wir gehen also von dem Psychischen, das wir kennen, aus, analysieren die gesammelten Beobachtungen und experimentellen Daten und nähern uns allmählich der Feststellung etwaiger einheitlicher Zustände und deren regelmässiger Aufeinanderfolge als einem fernen Ziele. Wir gehen immer von einem schon kontinuierlichen Psychischen aus. Es ist also keine Aufgabe der Psychologie, das erlebte Psychische am

Ende einer Untersuchung wiederherzustellen. Es genügt, gezeigt zu haben, dass die Beiträge zu seiner Analyse begründet sind."

[14] Ach, 209 f.

[15] Messer, 107. I have already said that I interpret Messer in this way, but that I do not find him clear.

[16] J. von Kries, Ueber die Natur gewisser mit den psychischen Vorgängen verknüpfter Gehirnzustände, *Zeits. f. Psych. und Physiol. d. Sinnesorg.*, viii., 1894. *e.g.*, 4, 17. Towards the end of the paper, von Kries points out that his own notion of 'connective adjustments' agrees very well with Exner's view of the part played by inhibition and facilitation in the processes of attention, reaction, etc. (S. Exner, *Entwurf zu einer physiol. Erklärung d. psychischen Erscheinungen*, i., 1894). He goes on, however, to say: "auf der anderen Seite aber kann ich mich doch der Anschauung nicht entschlagen, dass die Psychologie noch eine ganze Reihe von Problemen stellt, für welche die physiologischen Vorstellungen eine ähnliche Annäherung noch nicht gestatten. So scheint mir schon ein Verständnis der dispositiven Einstellungen . . . auf grosse Schwierigkeiten zu stossen. Ebenso ist es mir fraglich, ob es gelingt, von dem besonderen, dem Urteile zu grunde liegenden Zusammenhange genügend Rechenschaft zu geben" (32). Reference is made, further, to Ziehen's 'constellation' (*Leitfaden der physiol. Psychol. in 14 Vorlesungen*, 1891, 119; 1906, 186 ff., etc.; *Introduction*, 1895, 213: cf. Ach, 248) and—to the discussions in B. Erdmann's *Logik*.

In a memoir entitled *Ueber die materiellen Grundlagen der Bewusstseinserscheinungen*, 1898, von Kries questions the possibility of transferring to the centre explanatory concepts that are derived from observation at the periphery, and presents a detailed criticism of what he terms the *Leitungslehre* or *Leitungsprincip* (13). He suggests that there may be a differentiation within the cell, and that such an intracellular function may give the key to mental phenomena which associationism is inadequate to explain (60).

O. Gross (*Die cerebrale Sekundärfunktion*, 1902) regards the persistence of excitatory function (*Nachfunktion, Sekundärfunktion*) as of determining influence upon the processes of thought.

[17] Watt (420) refers only to Ebbinghaus (*Psych.*, i., 1902, 682; i., 1905, 719), whom he wrongly accuses of identifying *Aufgabe* with *motorische Einstellung*: Ebbinghaus speaks of "Fälle sensorischer Einstellung." It is a little curious that Ebbinghaus does not refer to von Kries in i., 680 (i., 717); but he had mentioned him before, in connection with a reference to Ziehen's constellation, in i., 664 (i., 698).

The *Einstellungen* of von Kries are referred to by Ach, 248; Messer, 84, 109; Bühler, 325, 356 f.

[18] "Meaning," says Stout, " . . . is in the scale of evolution prior to the development of ideational consciousness" (*Philos. Review*, vii., 1898, 75). With that statement I heartily agree. And when I call 'motor theories' one-sided (as I called the motor theories of attention one-sided, in *Feeling and Attention*, 311), I do so only because they seem, as a rule, to forget that ideational consciousness has, as a matter of fact, developed. I take a typical instance. "In each and every case," Bolton writes, "the object becomes what it is

conceived to be by acting upon it as you would act upon
the object which it is commonly conceived to be. What
the object means is determined by the adjustment that
is made to it" (*Psychol. Review*, xv., 1908, 169). And
he appeals to the lower animals, and the child, and the
Indian, as if the child and the poor Indian had no ideas
whatsoever.

I take it that meaning began to find conscious representation in this kinæsthetic way. But then came ideas,
and meaning found representation in all sorts of ways.
If the kinæsthetic way is still preferred, under certain
circumstances or by certain individuals, that may be
due either to persistence of type or to the action of the
mental law of growth and decay. Descriptive psychology must work out the details and the percentages. I
shall accept the percentages with an open mind; but I
protest against a psychology which ignores that tre-
mendous event in our mental history,—the appearance of
the image. I believe, too, that if Bolton were to go
a little more deeply into the psychology of the child and
the Indian, he would find plenty of occasions (especially
in the acquisition of new meanings) when motor adjustment is entirely secondary. Cf. Messer, 86, and the
references there given.

[19] Pillsbury writes (*Psychol. Review*, xv., 1908, 156):
"we always see the meaning as we look, think in meanings as we think, act in terms of meaning when we act."
If I may wrest this sentence to my own purpose (and
I do not think that Pillsbury's idea of meaning is far
removed from mine), it forms the obverse of the statement in the text.

[20] So Watt, 317 f.: "Vp. I. 'Die volle Bedeutung des

Wortes war schon bei der blossen optischen Wahrnehmung da. Es ist mir nicht zum Bewusstsein gekommen,
dass ich das Wort ausgesprochen hatte, oder dass die
Bedeutung in irgendwelcher Vorstellung explicite gegeben war.' Aber 'ein unwillkürliches, innerliches Aussprechen des Reizwortes und zwar, wie ich es selbst
aussprechen würde, und damit gleichzeitig verbunden das
Verständnis.' 'Es scheint, als wenn dieser Komplex von
Schrift-, Sprech- und Lautbild das Verständnis voll-
endete. Sonstige Repräsentation des Verständnisses
gab es nicht.' " Messer, 71 f.: "Gewöhnlich tritt nun bei
den Vp. das Verstehen mit dem Lesen, also dem
sinnlichen Erfassen des Wortbildes gleichzeitig auf,
verschmilzt jedenfalls mit ihm zu einem nicht weiter
analysierbaren Erlebnis: 'das Reizwort kommt, und ich
bin mir über die Bedeutung klar'—wie einmal Vp. II.
aussagt"; Messer then goes on to discuss the various
Nuancen which verbal meaning may display, up to the
point at which it "als ein besonderes Erlebnis sich von
der Auffassung der Reizworte abhebt": cf. Bühler, *Arch.
de Psych.*, vi., 1907, 381 f.; Wreschner, 6, 103 ff.; E.
H. Rowland, *The Psychol. Experiences connected with
the Different Parts of Speech*, 1907, 2 ff.

I have already referred (Lecture I., Note 7) to the
negative result of Ribot's study of general ideas. Bagley also reports a few cases in which 'only the auditory
experience of the sentence' was in consciousness (*op. cit.*,
108); these cases are so few that we cannot, with Bühler
(*Arch. f. d. ges. Psych.*, xii., 1908, 110), ascribe their
occurrence to a general defect of method. Binet has
missed the gesture-side of the word; "un mot, en effet,
ne signifie rien par lui même, . . . il n'est qu'un élément

brut, inerte, comme le bruit du vent" (*Année psychol.*, xiv., 1908, 334).

[21] I have referred to this experience in a letter to Huey, published in *The Psych. and Pedagogy of Reading*, 1908, 182 ff. It made a deep impression on me at the time. What actually happened, in experimental terms, was that I had to record a 'yes' or 'no' according as the grey shown was or was not recognised as a grey that had been shown earlier in the series. I found myself, then, writing 'yes' without the least apparent reason for doing so. My nervous system was 'recognising' for me.

Störring mentions something similar, in his Exper. und psychopathol. Untersuchungen üb. d. Bewusstsein d. Gültigkeit (*Arch. f. d. ges. Psych.*, xiv., 1909, 1 ff.). His observers distinguished, from the 'Bewusstsein der Sicherheit oder Gültigkeit,' something that they termed 'objektive Sicherheit,' 'Bewusstseinszustand der Sicherheit,' 'eine Seite der Prozesse,' 'Charakter der Sicherheit'; Störring himself calls it 'Zustand der Sicherheit.' "Alle Vp. stimmen also darin überein, dass in den Schlussprozessen ein Etwas eine dominierende Rolle spielt, welches sich deutlich unterscheidet von dem Bewusstsein der Gültigkeit mit oder ohne Worte . . . Dieses mit den Prozessen gegebene Etwas ist so beschaffen, dass auf Grund der Frage nach der Richtigkeit und bei Hinblick auf dasselbe Bejahung eintritt" (9). Störring thus regards the 'Etwas' as conscious; later on (12 ff.), he attempts its closer definition. It is possible that my own introspection, in the case cited, was at fault, and that my 'recognition' was also based upon a conscious 'Etwas.' There is, however, one observer for whom the 'Zustand der Sicherheit' appears to have lapsed into a physiological disposition. "In der späteren Zeit, als diese Erfahrung der Vp. sehr geläufig geworden war, benutzt sie gelegentlich das Auftreten des Bewusstseins der Sicherheit auf Grund einer Frage nach der Richtigkeit als *Kriterium* dafür, dass die als objektive Sicherheit bezeichneten Bedingungen vorhanden gewesen sind. . . . So sagt sie gelegentlich: 'Objektive Sicherheit war vorhanden, das merke ich, indem ich auf Frage nach der Richtigkeit hin das Bewusstsein der Sicherheit bekommen habe'" (5). What holds here of assurance may also, one would think, hold of recognition.

[22] I can, in principle, fully endorse what von Aster says of the character of words and of the significance of intonation (*Zeits. f. Psych.*, xlix., 1908, 78 f., 92 f., 98 ff.), though I interpret the phenomena a little differently, from the standpoint of systematic psychology. I am as keenly sensitive to the fitness of words and of combinations of words as I am to the fitness of musical phrases (Lecture I., Note 11); and the fitness comes to me by way of audition, as quality and intonation of voice. I have a different voice, in internal speech, for every author whose style compels me to a rereading; so that style is for me, in primary experience, a matter of voice heard. Take, for instance, Mr. Quiller Couch's completion of *St. Ives*. On the side of plot, I have my visual schema; but my test of style is auditory: does the book continue to talk in the Stevensonian voice? The various characters in a novel speak, of course, in their own proper voices, as men and women and children, educated and uneducated; but they also all speak in the author's voice,—or, if they do not, they make me very uncomfortable.

I cannot represent these differences of quality and intonation by speaking or reading aloud; I am a very poor reader; but I hear them. They have nothing to do with the actual voice or presence of the writer; oftentimes, indeed, the imaginary and the real come into sharp conflict, and the imaginary has to fight for what is, nevertheless, a certain victory. I have never tried to classify the voices, as I have never asked the question whether my musical accompaniment in reading shows any constant character, whether the same or a similar composition attends the same or a similar topic, author, degree of difficulty. But I know that there are writers of uncertain voice, shrill or squeaky or uneven, and that there are writers of patchwork voice; if I read them, it is only for the matter that their books contain.

It is hardly necessary to say that these imaginal endowments do not give my musical or literary criticisms any objective value; they simply furnish the conscious data which find expression in my personal opinions; they are the imaginal equivalents of what, in other minds, may be 'motor' or 'imageless' processes.—

In commenting upon my 'attitudinal feels,' Professor Colvin called my attention to the fact that he had placed on record similar experiences of his own: see *Philos. Review*, xv., 1906, 308 f., 516; and cf. the later and more explicit statements in Methods of Determining Ideational Types, *Psychol. Bulletin*, vi., 1909, 236. Several other members of my audience at the University of Illinois testified to the importance of these 'feels' in their thought-experience. E. H. Rowland, discussing the conscious representation of prepositions (*op. cit.*,

24), writes to the same effect. "All the different prepositions can be expressed by some variety of 'huddle', and
indeed that is the only way they can be expressed and
have any significance." This study contains many note-
worthy observations, which the author has unfortunately
pressed with undue haste into the service of theory.

I owe to my colleague, Dr. W. H. Pyle, the suggestion to observe the sensible play of facial expression.
I have been surprised to note how widely the expression
varies, during reflective thought and silent reading, and
I am disposed to believe that the corresponding (cuta-
neous and kinæsthetic) sensations play a considerable part
in certain conscious attitudes. The observations are
easily made by means of a suitably placed mirror, and
their 'self-consciousness' soon wears off.

[23] Bühler emphasizes, and quite rightly, the critic's
need of first-hand experience (*Arch. f. d. ges. Psych.*,
xii., 1908, 111). I have worked through a large number of observations by myself, and have taken several
series under the direction of an experimenter. There
were, of course, many experiences that, under the particular conditions, I was unable to analyse, and was therefore obliged to leave with a mere indication of their
presence (incidentally, I gained a high degree of respect
for the skill and patience both of Bühler himself and of
his two observers): but there was nothing that drove me
to a thought-element. The results will be published
elsewhere.

It is always in order to make a reservation for possible individual differences (Ach, 216); and I have
recently received a somewhat severe lesson on that very
subject. I have elsewhere argued that consciousness

has two main levels of clearness, and no more than two, so that the step and wave diagrams, which represent a number of levels or a continuous rise and fall, are incorrect. A quantitative study of attention, carried out in the Cornell laboratory by L. R. Geissler, and soon to be published in *Amer. Journ. Psych.*, seems to show, however, that there are two distinct types of mind, the two-level and the many-level (or continuous?) : certain observers constantly report the one formation, and certain others as insistently report the other. It looks, then,—provided that Geissler's results find confirmation,—as if individual difference of mental constitution, the possibility of which I admitted more in jest than in earnest in *Feeling and Attention*, 228, were really the explanation of the divergent accounts of the attentive consciousness: Angell and Baldwin and Morgan may be of the many-level, as Geissler and Külpe and I myself are of the two-level type. Such a difference in the general configuration of consciousness would itself furnish the key to differences in literary style, in manner of presentation, perhaps even in mode and tendency of thought; its verification is thus a matter of some importance; and I must confess to a feeling of satisfaction that, if I have been wrong, the error has been discovered in my own laboratory and by a firm believer in the two-level theory.

Nevertheless, I dislike to 'hedge' in the matter of the thought-element: I do not at all believe that it exists. All that Angell urges against Stout (*Philos. Review*, vi., 1897, 651) tells with increased force against Bühler. Stout himself protests against the supposition that, "when I speak of imageless apprehension, I have in

view a total consciousness rather than a partial constituent of a total state which contains as another
constituent some sensation or image" (*ibid.*, vii., 1898,
75). Calkins, while she regards it as "abundantly
proved . . . that along with imagery and often in the
focus of attention, when one compares and reasons and
recognises, [there] are elements neither sensational nor
affective," yet declares that "it is unwise and unnecessary
to advance a larger claim," and to assert, with "Stout,
Bühler, Woodworth," that "the occurrence of imageless thought has been proved" (*Amer. Journ. Psych.*,
xx., 1909, 277; cf. *Introd. to Psych.*, 1905, 136).

Calkins' reference to Stout, in this passage, raises
the question: Who, as a matter of fact, believes in
the thought-element? The distinction which she draws,
between an independent imageless thought and a non-
sensorial and non-affective constituent of a conscious
complex, had already been urged by P. Bovet (L'étude
expérimentale du jugement et de la pensée, *Arch. de
Psych.*, viii., 1908, 9 ff., 35). "Y a-t-il des faits
psychologiques, distincts des images et des états affectifs,
et jouant dans les opérations de la pensée un rôle pré-
pondérant"? That is one question: we may call it the
question of meaning, or attitude, or awareness. "Ces
faits, les pensées, se rencontrent-ils dans la conscience
sans qu'aucune représentation leur serve en quelque sort
de support"? That is a different question, the question
of the thought-element.

I do not find that Stout answers this second question
in the affirmative, although he had the two questions
before him. I do not find that Messer has even now,
after the appearance of Bühler's work, separated the

two questions: he formally accepts the thought-element
(*Arch. f. d. ges. Psych.*, x., 1907, 421 f.), but in so
doing he brackets Binet with Ach, and refers to passages of his own work (Messer, 77-87, 177-180) which
are not to the point.   Bühler himself is, of course, explicit; and Bovet follows him (37).   Woodworth comes,
I think, nearer than Messer to a separation of
the questions: the first he answers, very definitely, in the
affirmative; the second I take him to answer, also in the
affirmative, in such passages as the following: "I should
. . . insist that such sensory content [as is unavoidable
from the continuous stimulation of the sense organs]
does not always lie in the field of attention, and that at
times it is so marginal as to elude introspection.   But
principally I should insist that something else does often
lie in the field of attention, that, in short, there is
non-sensuous content, and that in many cases it is
descriptively as well as dynamically the most important
component of thought" (*Journ. Philos. Psych. Sci.
Meth.*, iii., 1906, 703).—I should be inclined, then, for
"Stout, Bühler, Woodworth," to write "Woodworth,
Bühler, Bovet."

Binet remains.   I do not think that Messer is justified
in classing Binet with Ach: for, while Binet did not
either, in 1903, separate the two questions, his readers
have every reason to suppose (on the ground of passages
like 104 ff.) that, had he done so, he would have acknowledged the thought-element.   Curiously enough,
Binet now makes imageless thought a matter of feeling,
sentiment (A. Binet et T. Simon, Langage et pensée,
Année psychol., xiv., 1908, 333 ff.).   "Nous croyons
avoir mis hors de doute . . . qu'il y a une pensée sans

images, qu'il y a une pensée sans mots, et que la pensée
est constituée par un sentiment intellectuel." We have,
then, an independent thought-process (cf. note, 337 f.),
but it is an intellectual feeling. The specific element
in thought "est de la nature du sentiment. Ce serait
un sentiment intellectuel, et par conséquent (?) assez
vague dans sa nature, mais dont nous percevons la pré-
sence, et dont nous percevons surtout les effets. . . .
C'est la perception confuse, et souvent émotionelle, de ce
qui se prepare et se fait en nous, qui constituerait la
pensée. . . . C'est même ce sentiment qui dicte les mots
et suggère les images; et, à leur tour, images et mots
réagissent sur ce sentiment." This view has evident
points of resemblance to that of Wundt.

[24] Many writers insist on the distinction of genesis and
description, and I should be the last to quarrel with
them. But when the formations described are stages
in a genetic progression, cross-sections of a single course
which leads through growth to culmination and thence
to decay,—and when this genetic progression is traceable (as it is in the case of action) within the lifetime,
even within the adult lifetime of the individual,—then it
seems to me that to make different mental elements out
of the different mental stages is, at the least, unnecessary and inexpedient. "Quand même toute pensée serait
une image transformée," writes Bovet (35), "il n'en
faudrait pas moins marquer d'abord en quoi une pensée
se distingue d'une image. De même les caractères dis-
tinctifs de l'homme et du singe subsistent, quelque opinion qu'on ait sur la théorie transformiste." We must,
of course, distinguish the 'thought' from the 'image';
but that is not the issue; the issue, for Bovet as for us,

is the establishment of the 'thought' as a new mental element; and a 'transformed image' is still an image. And who ever saw a baby monkey develope into a man? The point is, if I may repeat it: Can the individual observer trace, in his experience, the passage from explicit imagery to conscious attitude? Personally, I think that I can. Why, then, should I introduce a new mental element?

[25] *Elem. d. Psychophysik*, i., 1860 or 1889, 242.

[26] Bühler distinguishes four views or theories of the nature of thought. Two of these—that "die Gedanken seien nichts anderes als eine Reihe von flüchtigen halb unbewussten Einzelvorstellungen," and that "die Denkerlebnisse seien etwas, was psychologisch gar nicht bestimmt werden könne, was vielmehr nur vor das Forum der Logik gehöre"—he dismisses as not worth discussion (324). The third, the theory of 'possibility,' has various forms. In general, "die Möglichkeitstheorien suchen eine Erklärung im Unbewussten. Das, was ausser sinnlichen Elementen im Denkakt bewusst ist, soll nichts anderes sein als ein Ausdruck dafür, dass im Unbewussten schon etwas angeregt ist, was im nächsten Augenblick ins Bewusstsein treten kann. . . . Auch hat man wohl die Fassung des Unbewussten als etwas Dunkel- oder Halbbewusstes mit im Auge gehabt, so dass die erregten Dispositionen ihren Vorstellungen gegenüber nicht als ideelle Möglichkeiten sondern eher als reale, schon partiell verwirklichte Möglichkeiten angesehen werden müssten." Of these theories Bühler remarks: "alle die Möglichkeitstheorien lassen über dem Möglichen das Wirkliche zu kurz kommen" (325 f.).

I share this view: but cf. von Aster, *Zeits. f. Psych.*, xlix., 1908, 85 ff.

The fourth theory, that of 'condensation' (*Verdicht-ung*), looks upon thoughts as "zusammengeschobene, verkürzte, in einem Akt zusammengefasste Vorstellungs-reihen, die durch diese Zusammenfassung ihren An-blick etwas geändert haben." This view Bühler rejects for two reasons. (1) "Wenn der Gedanke ein Verdicht-ungsprodukt aus Vorstellungen wäre, dann müsste er sich durch dieselben Kategorien bestimmen lassen wie diese Vorstellungen. Nun hat es für einen Gedanken aber gar keinen Sinn, nach seiner Intensität oder gar nach seinen sinnlichen Qualitäten zu fragen" (328). It might be replied that Ach expressly attributes intensity to the *Bewusstheit* (96 f., 101, 212 f., 218 f.); and that Messer ascribes intensity to the cerebral disposition that underlies understanding, and a corresponding clear-ness, *Deutlichkeit*, to the understanding itself (84).* On the side of quality, too, we might reply that it is not always easy to pick out the constituent qualities even in a tonal or organic fusion, a formation that stands, so to say, only next door to sensation; and that it will naturally be difficult to pick them out in a formation where ideas—themselves complex processes—are 'zusam-mengeschoben,' 'abgekürzt,' 'beschleunigt.' For this telescoping of ideas implies, of course, all manner of complex synergy in the cortex; it is not, in reality, the ideas that are telescoped, but cortical excitations that are crossed, cut short, interfered with, inhibited. The correlated conscious formation is therefore given under

---

* Certain points in Bühler's own discussion (330 ff.) distinctly suggest the occurrence of thoughts at various intensities.

the worst possible conditions for analysis, and we might conceivably have to rest content with verifying the process of reduction at large (from explicit imagery to 'condensed' thought), without being able to trace identical qualities from one level to another.—This is to answer Bühler on his own ground. If substitution as well as telescoping takes place, analysis may be rendered easier (as, *e.g.*, by the generic intervention of kinæsthesis) or more difficult (as by the intercurrence, in abbreviated form, of ideational processes whose presence we do not suspect and for whose search we consequently have no cue); but the principle of the rejoinder remains the same.

(2) Bühler's second and less direct argument declares that the laws of the course of thought (*Gedankenfortschritt*) are different from those of the connection (*Verbindung*) of ideas; "es wäre doch durchaus unbegreiflich, wie mit einer Abkürzung und Beschleunigung von Vorstellungsabläufen, die ihr Automatischwerden mit sich bringt, ʾeine Aenderung ihrer Gesetzlichkeit verbunden sein sollte" (327 f.). We might, however, very well admit that apperceptive differ from associative connections, that determining tendencies shape consciousness otherwise than reproductive tendencies, that the judgment (connection under *Aufgabe*) differs from the free play of association, and yet maintain that the formations connected are, in every case, ideas. Moreover, Bühler, in his articles Ueber Gedankenzusammenhänge and Ueber Gedankenerinnerungen (*Arch. f. d. ges. Psych.*, xii., 1908, 1 ff., 24 ff.), assumes or presupposes the elementary character of his 'thoughts': he is to show, by reference to mode of connection, that thought

cannot possibly be explained by condensation of ideas; but he is satisfied, when working out the thought-connections, to stop short at thoughts as final terms of analysis. The *Zwischenerlebnisbeziehungen* that constitute the 'thread' of a thought-connection and that may link ideas and feelings as well as thoughts proper (5), and the *Zwischengegenstandsbeziehungen* that constitute logical connection and oftentimes serve to introduce a thought or an idea into a true thought-context (7), these *Beziehungen* or relations are either secondary thoughts or just 'conscious relations' (5, 12). But it is still an open question, both on the hypothetical ground of Bühler's argument and on the wider field of systematic psychology, whether 'conscious relations' are simple or complex, ultimate or derivative. Again: Bühler makes much of the fact that the thought-connections of his memory experiments showed themselves independent of the associative law of temporal contiguity (29 ff.). It might be replied that many modern psychologists, in their doctrine of association, accept a law of 'similarity' as well as a law of 'contiguity,' and that an attempted explanation of these results in associative terms would naturally turn to the former rather than to the latter. More effective, I think, is the reply that the influence of temporal contiguity, in view of the great complication of physiological substrate which the condensation-theory demands, could never be comparable in its effect with a reinstatement or redintegration of the habitual pattern of the cortical excitation. So far, indeed, is the lack of influence from telling against the theory, that it might have been predicted from the theory. Lastly, I notice that Bühler grants the occurrence, in daily life, of mechanised thought-associations; and that, though the conditions of his experiments were distinctly unfavourable to their appearance, he nevertheless inclines to the view that he has found cases of 'iteration,' in which thoughts are reproduced as ideas are reproduced in an 'association by contiguity' (70 ff.). But this lapse to the ideational type of behaviour is, so far as it goes, an indication of the ideational nature of the thoughts themselves.

I do not find, therefore, that Bühler's two arguments —the direct argument from the absence of intensity and quality, and the indirect argument from the nature of thought-connections—are, either separately or in combination, decisive against the theory of condensation. Cf. Binet, 84 ff., 106, 154; Watt, 431 ff.; Messer, 77, 83 ff., 109, 187.

[27] M. F. Washburn, The Term 'Feeling,' *Journ. Philos. Psych. Sci. Meth.*, iii., 1906, 63. I may here call attention to the same writer's The Psychology of Deductive Logic, *Mind*, N. S. vii., 1898, 523 ff. The paper is briefly, almost schematically written, and I do not know whether the author still—after the advent of the *Aufgabe*-psychology—adheres to all of the positions which it takes; she outlines, however, a consistently imaginal account of concept, judgment, fallacy and inference.

[28] Woodworth, in *Essays Philos. and Psychol.*, 1908, 495 f.; Calkins, *Introd. to Psych.*, 1901 or 1905, 132 f., 136. Woodworth's discussion of the point appears to me to betray an unnecessary sensitiveness: the logician has nothing to say in the matter of conscious content. Calkins has translated logic into psychology, and in so

doing has involved herself in a contradiction. For if
the 'relational element' comes to consciousness as 'belonging to' its concomitant processes, then it comes not as an
element at all, but as a connection of two elements: the
relational element of 'like,' let us say, *plus* the relational
element of 'belonging to' or of dependence. One then
wonders whether the concomitant processes do not come
to consciousness with a relational element of possession,
of 'having [something] belong to them.'

The element of relation has found many supporters.
See, *e.g.*: H. Spencer, *Princ. of Psych.*, 1855, §81:
"What are these relations? They can be nothing more
than certain secondary states of consciousness, produced
by the union of the primary states. . . . The original
modifications of consciousness are the feelings produced
in us by subjective and objective activities [by our own
actions and the actions of surrounding things]; and
any further modifications of consciousness must be such
as result from combinations of these original ones"
(285). Spencer here comes curiously near to the doctrine
of *Gestaltqualitäten*. The passage is retained in the
second edition, except that the second sentence ends:
"arising through connections of the primary states,"
and that the third sentence has 'aroused' for 'produced'
(ii., 1871, 254: so also the third ed., ii., 1881, 254).
The second edition contains, further, the chapter on
The Composition of Mind, in which it is said that "under
an ultimate analysis, what we call a relation proves to
be itself a kind of feeling" (i., 1869, 164; so i., 1881,
164). Structurally, indeed, the relation appears as
the typical mental element: for it "may be regarded
as one of those nervous shocks which we suspect to be

the units of composition of feelings," whereas feelings
themselves are "composed of units of feeling, or shocks."
Spencer, however, shows the logical bias when he adds:
"Take away the terms it unites, and it disappears along
with them; having no independent place,—no individ-
uality of its own." And yet "its qualitative character
is appreciable"!

Huxley follows Spencer in postulating what he calls,
in Humian terminology, 'impressions of relation' (*Hume*,
1881, 69). In 1893, E. Schrader published a little
work entitled *Die bewusste Beziehung zwischen Vorstellungen als konstitutives Bewusstseinselement: ein Beitrag
zur Psychologie der Denkerscheinungen*, in which he
maintained a like position. We have already referred
to James, Calkins, Binet, Woodworth, and the various
members of the Würzburg school. Calkins (*Amer.
Journ. Psych.*, xx., 1909, 274 f.; cf. *Introd. to Psych.*,
1905, 136) lengthens the list to include Meinong,*
Ebbinghaus, Münsterberg, etc. But she can do this
only by forcing her own system and terminology upon
writers who have definitely adopted other terms and
other criteria: Ebbinghaus, *e.g.*,—who has three elements, by the way, and not two,—would have protested
vigorously against the statement that he held "the
doctrine of elements of consciousness which are neither
sensational nor in any sense coördinate with the affections." Angell, too, in a passage which Calkins does
not quote (*Psych.*, 1904, 205 f.), explicitly mentions
two views of relation, the attentional theory and the

* Bühler (341) also brings the phenomena of *Gestaltqualität*
under the rubric of his *Regelbewusstsein*; but the reference is
rather a suggestion than a claim.

theory of special feelings (of which latter the theory of 'relational elements' is given as a sub-form), and himself decides, with apologies for dogmatism, that "the consciousness of relation is a basal factor in all activities of attention." Judd, again, hardly seems to me to belong to Calkins' list, though I confess that I do not find his writing clear. Thus, in his 'What is Perception?' (*Journ. Philos. Psych. Sci. Meth.*, vi., 1909, 41), he remarks: "Once the possibility of recognising a wholly different type of explanation [than that of analysis into sensory elements] is admitted, the conscious process will be treated as a complex made up of sensory elements and other processes which are functional in character and deserving of a separate treatment. We shall then see that any particular phase of experience may be described either with reference to its sensory facts or with reference to its functional phases of activity." I do not gather that Judd accepts 'relational elements' as items of mental structure or of the 'composition of mind,' though I may have misinterpreted this and similar passages.

"Wundt," Calkins says (277), "can afford to deny relational elements because he illicitly and unwittingly holds them concealed within his heterogeneous class of 'feelings.'" It is difficult to see the force of the 'unwittingly.' And if the criticism be valid, is not Wundt more excusable than Ebbinghaus,—in whom Calkins has found an ally? For Ebbinghaus holds the relational elements illicitly *and wittingly* concealed in his heterogeneous class of 'sensations.' But Wundt can take care of himself. Why, however, does not Calkins refer to Lehmann? The *Hauptgesetze d. menschl. Gefühlslebens* (1892,

339 ff.) recognises a class of *Beziehungsgefühle*, in the technical sense of the word *Gefühl*, which includes many of the formations that we have learned to know as *Bewusstseinslagen* or attitudes. Here, then, the relational element is wittingly concealed in feeling. O facinus indignum!—

Many years ago, I myself wrote a bit of imagemongery on the subject of relation; worse yet, I found a logician to agree with me (The Psychology of 'Relation,' *Philos. Review*, iii., 1894, 193 ff.; J. E. Creighton, Modern Psychology and Theories of Knowledge, *ibid.*, 196 ff.). The relation-artists have, wisely enough, passed it by in silence; it represented a crude first attempt at analysis, and I can do better now. But I still hold to the opinion that my 'feelings of relation' are complex and sensory-imaginal in character. No revival-meeting of "enthusiastic upholders of the relational-element doctrine" can shake this conviction.

[29] *Lehrbuch d. allg. Psych.*, 1894, 349 f. "Wir können auch nicht zugeben, dass das 'Urtheil,' diese logische Angelegenheit, zu einer *psychologischen* 'Grund-classe psychischer Phänomene' gestempelt wird; eine 'Psychologie des Urtheils' ist uns ein Widerspruch in sich."

[30] The most recent investigator, Störring, offers not a definition but a 'characterisation' of judgment in the following terms: "ein Erlebnis, das sich mit dem Bewusstsein der Gültigkeit oder mit dem Zustande der Sicherheit verbindet, d.h. mit einem Etwas, das, ohne ein Bewusstsein der Gültigkeit zu sein, so beschaffen ist, dass auf Grund der Frage nach der Gültigkeit bei Hinblick auf jenes Erlebnis infolge dieses Etwas Beja-

hung eintritt" (*Arch. f. d. ges. Psych.*, xiv., 1909, 42).
It is the introduction of the 'state of assurance' (see
Note 21 above) that differentiates this characterisation
from the view adopted, *e.g.*, by von Kries: "Die Vertief-
ung der Psychologie, die neueren logischen Untersuchungen verdankt wird, hat . . . mit Recht dazu geführt,
das 'Geltungsgefühl' als eine besondere und vorzugsweise wichtige Eigenschaft in dem psychologishen
Thatbestand eines jeden Urtheils in Anspruch zu nehmen" (*Ueber d. mater. Grundlagen*, etc., 1898, 52).
The new characterisation will probably meet the old
objection that it is too wide; for there are plenty of
automatic operations whose validity we should affirm if
it were questioned, but which assuredly are not judgments in any distinctive sense. Cf. W. B. Pillsbury,
An Attempt to Harmonise the Current Psychological
Theories of the Judgment, *Psychol. Bulletin*, iv., 1907,
237 ff.

[31] Bühler, 345 f. (cf. 341); cf. Bovet, *Arch. de
Psych.*, viii., 1908, 26; Dürr, *Zeits. f. Psych.*, xlix.,
1908, 339. Messer (124, 132) brings the Wundtian
Gesamtvorstellung into direct connection with the psychology of *Aufgabe:* cf. Lecture IV., Note 25.

[32] For the experimental status of this distinction, see
Messer, 122 ff.; Bovet, 25 ff.

[33] Watt, 344. Watt refers, I gather with disapproval,
to Royce's comment that what Ribot in his work on
general ideas and Marbe in his work on judgment "both
examined, were relatively reflex processes that express
the mere residuum of a mental skill long since acquired by
their subjects": Recent Logical Inquiries and their

Psychological Bearings, *Psychol. Review*, ix., 1902, 114; cf. Bühler, 301.

Watt accordingly discounts (412) the criticism passed by Wundt upon Marbe's work (*Physiol. Psych.*, iii., 1903, 580 f.). Messer also moderates that criticism: 111 f., 126. See, however, Bühler, 302; Dürr, *Zeits. f. Psych.*, xlix., 1908, 314.

[34] Woodworth, in *Studies in Philosophy and Psychology*, 1906, 351 ff.; cf. *Le Mouvement*, 1903, 308 ff., esp. 330 ff.; E. L. Thorndike, *Elements of Psych.*, 1905, 281 ff.; The Mental Antecedents of Voluntary Movements, *Journ. Philos. Psych. Sci. Meth.*, iv., 1907, 40 ff.

[35] Royce, *op. cit.*, 111 f.; cf. Dürr, *Zeits. f. Psych.*, xlix., 1908, 338. On the chaotic state of the doctrine of judgment, cf. Royce, 110 f.; Marbe, 13.

[36] I say nothing of the approach to judgment from the side of language (Wundt, B. Erdmann)—enormously important as this aspect of thought-psychology undoubtedly is—because I am concerned only with an experimental psychology. It is, however, probable, indeed almost inevitable, that suggestions for experimentation come from *Völkerpsychologie* as well as from logic. Cf. Dürr, *Zeits. f. Psych.*, xlix., 1908, 337 ff.; Bovet, *Arch. de Psych.*, viii., 1908, 47; W. H. Sheldon, Methods of Investigating the Problem of Judgment, *Psychol. Bulletin*, vi., 1907, 243 ff.

INDEX OF NAMES

References to the Notes begin with page 197

309

INDEX OF SUBJECTS

References to the Notes begin with page 197

312

CLASSICS IN PSYCHOLOGY

AN ARNO PRESS COLLECTION

Angell, James Rowland. **Psychology: On Introductory Study of the Structure and Function of Human Consciousness.** 4th edition. 1908

Bain, Alexander. **Mental Science.** 1868

Baldwin, James Mark. **Social and Ethical Interpretations in Mental Development.** 2nd edition. 1899

Bechterev, Vladimir Michailovitch. **General Principles of Human Reflexology.** [1932]

Binet, Alfred and Th[éodore] Simon. **The Development of Intelligence in Children.** 1916

Bogardus, Emory S. **Fundamentals of Social Psychology.** 1924

Buytendijk, F. J. J. **The Mind of the Dog.** 1936

Ebbinghaus, Hermann. **Psychology: An Elementary Text-Book.** 1908

Goddard, Henry Herbert. **The Kallikak Family.** 1931

Hobhouse, L[eonard] T. **Mind in Evolution.** 1915

Holt, Edwin B. **The Concept of Consciousness.** 1914

Külpe, Oswald. **Outlines of Psychology.** 1895

Ladd-Franklin, Christine. **Colour and Colour Theories.** 1929

Lectures Delivered at the 20th Anniversary Celebration of Clark University. (Reprinted from *The American Journal of Psychology*, Vol. 21, Nos. 2 and 3). 1910

Lipps, Theodor. **Psychological Studies.** 2nd edition. 1926

Loeb, Jacques. **Comparative Physiology of the Brain and Comparative Psychology.** 1900

Lotze, Hermann. **Outlines of Psychology.** [1885]

McDougall, William. **The Group Mind.** 2nd edition. 1920

Meier, Norman C., editor. **Studies in the Psychology of Art: Volume III.** 1939

Morgan, C. Lloyd. **Habit and Instinct.** 1896

Münsterberg, Hugo. **Psychology and Industrial Efficiency.** 1913

Murchison, Carl, editor. **Psychologies of 1930.** 1930

Piéron, Henri. **Thought and the Brain.** 1927

Pillsbury, W[alter] B[owers]. **Attention.** 1908

[Poffenberger, A. T., editor]. **James McKeen Cattell: Man of Science.** 1947

Preyer, W[illiam] **The Mind of the Child:** Parts I and II. 1890/1889

The Psychology of Skill: Three Studies. 1973

Reymert, Martin L., editor. **Feelings and Emotions:** The Wittenberg Symposium. 1928

Ribot, Th[éodule Armand]. **Essay on the Creative Imagination.** 1906

Roback, A[braham] A[aron]. **The Psychology of Character.** 1927

I. M. Sechenov: Biographical Sketch and Essays. (Reprinted from *Selected Works* by I. Sechenov). 1935

Sherrington, Charles. **The Integrative Action of the Nervous System.** 2nd edition. 1947

Spearman, C[harles]. **The Nature of 'Intelligence' and the Principles of Cognition.** 1923

Thorndike, Edward L. **Education:** A First Book. 1912

Thorndike, Edward L., E. O. Bregman, M. V. Cobb, et al. **The Measurement of Intelligence.** [1927]

Titchener, Edward Bradford. **Lectures on the Elementary Psychology of Feeling and Attention.** 1908

Titchener, Edward Bradford. **Lectures on the Experimental Psychology of the Thought-Processes.** 1909

Washburn, Margaret Floy. **Movement and Mental Imagery.** 1916

Whipple, Guy Montrose. **Manual of Mental and Physical Tests:** Parts I and II. 2nd edition. 1914/1915

Woodworth, Robert Sessions. **Dynamic Psychology.** 1918

Wundt, Wilhelm. **An Introduction to Psychology.** 1912

Yerkes, Robert M. **The Dancing Mouse** and **The Mind of a Gorilla.** 1907/1926

DATE DUE